MW01252961

Uncertainty, Diversity and The Common Good

Uncertainty, Diversity and The Common Good

Changing Norms and New Leadership Paradigms

Edited by
STEFAN GRÖSCHL

GOWER

Gower Applied Business Research
Our programme provides leaders, practitioners, scholars and researchers with thought provoking, cutting edge books that combine conceptual insights, interdisciplinary rigour and practical relevance in key areas of business and management.

Published by
Gower Publishing Limited
Wey Court East
Union Road
Farnham
Surrey
GU9 7PT
England

Gower Publishing Company
110 Cherry Street
Suite 3-1
Burlington
VT 05401-3818
USA

www.gowerpublishing.com

Stefan Gröschl has asserted his moral right under the Copyright, Designs and Patents Act, 1988, to be identified as the editor of this work.

British Library Cataloguing in Publication Data
Uncertainty, diversity and the common good : changing norms
   and new leadership paradigms.
   1. Social responsibility of business. 2. Leadership.
   3. International business enterprises--Management--Social
   aspects. 4. Corporations--Sociological aspects. 5. Common good.
   I. Groschl, Stefan.
   658.4'08-dc23

ISBN: 978-1-4094-5339-0 (hbk)
       978-1-4094-5340-6 (ebk)
       978-1-4724-0808-2 (epub)

The Library of Congress has cataloged the printed edition as follows:
Groschl, Stefan.
   Uncertainty, diversity and the common good : changing norms and new leadership
paradigms / by Stefan Groschl.
      pages cm. -- (Applied research - governance and leadership)
   Includes bibliographical references and index.
   ISBN 978-1-4094-5339-0 (hbk.) -- ISBN 978-1-4094-5340-6 (ebk.) -- ISBN 978-1-4724-0808-2 (epub)
   1. Leadership. 2. Social responsibility of business. 3. Industrial management--Social
aspects. 4.
Globalization--Social aspects. I. Title.
   HD57.7.G765 2013
   658.4'092--dc23

                                                              2012046576

Printed in the United Kingdom by Henry Ling Limited,
at the Dorset Press, Dorchester, DT1 1HD

Contents

List of Figures

List of Tables

About the Editor

Stefan Gröschl is Co-Chair of Leadership and Diversity at ESSEC. He has published four books on leadership, international human resources management and diversity issues. Dr Gröschl is widely known as a diversity management expert and has shared his expertise in a wide range of academic and public arenas. His research has been published in numerous book chapters and articles in both the trade and academic press. His assignments have taken him to a wide range of academic institutions in Mexico, Taiwan, Spain, New Zealand, Germany, Bahrain and France.

About the Contributors

Celia de Anca

Celia de Anca is currently the Director of the Centre for Diversity in Global Management at IE Business School. She was previously the Director of Corporate Programmes at the Euro-Arab Management School (EAMS), Granada. She has also worked for the Fundación Cooperación Internacional y Promoción Ibero-América Europa. (CIPIE) and at the International Division of Banco de Santander. She has a master's degree from the Fletcher School of Law and Diplomacy (Boston), and from the Universidad Politécnica de Madrid. She holds a degree and PhD from the Universidad Autónoma de Madrid, with a comparative thesis on Islamic, ethical/ecological investment funds and on the London Market. She is the author of *Beyond Tribalism*, Palgrave Macmillan 2012, and co-author of *Managing Diversity in the Global Organization*, Macmillan 2007. She has had articles published in specialized journals, in addition to regular articles in the press. She was an external advisor of the Merrill Lynch's Diversity & Inclusion Council up to 2009. She is a member of the Ethics Committee of InverCaixa's Ethics Fund, Spain and a member of the International Scientific Committee of the University Euromed in Marseille, France. She is also a member of the Executive Committee at IE Business School. She has received the award of Women Executive of the Year 2008 by the Business Women Association of Madrid (ASEME).

Salvador Aragón

Salvador Aragon is Professor of Strategy, Information Systems and Innovation at IE Business School. In addition, he combines this academic activity with the role of Chief Innovation Officer at IE Business School. He holds a MBA from IE Business School and he has a degree in Industrial Engineering from University of Navarre, Spain. His research has been focused on the role of information technologies in the business organization, their relevance as an engine for innovation and transformation. Furthermore, Professor Aragón has researched the concept of innovation governance as a way to manage and to spark innovation within organizations.

Laurent Bibard

Laurent Bibard is Professor at ESSEC Business School, Paris Singapore. He was Dean for MBA Programs at ESSEC (2005–2009), and is currently Full Professor, Management Department. Laurent is educated in Management (PhD in Economics) and Philosophy (PhD in Political Philosophy). His researches benefit from this two-fold education, questioning management from a philosophical perspective, and thought on the basis of experience and practice. Some of his recent researches concern organizational vigilance interpreted as the organizational conditions favouring collective as well as individual mindfulness on one hand, and gender relations on the other hand. Professor Bibard is a thorough consultant, accompanying leaders and organizations in changing environments. He was invited to many prestigious universities in Germany (Mannheim), Canada (UQAM) Japan (Keio Business School, Keio University) and so on. His publications include 'Management and Philosophy: What is at Stake?' (*Keio Business Forum*, March 2011, Vol. 28, no. 1, pp. 227–243) and 'Towards a Phenomenology of Management: From Modelling to day-to-day Moral Sensemaking Cognition' (*Moral Foundations of Management Knowledge*, Djelic & Vranceanu ed., 2007). Two Laurent books are currently being translated, *Sexualité et Mondialisation* (*Sexuality and Globalization*) into English, and *La Sagesse et le Feminine* (*Wisdom and Feminity*) into Japanese.

Nicholas Capaldi

Nicholas Capaldi is Legendre-Soulé Distinguished Chair in Business Ethics at Loyola University, New Orleans, where he also serves as Director of the newly-created Center for Spiritual Capital. He received his BA from the University of Pennsylvania and his PhD from Columbia University. His principal research and teaching interest is in public policy and its intersection with political science, philosophy, law, religion and economics. He is the author of eight books, over 100 articles, editor of six anthologies, member of the editorial board of six journals, and has served as editor of *Public Affairs Quarterly*.

Laurence de Carlo

Laurence de Carlo is Professor at the Public and Private Policy Department, ESSEC Business School, France. She studies interactional and facilitation dynamics in complex decision processes in Planning and Environment. She also deals research on the pedagogy of negotiation, consultation and facilitation in these complex decision processes. She has published on these topics using concepts such as paradox and ambivalence, potential space for creativity, acceptance of conflicts, fantasy and illusion versus reality, and rationality bounded by unconscious phenomena. Her research appears in several collective books and in the *Negotiation Journal*, *Conflict Resolution Quarterly*, *International Studies of Management and Organization*, *Revue Française de Gestion*, *Négociations*, *Espaces et Sociétés*, *Recherches Qualitatives* and so on.

Conchita Galdón

Conchita Galdón is vice-director of the Center for Diversity in Global Management at IE Business School. At the IE center for Diversity she has been responsible for research and applied projects on multicultural diversity, mentoring for women, women entrepreneurship and leadership among others. She holds a Master's Degree in Public Administration and International Development from Harvard Kennedy School, where she got intensive training in advanced multi-party negotiation and conflict resolution.

She holds a BA in Economics from Universidad Autónoma de Madrid, Spain. She has been chair of a project for the prevention of social risks among youngsters. Later she worked as an intern at the UN Headquarters. At Santander Bank she was Economic Analyst for Latin America at the Latin America Division. Concepción collaborated as Intern assistant to the Ministry of Finance of Liberia. At present, as well as working at the Center for Diversity in Global Management, she is co-founder and CEO of global non-profit social venture Fundacion Puentes Global.

Stefan Gröschl

Stefan Gröschl is Co-chair of the ESSEC Leadership and Diversity Chair. He has published four books on leadership, international human resources management and diversity management-related aspects. Stefan is widely known as a diversity management expert and has shared his expertise in a wide range of academic and public arenas. His research has also been published in numerous book chapters and articles in both the trade and academic press. His work has brought Stefan to assignments in a wide range of academic institutions in Mexico, Taiwan, Spain, New Zealand, Germany, Bahrain and France.

Vipin Gupta

Vipin Gupta is Professor and Co-director of the Global Management Center at the California State University San Bernardino. He has made significant contributions to the science of culture, sustainable strategic management in the emerging markets, managing organizational and technological transformations, and entrepreneurial and women's leadership, and is a pioneer in the field of culturally sensitive models of family business around the world. He has authored or edited 16 books, including the seminal GLOBE book on culture and leadership in 62 societies, 11 on family business models in different cultural regions, two on organizational performance, one on the MNCs in China, and an innovative strategy textbook. He has published about 150 articles as book chapters and in academic journals, such as the *Journal of Business Venturing*, *Journal of World Business*, *Family Business Review*, *International Journal of Cross-cultural Management* and *Asia-Pacific Journal of Management*, among others. Dr Gupta has been a Japan Foundation fellow and a recipient of the Society for Industrial Organizational Psychologists' coveted 'Scott M. Myers Award for Applied Research – 2005'.

Ciara Hackett

Ciara joined QUB in August 2012, having previously taught at National University of Ireland Galway (NUIG). She completed her PhD in 2009 on the area of CSR and regulation in Ireland. At NUIG, she taught Tort Law, Jurisprudence, Advanced Legal Research and Methods, Corporate Governance and Corporate Social Responsibility. Her research explores a diverse range of issues in the areas of regulation, corporate governance and corporate social responsibility as well as legal theories of development. She is currently engaged in a number of projects in the areas of Corporate Social Responsibility, Tort Law and Corporate Governance. Her interests lie in the need to regulate on certain aspects of CSR in order to align national interests with corporate agendas. Current interests looks at the role of diversity, the potential for diversity quotas with the area of board composition and specifically via persons with a disability.

Hae-Jung Hong

Hae-Jung Hong is currently a Post-Doctoral fellow at Rouen Business School in France, and held a Visiting Research Fellow in the Strategy Department at INSEAD Fontainebleau and was a Lecturer in the Management Department at ESSEC Business School in Paris in 2011–2012. She received her MBA in Hospitality Management and PhD from ESSEC Business School. She has participated in teaching executive programmes at INSEAD Fontainebleau and Abu Dhabi campuses, MBA courses at the ESSEC Business School,and Grande Écoles programme at the Rouen Business School. Hae-Jung Hong's current research projects focus on multiculturals as the new workplace demographic and their roles impacting global team effectiveness.

Bas de Leeuw

Bas de Leeuw is Managing Director of the World Resources Forum (WRF), based in Switzerland. Before joining the WRF in 2011 he was Executive Director of the Donella Meadows Institute, based in Vermont, USA. He has been a diplomat for the United Nations Environment Programme (UNEP), in Paris, France, from 1998 to 2009, where he set up and managed a number of global initiatives, such as the Sustainable Consumption Program, the Marrakech Process on Sustainable Consumption and Production, the International Life Cycle Panel, and the International Resource Panel. He served as the Head of the Strategy Unit and as Head of the Integrated Resource Management Unit, and was Head of the Secretariat of both the Life Cycle Panel and the Resource Panel. He also set up the UNEP/Wuppertal Institute Centre on Sustainable Consumption and Production and represented UNEP in its Board. He has also worked as a national expert for the OECD and has held various positions in the Dutch Government (Ministry of Economic Affairs respectively Ministry of Housing, Spatial Planning and Environment) between 1985 and 1991.

Gregory A. Norris

Greg Norris is Adjunct Lecturer with the Harvard School of Public Health, where he teaches life cycle assessment (LCA), works in the Center for Global Health and the Environment, and advises graduate students in related research. He is also Visiting Professor with the Applied Sustainability Center at the University of Arkansas, where he serves as Director of Research for The Sustainability Consortium. He founded New Earth, a non-profit institute developing and deploying technologies that enable people around the world to drive sustainable development 'from the bottom up'. Its projects include Earthster (www.earthster.org), an open source platform for product-level sustainability assessment; Handprinter (www.handprinter.org), which helps people take actions at home and at work which more than compensate for their environmental and social 'footprints'; and the Social Hot Spots Database (www.socialhotspots.org), a transparent data source on supply chain impacts and opportunities for improving human rights, working conditions, community and other social impacts. In 1996 Norris founded Sylvatica, an international life cycle assessment institute (www.sylvatica.com) which consults on LCA to the UN, governments in the US and abroad, a variety of Fortune 500 companies, industrial associations, and smaller companies and the non-profit sector. He is a member of the Royal Government of Bhutan's International Expert Working Group, comprised of 60 experts from around the world commissioned to draft a new global development paradigm during 2013–2014 to promote well-being and happiness as a global goal through effective and pragmatic international public policies. He is an editor for the *International Journal of LCA*, the *Journal of Industrial Ecology* and *Greenhouse Gas Measurement and Management*.

Isabel Rimanoczy

Isabel Rimanoczy is a Legacy Coach (www.legacycoaching.net) who has over 25 years' experience working in North America, Latin America, Europe and Asia with multinational corporations in the areas of coaching and executive development, and specifically helping adults to navigate transitions, to learn and to change. A frequent speaker and presenter at international conferences, she has authored chapters in several books and over 130 articles that have appeared in North American, Latin American and European business publications. She co-authored the book *Action Reflection Learning: Solving Real Business Problems by Connecting Learning with Earning* , *Circles of Dialogue* , and recently authored *Big Bang Being: Developing the Sustainability Mindset*; based on her doctoral research at Columbia University. Isabel is a Visiting Professor at Fairleigh Dickinson University and Fordham, New York, where she teaches the Sustainability Mindset seminar. In 2009 she co-founded the charitable 501 c (3) organization *Minervas, Women Changing the World* to inspire, support and connect women making a difference. She has an MA in Psychology from the University of Buenos Aires (1984), and earned her MBA from the University of Palermo (1993) and her doctorate at Columbia University (2010).

Ciara Sutton

Ciara Sutton is a Research Fellow and lecturer at the Department of Marketing and Strategy, Stockholm School of Economics, and the Area Principal of Strategy and International Business at SSE Russia. She conducts research on strategy and identity in the venture capital and private equity industry in Sweden, as well as work within the field of cross-cultural management and global leadership. She was awarded the Wallander scholarship for promising young researchers in 2009. She is currently co-authoring the European edition of the strategy textbook *Crafting and Executing Strategy: The Quest for Competitive Advantage*. Ciara has wide experience teaching at undergraduate, masters and executive levels and works regularly as a coach in organizational change projects.

Junko Takagi

Junko Takagi is currently Associate Teaching Professor of Management and Chair of Leadership and Diversity at ESSEC Business School. She did her post graduate studies in Canada and the US and has a PhD in Sociology from Stanford University. Her recent research interests include identity issues in multicultural settings investigating the phenomenon of culture work on the part of multicultural individuals, global leadership focusing on leaders of global teams, and gender issues in the workplace and in particular the role of women in top management on other women in the organization. Junko has contributed to international journals and books on these and other topics, and consults with multinational firms on diversity issues.

Lena Zander

Lena Zander is Professor at the Department of Business Studies, Uppsala University, Sweden, and an Honorary Research Associate at the Victoria University of Wellington, New Zealand. Lena conducts research on cross-cultural management, global leadership, multicultural teams, as well as developing international management theory from a cultural perspective. She has published in books and journals such as *Journal of International Business Studies*, *Journal of World Business*, *International Business Review*, *Scandinavian Journal of Management* and *Advances in International Management*. Lena is currently co-editing a *Management International Review* special issue on 'Leveraging Values in Global Organizations'. She is an associate editor of *Academy of Management Perspectives*, and serves on the editorial review boards of *Journal of World Business*, *Journal of Leadership and Organizational Studies* and the *International Journal of Cross Cultural Management*. Lena has won multiple best-dissertation, -paper and -reviewer awards at AIB, ANZAM and AOM.

Foreword:
Empowering Individuals is the Core of Modern Leadership

New paradigms and ways of thinking are needed, since we cannot solve problems by using the same kind of thinking we used when we created them.

This quote from Albert Einstein can be found in the chairman's statement of last year's World Resources Forum (WRF).[1] It was one of the key recommendations of the forum for establishing a green, resource-efficient economy. It has to be recognized, the statement goes on, that not everything that counts can be counted and not everything that can be counted counts.

Einstein (once a student and professor in Zurich close to where the WRF has its roots) was very much a presence in the Swiss mountain resort Davos, where over 400 experts and policymakers from more than 40 countries met to discuss the current status and future of our natural resources. It was remarkable to hear these words, advocating a blending of 'hard' and 'soft' scientific approaches, in a conference which until then had been concentrating on the global state-of-the-art of engineering and technical sciences.

Sure, the engineers and economists were there with their analyses, data, graphs, projections and trends, and they were appreciated for sharing their insights and for their willingness to discuss. But some other people, such as psychologists, sociologists, philosophers and non-governmental organization (NGO) leaders were applauded as well. They shared a common search for values, emotions, mindsets and underlying driving forces for consumption. And their insights also made it into the final report.

The chairman's statement ends with the usual phrase that the recommendations of the conference are directed towards governments, business and civil society, but then surprisingly adds that this 'also serves as a commitment to ourselves in our capacity as individuals and [hence the] most valuable resources of the planet'.

Last year's conference marked the beginning of a transformation process towards a more holistic gathering where sustainability is not merely seen as a technical issue. In this way it is reflecting what can be seen all over the world, in meetings, workshops, conferences and even official UN negotiations on sustainability, increasingly the behavioural aspect is seen as the missing link between analyses – knowing what is at stake – and implementation – doing something about it.

Obviously, change is needed. For that an individual needs to be aware of a problem, have the intention to solve it and be able to do so. Politicians and business leaders are no different. Knowing this, one finds it in fact remarkable that the two worlds of hard

---

1   Shaping the Future of our Natural Resources – Towards a Green Economy. Highlights of World Resources Forum, Davos, Switzerland, September 19–21, 2011. Can be downloaded from www.worldresourcesforum.org.

and soft skill scientists have met and worked together so seldom. The same is true for educational programmes, which sometimes fail to combine the two disciplines as well.[2]

We have come a long way since 1992, when in Rio de Janeiro the Agenda 21 was born during the UN Conference on Environment and Development.. Ten years later, in 2002, the Johannesburg World Summit on Sustainable Development added 'sustainable consumption' as a major approach to the existing environmental strategies and activity plans, based upon the pioneering work from, among others, the United Nations Environment Programme (UNEP). Some years earlier this small but inventive UN organization had recognized that its successful 'Cleaner Production' programme alone would not do the trick. It is no use to produce clean products if you cannot sell them, if they do not fulfil any of people's real needs, and if you cannot use the underlying driving forces of consumption for exploring far more efficient and effective ways of bringing about quality of life for all. That is how 'sustainable consumption' emerged as a holistic programme which since then has inspired government and business leaders, as well as researchers and NGOs, to start redefining leadership.

Now, again ten years later, in 2012, we can safely say that the world at least has developed the key strategies to make meaningful progress: Sustainable consumption and production, sustainable resource management, circular economy, green economy ... all of them in fact aiming at one and the same thing: Achieving a balance between economic, ecological and social aspects of the ways our society defines and fulfils its needs. Or in other words: Live our lives causing less pollution, using fewer resources, and at the same time securing decent lives not only for ourselves, but also for others.

Achieving this, we increasingly have come to recognize, is not a mechanical technical process, but rather a quest, where one cannot rely too much on models and calculations. Instead one must rely on one's own heart and intuition, and trust the hearts and intuition of others.

It has to be said, though, that politicians have not achieved significant progress over the last decades in implementing at least the basic tools for success: Proper legislation, major tax shifts from labour to resources, and a drastic revision of government procurement programmes. Many business leaders, however, stepped up to the plate. Countless are the initiatives of individual companies, as well as organizations such as WBCSD (World Business Council for Sustainable Development), going far beyond cleaner production or eco-design, and entailing redefinitions of products, product service systems and business models, as well as new ways of communicating with clients and the public, involving them through the social media, and empowering their staff through in-house or external awareness and training programmes.

Business is indeed key for sustainable development. New leadership styles are needed, in which data and calculations are given the place where they belong: At the bottom of the decision-making pyramid. Not automatically leading to conclusions, but rather to be interpreted and handled by human beings, who are so much more than decision-making machines. People have feelings, dreams and intuition to add to the data. Being capable of handling the potential of people, in such a way that the company can be profitable and fulfilling at the same time, is at the basis of success for today's leaders.

---

2   Wäger P. and de Leeuw B., World Resources Forum, Towards a Resource Efficient Green Economy, in GAIA 20/4 (2011).

Companies are no longer judged on financial performance alone by their stakeholders. Increasingly people do want to know where the product they buy is coming from, and how it was made. The world behind the product, as it was once called, keeps emerging and, thanks also to the modern, social media and information and communication technology, those human, 'soft' factors in purchasing decisions are here to stay.

This requires from companies a real human face. This requires also that chief executive officers (CEOs) need to be seen as people, house fathers and mothers with emotions and values, and need to act as such. This requires that leadership styles with exactly those elements – some call it 'inclusive' leadership – need to be developed, recognized, strengthened, taught and practiced.

After all, where at the practical level the old distinction between work and personal life was already blurring – by the increasing use of modern information and communication technology – the same will most likely increasingly apply at the mental level. With all the knowledge we now have about the world behind our company it will increasingly become odd to behave differently when we are at work, as compared to when we are a father or mother, child, brother, sister or friend at home.

Who would nowadays understand such contradiction as the following: We talk on the weekend with our friends, during a walk on the beach, about oil spills, or other ecological or social disasters, agreeing that this all should stop. Why should we forget about all that the moment we enter our office on Monday morning? As if we need to throw a switch, disable our humanity for a while, thinking we should behave and act differently only because we represent a company, which surely can do something about a more sustainable future, but apparently needs to wait for its competitors to do the same.

Sustainability needs to become integrated in all business decisions. Leaders who put their staff at ease and even encourage them to continue behaving as human beings, whilst at work, will without any doubt see that they unlock a vast reservoir of creativity and solutions.[3]

Empowering individuals, stimulating diversity, encouraging out of the box thinking as well as trusting and using feelings and intuition is not an add-on, rather the core of modern leadership which will bring us closer to a sustainable future. This book contributes to this discussion with a rich pallet of thoughts, concepts, methods, views and inspiration.

Bas de Leeuw
Managing Director
World Resources Forum, Switzerland

---

3   This paragraph is based upon a training talk for bank employees, excerpts can be accessed on the web, see http://www.youtube.com/watch?v=E2Q9rgll3jM.

Introduction

STEFAN GRÖSCHL

In 1972, in Stockholm, the United Nations Conference on the Human Environment declared that:

> ... We see around us growing evidence of man-made harm in many regions of the earth: dangerous levels of pollution in water, air, earth and living beings; major and undesirable disturbances to the ecological balance of the biosphere; destruction and depletion of irreplaceable resources; and gross deficiencies, harmful to the physical, mental and social health of man, in the man-made environment, particularly in the living and working environment ... A point has been reached in history when we must shape our actions throughout the world with a more prudent care for their environmental consequences. Through ignorance or indifference we can do massive and irreversible harm to the earthly environment on which our life and well-being depend. Conversely, through fuller knowledge and wiser action, we can achieve for ourselves and our posterity a better life in an environment more in keeping with human needs and hopes (pp. 1–2).

What has happened since 1972? How have societies reacted to these warnings and appeals, and in particular, how have private businesses addressed ecological and socio-economic challenges and *uncertainties* throughout the past 40 years? Many organizations and commentators would respond positively – referring to technological advancements, economic value creation and the expansion of material consumption in societies.

While these developments are undeniable and significant for humankind and its well-being, progress has been inequitably distributed and has had profound environmental and societal implications: The United Nations Environmental Program (UNEP) (2011) concluded that 'overexploitation, pollution, land-use change, and loss of biodiversity rose toward the top of the list of major international environmental concerns'. According to the World Meteorological Organization's 2011 report (WMO, 2011) in 2010, global CO_2 and methane emissions have reached record highs since pre-industrial time. With no significant system innovations and instead, conducting business 'as usual', future usage of natural resources and emissions will exceed 'all measures of available resources and assessments of limits to the capacity to absorb impacts' (UNEP, 2011: 29). According to the United Nations' Millennium Project, in 2006 more than one billion people globally lived on less than one US dollar per day. The inequitable distribution of wealth and income poverty is not restricted to underdeveloped or developing countries. In developed countries such as the US, 'the richest one percent of all Americans have a greater net worth than the bottom 90 percent combined' (Kristof, 2011). Beside income poverty, globally 270 million children suffer from long-term malnourishment and micronutrient deficiency. Every 3.6 seconds a person dies of starvation and the large majority are children under the age of five (Millennium Project, 2006). Despite all warnings and appeals throughout the past 40 years, it seems that never have we faced as many serious, imminent challenges for the future of human well-being as we do today.

The large-scale and often irreversible, environmental and socio-economic impacts on the well-being of human kind and its future generations require immediate and significant policy and behavioural changes of all stakeholders. At the very core of most of these actions and changes will be private businesses. Due to their size, global presence, wealth and/or innovative nature, multinational corporations have the lobbying and bargaining power that can influence policymakers and consumer behaviours when addressing the numerous socio-economic and ecological challenges. Business leaders will have to pose 'uncomfortable' questions about their future roles and that of their businesses within these critical times of *uncertainty* and insecurity. Can we continue to do 'business as usual' and can we apply a 'one-size-fits-all' approach in a world as *diverse*, complex and *ambiguous*?

Business leaders will have to reconsider the rules of the game, and to take into account not only economic but also socio-environmental parameters in order to address the needs of a world that is constantly evolving and thus, by definition, *unpredictable*. While many business leaders promote corporate socially responsible actions to address socio-environmental challenges, at an organizational level these initiatives remain marginalized and are not centred within the core of the business, and at global scale social purpose-driven actions have been embryonic, mostly voluntary, and often have been a disguise for their market and image-driven needs. Responding to the socio-environmental challenges and *unpredictability* meaningfully requires intelligences that enable managers to tackle the challenges of adaptation and change, and to develop a sustainable, lasting and consistent managerial approach. Creating enduring links between socio-environmental and economic activities requires a new model of responsible leadership that addresses conflicting issues and that brings together dimensions that are incompatible within existing paradigms.

In *Uncertainty, Diversity and the Common Good: Changing Norms and New Leadership Paradigms*, contributors from leading academic institutions around the world, from perspectives that embrace philosophy; sociology; psychology; ecological and environmental economics; management; and entrepreneurship, discuss different models of responsible global leadership. Contributors argue that we need new paradigms that will allow us to create continuity and meaning in times of change and the chapters in this book indicate what these new paradigms might look like, with particular regard to the issue of *diversity* as an asset with which to confront uncertainty. The chapters in this book tell of leaders working with *diversity* to create social change and new visions of leadership that are impacting social and cultural norms. This all leads to a discussion of the nature and diversity of leadership itself which will be helpful to academic researchers and higher-level students, as well as policymakers and practitioners.

In Part One, two chapters set the context by discussing the meaning of *responsible* as part of a new leadership model or paradigm, and the conceptualization of the *common good*. Bibard discusses the common good as understood by ancient Aristotelian philosophy versus modern philosophy. He elucidates how a *common good* may become possible again in the context of a global world and the legitimacy of profit-making in business. The author finds that the generally accepted prevalence of private interests hinders the notion of a possible shared fundamental interest in a *common good*. Bibard identifies three main reasons to be at the origin of the currently taken-for-granted legitimacy of profit-making. Through a detour to the birth of modern economics as such, he shows that individual self-interest is at the root of any economic calculation. The author concludes with a philosophical enquiry about the notion of *common good* and what it could consist of in today's world. In the first part of his chapter Capaldi looks at the *common good* from the Lockean Liberty Narrative (Anglo-American business world) and the Rousseau/Marx equality narrative (European business community). In the second part Capaldi discusses American Exceptionalism and how a particular religious and cultural context informs business practice and achieves the *common good*.

Part Two and its chapters focus on the conceptualizing of global leadership and social responsibility. Sutton and Zander find a great complexity in the responsibility of multinational firms when addressing global corporate responsibility, as global companies exist in a matrix of institutional structures, organizational interests and societal norms. Reconciling this matrix of oftentimes conflicting and overlapping contextual domains of corporate social responsibility (CSR) is the responsibility of global leaders, the authors argue. This chapter conceptually outlines how CSR domains in varying national and cultural contexts can be reconciled by global leaders, who act as boundary spanners, bridge makers and blenders. Hackett addresses the role of corporate leaders in furthering the social agenda, and suggests that the shifts in the global governance structure and the rise of the corporation as a global leader has inspired or required corporate leaders to assume the mantle of social responsibility and 'fill the gaps' voided by national governments. Based on the premise that leaders are assuming responsibility beyond mere profit maximization, the author questions the motivation for this role change and suggests that there is a delicate balance between the corporate objective and profit maximization. The chapter ends on a discussion of the question why corporate leaders should actually be more responsible. In their chapter de Anca, Aragón, and Concepcíon Galdón develop a conceptual framework of diversity innovation in complexity. The authors argue that leaders in today's fluid organizations should use the power of diversity to promote innovation by leveraging the formal and informal connections that are created within the companies in which they operate. The authors examine the hypothesis that identification flows from the individual to the organization and vice versa through various communities, voluntarily chosen or assigned externally, which each individual feels connected with. This connection occurs on the basis of identity categories acting as affinity elements that are different for each individual and group relationship. Drawing on Akerlof's statement that the identification of workers with the company increases profitability, this chapter explores the mechanisms through which identity flows in the different cultural contexts.

In Part Three the contributions shift the focus from conceptualizing the key themes and terms of this book to the more applied aspects and implications of global leadership and social responsibility. In his chapter, Gupta uses three models of socially responsible leadership to discuss organizational and societal conditions that are likely to influence how the dimensions associated with these models are implemented. Based on this framework, Gupta presents a leadership case study from India, and analyzes how it has transposed dimensions of socially responsible leadership while navigating the pluralistic complexities in a global world.

Takagi and Hong investigate global leadership as it applies to the management of global teams, and focus on team leaders' perceptions of teamwork in a global context and their experiences leading global teams. Based on a qualitative study of the leaders of Cosmo, a French multinational firm, the authors analyze team leaders' perceptions of teams, teamwork and cultural diversity, and their experiences leading global teams. Team leaders at Cosmo are faced with the multiple daily challenges of working with cultural diversity and trying to ensure team performance. The authors look at what are the perceptions of leaders of global teams regarding cultural diversity, its contribution to team performance, and the skills needed to deal with cultural diversity on a daily basis.

Part Four and its two chapters provide perspectives from stakeholders such as consumers and employees. Norris discusses how corporate leaders can address wasteful consumption and the maximization of consumption efficiency by engaging and encouraging consumers to make changes in their behaviour. The author introduces the concept of handprinting, which presents a means for true leaders in social responsibility to engage consumers – and their own employees – in a positively-framed approach to sustainable consumption, which has the potential to bring transformative change. In his second contribution to this book, Bibard argues that due to the current worldwide crisis, leadership may confront serious difficulties based on the lack of confidence and trust in organizations. If companies are to manage crises in times of uncertainty, they urgently need reciprocal trust between their employees, managers and leaders. Bibard traces back the main components of leadership to some of their historical and philosophical roots to identify how to favour internal confidence in organizations.

In the final part of this book, two contributors address the duty of educators to develop and train future managers and leaders with a more responsible mindset, and with the abilities to deal with the often seemingly conflicting and incompatible challenges of expanding economic activities and producing social progress, while reducing the rate of resource use and the environmental impact of such use (decoupling). In her chapter, Rimanoczy describes exploring the processes that business leaders go through as they learn to identify and champion sustainability initiatives. In this exercise, leaders describe the knowledge and support they found, and identify the mindset, competencies and attitudes that helped them in that learning process. Understanding all this might help educators to promote the concept of sustainability and to develop leaders to champion appropriate initiatives. De Carlo's chapter focuses on water management seminars, with the knowledge based strongly on practice, and moving away from the traditional focus on theory and methods. The author's constructivist teaching approach provides students with the ability to formulate their own knowledge and methods of water management, and their own leadership models.

I would like to thank all the writers for their enriching contributions, and our Chair partners Deloitte and L'Oréal for their support. I would also like to thank Joel Bothello for his contributions and work throughout the formatting process. Last but not least a huge 'Danke Schön' to Merle Piest for her great organizational abilities to make this book happening!

References

UNEP 2011. *Decoupling Natural Resource Use and Environmental Impacts from Economic Growth.* A Report of the Working Group on Decoupling to the International Resource Panel. Fischer-

Kowalski, M., Swilling, M., von Weizsäcker, E.U., Ren, Y., Moriguchi, Y., Crane, W., Krausmann, F., Eisenmenger, N., Giljum, S., Hennicke, P., Romero Lankao, P., Siriban Manalang, A.

United Nations Conference on the Human Environment. 1972. Available at: http://www.unep.org/Documents.Multilingual/Default.asp?documentid=97&articleid=1503 (accessed July 2012).

World Meteorological Organization. 2011. *Greenhouse Gas Concentrations Continue Climbing*. Press Release 934.

United Nations' Millennium Project. 2006. *Fast Facts: The Faces of Poverty*. E3-1.

Kristof, N.D. 2011. America's Primal Scream. *New York Times Sunday Review*, 15 October, p. 15.

PART I

Conceptualizing the Common Good

1 Business and the Common Good: Some Fundamental Issues

LAURENT BIBARD

Introduction

Observing that globalization leads to hyper competition is quite trivial. Observing that competition leads to companies making decisions which potentially endanger the notion of the common good becomes trivial as well. After years of the belief that capitalism had overcome all possible internal as well as external contradictions, the question of the extent to which companies – private companies – contribute or damage the common good again looms ahead. The renewal of the questioning has been prepared by the emergence of ethics, sustainability and corporate social responsibility (CSR) topics in business. As a result, nobody can look indifferently at these topics anymore.

Nevertheless, a second preoccupying issue looms ahead. The question of what the common good consists of cannot be avoided. As states are submitted to financial evaluations, as a tendency of making war for scarce resources intensifies, as energy and water are dangerously less and less available, the way of conceptualizing 'common good' becomes no longer evident.

Strangely enough, companies and people's private interest – which no doubt contribute to the resource scarcity that is a function of human desires – contribute to a situation where the notion of 'common good' is objectively in question. In other words, the dynamic which endangers the notion of common good, simultaneously makes the notion of common good uncertain if not dubious. One could expect that the dangers provoked by the uncontrolled increase of mercenary behaviour would favour a parallel defence of a common good and public values, such as the defence of ethics, sustainability and CSR. This is only partially true. Another consequence of the increasingly taken-for-granted legitimacy of private interests is a similarly taken-for-granted carelessness about the notion of a possible shared fundamental interest in a 'common good'. In practice, people lack more and more education about the possibility and relevance of a defence of such a notion. Some of them try to defend the theoretical and practical relevance of the notion and its aim.

As in management, it is necessary to take some distance to evaluate how best to tackle the problem. I do so by: 1) starting from a brief glance at economics since the seventies, 2) making a detour through the birth of modern economics as such, 3) enlarging definitively the scope of our questioning through a philosophical enquiry about the notion of 'common good'.

I. On the Recent History of Economics and Management: The Legitimacy of Profit-making

Three main reasons may be identified as the origin of the current taken-for-granted legitimacy of profit-making: The first is the continuously deepening economic crisis since 1973. The second is the fall of the communist regime and the end of the Cold War, and the third is a theoretical statement on profit-making legitimacy. Before giving these reasons, it is worth underscoring the fundamental legitimacy of profit-making considered apart from its current dominant increase as alluded to in our introduction. Such a fundamental legitimacy may be put the following way: The objective of people taking care of poor people should never be that everybody becomes poor. It should be to enrich everybody. In other words, it is not by getting poorer that people may possibly contribute to others' enrichment. Even considering an increasing scarcity of worldwide resources, the means for a worldwide stabilized economy do not depend on a general impoverishment. At any rate, the question of what being rich and poor means needs to be discussed.

1) A CONTINUOUSLY DEEPENING ECONOMIC CRISIS

The consideration of the economic crisis depends on two circumstances which make quite uncertain our understanding of it: The so-called crisis started due to a petrol cost increase, which endangered the Western countries stability. The contemporary worldwide economic crisis was originally a Western crisis, provoked by a (geo-) political decision. Second, the crisis was all the more significant in that it followed a quite 'naïve' long-lasting growth period.

The emergence of a worldwide economic crisis which has lasted since the 1970s depended on a previous naïve sentiment that economics could grow without limits. Such a naïvety was of course conditioned by the growth duration. Any stable situation creates its own evidence and tacitly admitted paradigms. The Western understanding of its economical, political and moral legitimacy predominantly depended on its success and domination.

Such a taken-for-granted understanding was intensified by the sentiment of legitimacy provoked by the Cold War. Having an enemy always reinforces the sentiment of being right. Being right 'against' is much stronger than being right for the sake of being right. The question of what 'being right for the sake of being right' means is certainly quite difficult to answer. This would mean answering to the question of what does this 'natural right' consists of.

Be that as it may, the enormous surprise caused by the petrol prices certainly created the conditions for a loss of naïvety. Since this political decision, the world would never remain the same as it had previously – as it used to be depending on the point of view of the most important Western country, the United States of America. The very moment when Western countries lost their peace, a possibility of awareness appeared.

2) THE END OF THE COLD WAR

This possibility was nevertheless lost quite soon. The end of the Cold War contributed to an even more deepened naïvety. The collapse of the most powerful and unique enemy of the West, the Soviet Union regime, overwhelmingly evidenced the triumph of Western values, rights and relevance. One way or another, people more or less consciously – and most often rather unconsciously – integrated the taken for granted legitimacy of the capitalist/Western system – despite the radical crisis intensification. A bit less than 20 years after the Berlin Wall fell, the 2008 financial crisis made clear that nothing fundamental had been solved by and through the end of the Cold War sometimes understood as the End of History (Fukuyama 1992). In other words, history was not over. In fact, something else had been preparing, which would certainly open again the doors of an uncertain future. Such a reopening was announced on September 11, 2001.

3) A THEORETICAL STATEMENT ON PROFIT-MAKING

Let us take some distance from the facts and turbulences of history. A statement of outstanding importance was published in the *New York Times* in 1970. This statement came from the economist Milton Friedman, stating: 'The Social Responsibility of Business Is To Increase Its Profit.' Surely Friedman's argument is at least partially – if not absolutely – right. The first fundamental and inevitable sustainability people must aim at is the corporate one, if they are to support environmental, social and political sustainability. As long as the worldwide system remains a capitalist one, the first duty of corporations is to last as long they can. The duty of society is then to observe their sustainability, and to ratify their failure when they go bankrupt – that is all. At any rate, corporations are necessary for producing services and goods, and it is an inescapable fact that they are the most important, if not the most decisive, global economic actors. Considered in this perspective, their minimum social responsibility is to increase their profit.

The Friedman statement nevertheless provokes a kind of a confusion due to the understanding it imposes on economics. The clear separation between economics and politics and the dominant support of a profit-oriented economy radically favours an indifferent if not cynical behaviour towards the notion of a possible common good. Politicians are accountable for their actions – for their intentions and for the consequences of their actions. Politicians are the ones to make a possible common good relevant and effective. Businessmen could legitimately not care less about politics.

This might be theoretically true. Grounded on an orthodox theoretical understanding of economics, the subsequent clear separation of economics and politics conforms to a necessary clarity concerning the distinction between private and public interests. If humans are to defend the notion and reality of private property, they need to separate clearly economics from politics and vice-versa.

Such a separation may be theoretically solid. Kant nevertheless quite emphatically stated that what may be true in theory does not necessarily apply in practice: The statement is but evident (Kant 1970). What as a researcher Milton Friedman made public is a theoretical statement; one which was published in a highly important American mass media – a highly important American newspaper distributed worldwide. The Friedman statement had at least slight practical consequences. These practical consequences may be summed up by saying that most businessmen were ready to hear that their unique social responsibility was to increase their profit. They were ready to limit their responsibility to their egoistic interest. Since the Friedman statement, businessmen and businesswomen would aim at increasing their profit exclusively, on the basis of an outstanding scholar's benediction. Before I go further, let us ask to what extent scholars should question the relevance of a publication before making public their statements. The answer to this question can certainly not be a naïve one.

II. On the Origins of Modern Economics

Were we to understand globalization in a relevant way, we should for now on get rid of the very first possible interpretation of it: Western culture spreading worldwide. This interpretation was certainly true for a while – perhaps as long as a few centuries. Yet globalization must now be understood as a tension between Western culture and the 'others', if not more radically as a tension between some principles and attitudes respectively grounded on the assumption that humans can do everything in this world, and on the other hand, that they cannot; 'doing everything' here means having the world under control, for the sake of humanity. Such an assumption must be traced back to the emergence of the European humanist paradigm. The European humanism is understandable as the decision to take control of 'nature' instead of 'God', for the very sake of human life (Bibard 2005). Humanism became an at least partially worldwide basis for the current globalization dynamic for two main reasons: 1) It was initially politically driven, as exemplified by colonization, and 2) It contained deep human or universal roots which made it somewhat fascinating for people confronted by it with respect to science and technologies.[1] One of the aspects of it which grounds the contemporary liberal approach of humans is the related political philosophy. In other words, the current understanding and shaping of economic life is, for now, grounded on some fundamental philosophical assumptions concerning humans' political or collective life. This is particularly the case for Friedman's statement on CSR.

An ancient understanding of economics made it basically dependent on the family life. The etymology of 'economy' (oiko-nomos), traces back to the household, traditionally mastered by women. Economics are naturally no longer limited to such an understanding. But a specific radical change occurred during the so-called 'Renaissance' and the period surrounding it, when new bases for the understanding of politics were made clear. These bases were particularly made clear by the philosopher Thomas Hobbes, who presented his understanding of politics at least in two books, *De Cive* and *Leviathan* (Hobbes 1982, 1985).

Regarding the latter text in particular, what Hobbes makes clear on politics is the following: Humans do not spontaneously live together, or collectively. Rather, they live as individuals, isolated or separated from each other, and they long for goods and resources. Such a life is deeply conditioned by fear and desire – the fear of a violent death and the desire for a long and peaceful life – admittedly reproduced. As humans sooner or

---

1   On this aspect of the beginning 'humanism', see Descartes 1956, Part VI; on a thorough understanding of sciences and technologies from both a theoretical and an empirical perspective, cf Latour 2004 and 1988. For an economical approach of sciences and innovations, cf Callon 1992 and Freeman and Soete 1997.

later aim at the same means (food, females, land and so on[2]), they sooner or later fight for life, fighting against scarcity (Hobbes 1985), but as well fighting for recognition. Humans are full of 'vanity', they want to be recognized by other humans depending on the way they understand themselves (Hobbes 1985). Sooner or later, humans become aware of the general war which characterizes their spontaneous world. The 'natural state' of humanity is a state of a kind of 'civil' war – apart from the fact that any 'civil' state does not exist. The 'natural' humans' state is but a violent existence, based on everyone's right if not duty to live, and to defend himself/herself for that unique purpose – the mere struggle for life.

Added to them being full of desire, fear and vanity, humans are rational (Hobbes 1985). They sooner or later have the sentiment that they should get rid of a continuously fighting life. Not only is such a life dangerous, but it is as well radically uncertain, and last but not least, it represents a huge waste of time. They decide to delegate their right and strength for defence to a unique entity – the 'Leviathan', which will become the modern 'State', defined by the very monopoly of the use of violence. The Leviathan is defined as the only entity, structure, human or assembly of humans entitled to define as well as to apply the rules dedicated to a collectively secure and peaceful life. The fundamental convention made by humans in order to dispose of the necessity to fight in order to live defines the first and original 'social contract'.

Beyond all its possible nuances, the modern understanding of political life is grounded on the notion of a previous and constitutive 'social contract'. Such an understanding of the roots of political life has a wide range of consequences among which are the following ones:

1. The notion of 'natural state' is actually an artefact: No philosopher ever pretended such a human condition ever existed empirically.
2. The notion nevertheless makes room for an anthropology which includes as its core content the modern understanding of rationality. This modern understanding is actually an economical one.
3. The economical understanding of human rationality does not necessarily involve a notion of any common good for the sake of a common good as such.
4. The modern understanding of politics based on the artefact of 'natural state' is future-oriented.
5. The current issues on the tension between business and common good may radically result from such an understanding.

Let us consider briefly these points.

1. THE 'NATURAL STATE' NOTION IS AN ARTEFACT

When describing the human 'natural state', Hobbes makes clear that he considers humans as individuals, equal to each other, free, and rational. Contrary to what occurred in the former Aristotelian understanding of politics which Hobbes opposes, humans are not

---

2   Looking for a female results from the vital male instinct of reproduction. Such an instinct may be considered feminine as well as masculine. The differentiation between male and female has no sense on Hobbes' political philosophy perspective, despite an implicit 'male' understanding of the world. I present a brief analysis of this issue in my forthcoming 'For a Contemporary Problematisation of Sexuality' (Bibard 2012).

any more supposed to relate to each other through various so-called 'natural' bounds.[3] In Hobbes's perspective, humans are considered independently of their physical features, for example independent of their sex, ethnic group and age. This is of course not made that clear in Hobbes's writings. It is nevertheless the fundamental Hobbes assumption, which is particularly visible when Hobbes argues about humans' 'natural' equality (Hobbes 1985). Let us keep in mind the main stake of Hobbes's assumption: Getting rid of 'nature'. Hobbes talks all the more of a supposed 'state of nature', or 'natural state', that the 'state' he depicts as being the original one is radically at odds with an intuitive spontaneous understanding of humans. Would humans be spontaneously rational, equal and free individuals, there would be no need for any political organization for their collective existence. 'Anarchy' understood as a 'gods' democracy' on Rousseau point of view,[4] would immediately be possible.

2. ON RATIONALITY AND ECONOMICS

The dynamics through which humans shift from the so-called initial 'natural state' to 'society' or to the 'social contract' is based on a universally shared individual rational choice. Rationality is at first concerned as driving the sentiment that life is too costly: defending one's interests is too much of a burden for individuals who spend their whole life struggling for the sake of sustainability and fleeing from violent death. The possibility to delegate one's rights to live – and subsequently one's duty to defend oneself – to a third, impartial and disinterested judge, which would play the role of the Leviathan, is based on a calculation. This calculation results from a comparison of delegation versus the related costs of a spontaneously given 'natural' life. Rationality is involved as soon as individuals are supposed to understand that they can, at any rate, make the choice of delegating their power to a third judge if everybody does the same. Would an individual make such a choice remaining the only one in doing so, or someone among some others, the others would sooner or later submit if not enslave them. A necessary condition for a possible social contract is that everybody makes it at once.

   The individual's self-understanding is at the root of any economical calculation. Hobbes grounds his understanding of politics on a new understanding of humans' 'rationality', envisaged in the context of his previous notion of the 'natural state'. 'Rationality' had previously been approached on the basis of theology, as the human capacity to understand the whole – and ultimately 'God'. Rationality will from now on be approached on the basis of an individual self-interest. Politics will definitely be understood as the servant of individual lives. This traces back to John Locke's understanding of Hobbes's political philosophy. This is the core understanding which interests us in the context of the questioning about the relations between business and the common good.

   Before shifting to the next point, let's remind ourselves that another interpretation actually remains possible in the horizon of the Hobbes's understanding of the so-called 'social contract'. One of Hobbes's intentions was to help resolve the chaotic English civil war. Hobbes's intention was to lay the foundations of a new political stability. He

---

3   Such spontaneous bounds were taken for granted by the previous political philosophy, which is not only a Western philosophical option, but rather a universal one. Exceptions are quite scarce and deserve close attention; cf Christianism and Buddhism for instance. It is of some importance to have in mind that Christianism is at the root of Hobbes thought.

4   On Rousseau's opinion, democracy is only possible for gods (on this crucial point, cf Strauss 1947).

thought this could be reached by making clear the legitimacy of the State. In Hobbes's context, such a legitimacy could not be reached except through people identifying themselves with the authority. Such identification would radically be guaranteed making clear that people are ultimately at the root of their own States. The modern wide range of expressions and aspects of tyrannies and dictatorships directly result from Hobbes's political understanding of an unquestionable State sovereignty. In other words, the contemporaneous possibility of extremes and extremisms – be them on one hand 'liberal' or resulting on the other from a priority given to the power of the State – rests on the 'modern' understanding of politics as established by Hobbes.

This interpretation of Hobbes's political philosophy consequences makes even more urgent a clarification of our understanding of the notion of a possible 'common good'.

3. ON THE NOTION OF A POSSIBLE 'COMMON GOOD'

Our questioning of the relation between business and the common good is done so in the context of an intensification of worldwide liberalism, parallel to increasing claims against it. The increasing claims against liberalism are claims against the enrichment of some people who play with the financial system. Freed from any internal or external regulation, the worldwide financial system makes room for an exclusively profit-oriented logic, which sooner or later contradicts the industrial and service systems. Economics understood as the whole sphere of agro-industry, industry and services as well as the financial-related system is potentially if not structurally self-contradictory. This self-contradiction is significant, exemplified through the enrichment of some very happy few while the vast majority of humans get poorer and poorer. The claims against globalization understood as the triumph of a worldwide liberalism (Fukuyama 1992), is a claim for a renewed common good – versus the 'common' good exclusively dedicated to a very happy few.

The difficulty is that this claim is itself sooner or later based on Locke's understanding of Hobbes (Locke 1690). The Locke understanding of Hobbes laid the foundation for modern liberalism. Modern liberalism's main statement is that the State's unique and highest objective and missions are to defend individuals' private interests, represented by their property. The modern liberalism is sooner or later economical (Strauss 1953). Economics understood as the basis of politics makes room for the spontaneous defence of private interest; thus there is a huge difficulty in approaching the notion of a possible common interest, if not a common good. The notion of a possible common good is implicitly abandoned by the modern political science established by Hobbes and his successors.[5] The original meaning of 'politics' concerns collective life for the sake of collective life (Aristotle 1998). One of the most important consequences of the emergence

---

5   It is worth taking into account that the former 'ancient political *philosophy*' was replaced by the 'modern political *sciences*'. The replacement of 'philosophy' by the 'sciences' means a replacement of a normative approach of politics by a structural or a 'technical' one which aims at remaining 'neutral' in order to guarantee its objectivity. The difference between philosophy and sciences is that sciences may be of some help for tyrants as well as for democrats. In other words, while making room for an intensified and legitimate private life for the sake of a private life is correlated to the considerations of politics as a technical issue – the ultimate objective of which is to make room for people's private choices, orientations, options – political philosophy may look dangerous, because it aims sooner or later at telling people how they *should* live. Modern political sciences are dangerous because they potentially address the technical problem of how to govern for the sake of any kind of governor, and in the name of their necessary axiological neutrality. The axiological neutrality of modern sciences is correlated to the understanding of humans as essentially free (cf Klein 1992 in the horizon of Klein 1986. On mathematics as correlated to history and their evolution, cf Kline 1980).

of the modern political science is to prevent people from accessing an understanding of what 'politics' means. People's claims against the worldwide spread of liberalism are still based on individual interests. People do not claim intentionally for a common good. They claim for an extended good for their own peculiar situations. This claim is, in the current global context, of utmost legitimacy, yet far away from an awareness of what a possible 'common good' would consist of.

4. A FUTURE-ORIENTED ANTHROPOLOGY

The above-mentioned situation is all the more problematic, given that the involved anthropology in the 'natural state' approach of the origins of politics is actually future-oriented. Whatever the reasons, human equality, freedom, individuality and rationality are from now on claimed as characterizing humans as they *should* be considered. Such a consideration would guarantee a universal and reciprocal recognition of each individual, independently of their sex, ethnic group, age and so on; in other words independently of any presupposed 'nature'. This anthropology is the anthropology at the roots of the Western notion of 'human rights'. It is a future-oriented anthropology, which is supposed to represent what History should drive towards (Kant 1963). Strikingly enough, when making up their minds for the original covenant, humans are supposed to overcome the difficulty related to this anthropology. They are supposed to overcome violence, scarcity, continuous struggle for life, in other words 'natural' civil wars. Violence, scarcity, continuous struggle for life, 'natural' civil wars seem to be necessarily related to the anthropology of the human rights – would the accomplishment of humanity as resulting in a universal agreement on the modern anthropology provoke and drive humans to a ceaseless worldwide civil war?

5. THE CONTEMPORARY PROBLEMATIC

The above question is neither secondary nor provocative for the sake of being provocative. The above question is driven by the need of an understanding of the conditions for a possibly current common good. The aforementioned tension between the two main possible interpretations of Hobbes political philosophy allow us to discover to what extent our situation is delicate. Our contemporary access to a notion of a possible common good is mostly prevented by the inheritance of the modern, fundamental political science paradigms.

We thus need a further step in our enquiry to grasp what and how a common good may become possible again in the context of a global world. Strikingly enough, the very period when the world technically becomes the anticipated and aimed at 'global village', the notion of a 'common good' has potentially disappeared from our understanding on the whole.

III. On Politics and 'Common Good' As Such

The current state-of-the-art of our enquiry is that business and a possible 'common good' are fundamentally contradictory. Making business – or profit-making – is frontally opposed to any notion of a common good. It is worth underscoring that in many if not all traditions, the notion of any 'good' involves the notion of being 'common' or shared. Nothing which would be considered as 'the good' could concern a separated part of the whole. If any notion of 'good' is to show relevance and signification, it necessarily concerns the whole, or is common to everything here and now. The 'good' is necessarily a 'common good'. Thus, any human activity or project aiming at helping a private, or separated interest, is necessarily a 'bad' one. Business and 'goodness' are separated as are evil and good.

This is nevertheless certainly false. For how could the 'good' remain separated from the bad or from evil, without suffering – as separated – thus becoming itself bad or evil? The 'common' good necessarily includes the possibility of any 'internal'; here, the possibility of private interest and business. Business is a part of the common good. This perspective on (common) good and evil is far from being absurd and isolated. The most important Western philosophers such as Aristotle and Hegel defended an understanding of economics and business grounded on it (Aristotle 1998, Hegel 1991, cf Hegel 1953). In such a perspective, separation – the defence of private interest for the sake of private interest – is part of the whole. It is as such an inevitable aspect of the whole, and as far as we are concerned, of any public or 'political' life. A political life which would not make room for a minimum of private life and private interests would even be radically contradictory to the very possibility of any meaningful public life (Plato 1968) [6]. The question is of course to what extent should politics make room to private interests as such, or to what extent should business be taken into account for a simultaneous and balanced understanding of the common good.

Such a question represents by itself a revolution towards the contemporary admitted question on business and the common good – because the point of departure of the question is not business as taken for granted, but the common good. Taking for granted that people should look after the common good previous to any other kind of preoccupation, objectives and projects presuppose a dominance of the common good on any possible private interest or profit-making. Such a presupposition was the dominant one until the emergence of modern political science.

Ancient political philosophy contrasted to modern political science may be featured on the basis of the following structural assumption. This structural assumption is that humans spontaneously – or 'naturally' – belong to communities, and that their lives are naturally collective if not political (Aristotle 1998). On an ancient political philosophy perspective, collective life is the normal, natural, spontaneous life of humans, who are always 'already' embedded in roles and social games, playing determined parts such as father, employee, statesman, wife, child and so on. In Aristotelian words, humans are spontaneously politic, or 'political animals' (Aristotle 1998). In such a context, the 'common good' is understood as the good of the 'city' or the political good for the sake of itself, whereas 'business' or private interests and the extent to which they are respected and preserved depend on political decisions. In the ancient political philosophy perspective, the extent to which private interests are free results from a political option, whereas in the modern political science perspective, the whole political life is sooner or later considered as the servant of private interests.

---

6   In his *Republic*, Plato makes clear the conditions for a public or just life considered for the sake of itself (Plato 1968). One of his conclusions is that such a republic or such a regime is potentially tyrannical, due to its radical transparency. An 'absolutely' just regime certainly could be radically unjust or humanly impossible.

THE ANCIENT POLITICAL PHILOSOPHY PERSPECTIVE AND ITS DIFFICULTIES

The above-mentioned ancient political philosophy perspective is far from being isolated. It actually represents the general approach of politics before the emergence of the modern one. Politics, or the mere possibility of any common good, is approached on the basis of 'natural' life, understood as a shared heterosexual life. Male and female connections, making possible the human reproduction and existence, are supposed to represent and shape the basis of any further bigger collective human entity (from families to worldwide globalization through clans, villages, cities, countries, empires and so on). In other words, sex (understood as heterosexuality leading to reproduction), is considered as the root of politics. This approach of politics is inseparable from a series of related observations, assumptions and consequences which deserve some attention.

A WORLD WITH INTERNAL DIFFERENCES

In Aristotle's perspective – which is here the main reference – humans are not supposed to be equal to each other. In the Aristotelian point of view, women are inferior to men, as slaves are to masters and children to parents (Aristotle 1998). It is nevertheless quite less known that such hierarchies in the human world, even if 'natural' or inescapable, are never as stable as believed. In Aristotle's opinion, it is sometimes extremely difficult to assert surely that somebody is inferior to somebody else – a slave to a master or a woman to a man (cf Aristotle 1998). Naturally, such a difficulty makes room for reasonable doubts, even if this does not appear that clearly in Aristotle writings.[7] Doubt does not concern the reality and relevance of hierarchies, but who is inferior to whom, in which circumstances, to what extent and how long.

   This may still be put another way. Humans need authority. They are to be driven or to drive. The question is who is to be driven and who is to drive others, and in which circumstances. In other words, leadership is necessary, but the answer to the question about who should lead whom when, how and how long cannot be answered easily. Giving an answer to this question depends on practice as well as on theory (Aristotle 1985). Surely enough, humans need sometimes to lead and sometimes to be led. This may vary depending on people, on the steps of life, on social and organizational circumstances. But the necessity for leaders is not questionable.

THE NEED FOR EDUCATION

The above point is all the more important in that it concerns one of the most important human phenomena: Education. One of the most problematic long-term consequences of the modern political science perspective is that, given that humans are spontaneously equal to each other, education is ultimately not justified. For on the basis of what privilege would an adult educate a child? What sense would the notion of education make when admitting that children are spontaneously equal to adults? A series or arguments may ground a doubt concerning the relevance of education: Surely adults do not show the duly required maturity to pretend educating children; they show themselves as problematic, incapable to rule people, with perverted behaviour and so on. In other words adults are

---

7   On this aspect of Aristotle presenting his thoughts, cf Strauss 1952, cf Cropsey and Strauss 1987.

but old children, tyrants and unaware people. The adults' incapacity to run the world may be an added argument in favour of asserting children's equality to them, and the establishment of laws which aim at protecting them from their parents. It is nevertheless absolutely indispensable that children be educated and be helped to acquire the right skills and maturity to participate in shaping their world in due time. Again here, the question may be asked: To what extent is education needed, and what does it mean? What is the kind of spontaneous strength children have, and what must be given to them in order to make them the most free and responsible – taken for granted these objectives are the right ones for an education?

A REGULATED ECONOMY

A third – but not least – point is made by Aristotle in the very first book of his *Politics*. Economy and finance should be maintained under control, due to the otherwise absurd development of money-making for the exclusive sake of money-making (cf Aristotle 1998). Money-making is necessary to ensure the right working of the household. Economics are considered by Aristotle on the basis of the etymology of 'economics': The laws or rules of the household. Economics concern humans' private life. The private life is limited to the family life. Otherwise, humans live in the 'city', which is concerned by politics. On the basis of the very comparison of fathers to kings (Aristotle 1998), Aristotle thoroughly distinguishes their respective roles, perimeters and ways. Should a king try to govern like a father, his reign would be a tyranny. Not because of running the city as a father – fathers' authority or leadership is not necessarily tyrannical – but because public and private lives are not the same. Public life needs an adapted leadership which is 'naturally' superior to the private leadership. Such superiority results at least from the size of the governed or ruled entity. A family is necessarily smaller than a city, a city concerns the common good, a family the private one. A city cannot be ruled on the basis of a family government.[8] On the other hand, political life should itself be maintained under control. Aristotle is supposed to have bred Alexander the Great, and Aristotle was radically opposed to Alexander the Great's ambition and conquests. Aristotle thought a city should remain small if it is to remain governable. Politicians should remain moderate. The whole Aristotle book on politics is dedicated to a description of a moderate policy.[9]

Private life should be maintained under control of temperate politicians. Temperate politicians should control money-making, as money-making for the sake of money-making is sooner or later not only absurd, but dangerous. Money-making for the sake of money-making makes people forget about the ultimate ends of action. Action should be of some use for the common good, and the common good should be understood on the basis of a rigorous analysis of humans' ends. Such an analysis depends on an understanding of ethics. Money-making for the sake of money-making makes humans forget about the

---

8   Cf Plato's *Republic* on the qualitative difference between Books II to IV on one hand and V to VII on the other hand ; cf the Aristophanes' intention in his *Assembly of Women* presenting the new regime as a unique family regime (Aristophanes 1997).

9   Cf 'Aristotle', in *History of Political Philosophy* (Cropsey and Strauss 1987). The description of the 'perfect regime' in Aristotle's perspective is a description of a moderate city. This description is prepared by the praise of middle classes former to the presentation of the best regime. Middle classes are necessary for societies to prevent tyrannies. Significantly enough, Aristotle's *Politics* is the continuation of his *Nicomachean Ethics*. The core of Aristotle teaching on ethics concerns the equilibrium between extremes. Aristotle's ethics may be featured as ethics based on moderation and aiming at temperance (Aristotle 1985).

valuable and ultimate ends of action. This is visible through the seemingly but ridiculous 'natural' reproduction of money through speculation (Aristotle 1998). Money is not alive, nevertheless making money for the sake of money-making makes money look as a living being, which is absurd as well if not dangerous (cf Aristotle 1998).

The three above points make clear the differences between the ancient political philosophy understanding of politics and the modern political science one. Ancient political philosophy – which not only conditioned the understanding of politics in Europe but worldwide with some variations until the emergence of the European modern political science – considers political life on the basis of a normative approach. Politics should make possible humans' valuable and ultimate ends, not at all vanity and enrichment for their own sake. Aristotle identifies three main stages in humans' end: 1) The first ones concern the biological life pleasures (feeding, reproducing and so on), 2) the second ones concern political life as such, desire for power and recognition, 3) the third ones concern knowledge, or what he calls 'contemplation' (Aristotle 1985, Aristotle 1991). Politics should simultaneously orient and condition economics which concern biological needs and make room for education and ultimately human destiny, including knowledge or contemplation of the whole (Aristotle 1985, Aristotle 1998).

The fundamental difficulty of this ancient political philosophy approach concerns *freedom*. Not only are some humans supposed just to follow others, if not to be submitted to the others as slaves, but the very notion of liberty is not at the core of this understanding of politics. Such understanding – which actually is 'common good'-oriented – frontally contrasts the modern understanding of economics and profit-making. I will end my enquiry examining this issue.

Revisiting Politics: On Leadership Nowadays

The ancient political philosophy and the modern political science approaches represent two fundamental models which may help in correctly raising the right questions about politics – consequently about the business and common good tension. Politics for the sake of politics is as dangerous as business for the sake of business. The first one potentially represents any tyranny aiming at imposing a supreme power on people, preventing any kind of legitimate freedom. This amounts to considering people as children, unable to evaluate and take their own responsibilities on political or collective issues. On the other hand, making room for a radically free market, allowing people to make business as they want to the extent of their spontaneous private interests and desires would amount to assuming that the market is self-regulated. This assumption is ungrounded. The economic assumption of pure and perfect rationality is not an *empirical*, but a *theoretical* one. Economics considered as resulting from economic agents assumed to behave rationally does not result from observations, but from a normative approach to economics. Such a normative approach results from the Hobbesian assumption that people are spontaneously rational, equal to each other, and free individuals. Actually, people are not spontaneously rational, equal to each other and free individuals but tend to become such. Now, people tend to become rational, equal and free individuals on the basis of their inequalities and bounded rationalities, accepting conscious or unconscious slavery, ethnic group and 'natural' features. Actually, the ancient political philosophy anthropology is more relevant than the modern one. The modern anthropology assumes that people are spontaneously as they *should* be. It does not take into account humans' real condition or who humans are.

On the other hand, the ancient political philosophy anthropology limits its observations on the basis of the 'initial' empirical variety of people, and deduces a normative approach of humans based on such observations. Through its innumerable violence based on people's natural features, history evidences the danger of taking for granted humans' apparent differences. If norms be established on the basis of empirical observation of humans' diversity (ancient political philosophy), or if they be considered as an already-made reality (humans considered as immediately rational, equal, and free individuals), they create political and economical confusion and disorder.

Let us examine the fundamental leadership issue on the basis of the above observation. Hegel observed that human history started with an idea of liberty limited to one individual. In his opinion, history could be interpreted as a continuous even if somewhat violent progress towards a completion of liberty for *any* human. The 'end of history' would on this perspective consist in a universal freedom. Not only one individual, nor some humans, but everybody would enjoy a radical freedom, based on a universal recognition of each individual (Kojève 1980). Such an 'end of history' would mean that everybody is their own leader. Let us try to imagine what such an understanding would mean for organizational life. It would mean that, despite structures and hierarchies, everybody is sooner or later a leader – for themselves and for others. How can organizations reach a level of maturity that is able to guarantee that everybody feels themselves as accountable leaders of a limited perimeter? This amounts to the following question: How does that universally shared awareness become possible?

Envisaging a universal awareness and sense of responsibility depends on an approach of organizations which pays attention to the necessity of a high reliability – independently of the organizational objectives or supposed mission (Weick and Roberts 1993). Such an approach has of course to do with a theory of motivation at work, which questions people's commitment and simultaneous capacity to doubt. A capacity to doubt is as well a capacity to question reality, in the horizon of a self-understanding which takes for granted that everybody is accountable for their job, as well as for the collective stakes of organizations (cf Weick 1988, Weick 2010 on the Bhopal disaster). A universal awareness requires that everybody simultaneously internalize some skills and competencies which guarantees their normal contribution to the organization, and at the same time that everybody internalizes the fundamental right – if not duty – to question reality and actions when apparently necessary. The practical question is of course to what extent reality or actions may sound potentially problematic or wrong – in other words questionable (cf Weick 1990, Crozier and Friedberg 1980, Cyert and March 1963). What is at stake is an equilibrium between taken-for-granted routines, evidences, organizational culture and values, and a capacity to question evidences, taken-for-granted operations and practices, habits and implicit culture (cf Nelson and Winter 1982).

Taking into account seriously enough the Aristotelian understanding of politics makes us pay attention to the fact that organizations begin by the family units. Organizations begin by families, and concern progressively bigger and bigger entities, from clans and villages to nations and the whole world, through cities and corporations. In other words, taking into account the tension between competence and awareness in organizations means taking into account the tension between evidence and the capacity to question them when necessary. This must occur at any level, from the smallest and most private level (families, be them biological or institutional) to the largest and most public one (our global world). The tension between people's competencies and taken-for-granted values and culture, and the capacity to doubt and question actions and reality, concerns each step of the humans' collective as well as individuals' existence.

The very first place where human offspring learn to act as well as to question is the family – be it biological or institutional. The very place where humanity starts is the family, which results from heterosexual relations. Nowadays, heterosexuality is not any more necessary *neither* to have children, *nor* to defend any community. Independently of future discoveries in biotechnology, it is nevertheless so far thanks to heterosexual intercourse – natural or artificial intercourse – that humans come to existence. This observation has two important consequences: Heterosexuality remains necessary for human reproduction, and being offspring of heterosexual intercourse, humans involve the two sexualities, the masculine and the feminine one. Human life begins by a fundamental education depending on the understanding of both feminine and masculine specificities – be they integrated in individuals or actually represented by men and women.

Here we are at the roots of any possible human education. Significantly enough, we are at the root of any possible human desire – including the one to get rid of 'nature'. The modern development of business for the sake of business at least partly results from the modern decision to get rid of nature. Heterosexuality represents the so far fundamental inescapable 'natural' human feature which conditions humans' existence, learning and education. Revisiting what leadership means certainly depends on a renewed understanding of gender relations. Gender relations are the ones where revisiting the notion of leadership is the more urgent, the more necessary – and incidentally, ongoing.

Some previous statements above may drive to a renewed understanding of the tension between business and the common good understood as a gender tension. Certainly enough, the political stake did never change: People need to succeed in balancing liberty and structures. Collective life requires that people reach a right equilibrium between the imperative awareness about social – if not political – responsibility, and private self-interest. Such a balance would certainly benefit from an Aristotelian, moderation grounded approach of ethics. The most important work remains to be done: Re-learning about the tension between private and public good, which amounts to learning about gender relations management.

References

Aristophanes. 1997. *Assembly of Women*. Amherst: Prometheus Books.

Aristotle. 1985. *Nicomachean Ethics*, translated by T. Irwin. Indianapolis: Hackett Publishing.

Aristotle. 1991. *The Metaphysics*. Amherst: Prometheus Books.

Aristotle. 1998. *Politics*. New York: Oxford University Press.

Bibard, L. 2005. The Ethics of Capitalism, in *Ethical Boundaries of Capitalism*, edited by D. Daianu and R. Vranceanu. Farnham: Ashgate, 3–24.

Callon, M. 1992. Variety and Irreversibility in Networks of Technique Conception and Adoption, in *Technology and the Wealth of Nations*, edited by D. Foray and C. Freeman. London: Frances Printer, 232–268.

Cropsey, J. and Strauss, L. 1987. *History of Political Philosophy*. Chicago: The University of Chicago Press.

Crozier, M. and Friedberg, E. 1980. *Actors and Systems: The Politics of Collective Action*. Chicago: University of Chicago Press.

Cyert, R. and March, J. 1963. *A Behavioral Theory of the Firm*. New Jersey: Prentice Hall.

Descartes, R. 1956. *Discourse on Method*. New Jersey: Prentice Hall.

Freeman, C. and Soete, L. 1997. *The Economics of Industrial Innovation*. Cambridge: MIT Press.

Friedman, M. 1970. The Social Responsibility of Business is to Increase Its Profits. *New York Times*, 13 September.

Fukuyama, F. 1992. *The End of History and the Last Man*. London: Penguin.

Hegel, W. 1953. *Reason in History*. New Jersey: Prentice Hall.

Hegel, W. 1991. *Elements of the Philosophy of Right*. Cambridge: Cambridge University Press.

Hobbes, T. 1982. *De Cive: Or The Citizen*. Westport: Greenwood Press.

Hobbes, T. 1985. *Leviathan*. London: Penguin Books.

Kant, E. 1963. *On History*. New Jersey: Prentice Hall.

Kant, E. 1970. *Political Writings*. Cambridge: Cambridge University Press.

Klein, J. 1986. *Lectures and Essays*, edited by R. Williamson. Annapolis: St. John's College Press.

Klein, J. 1992. *Greek Mathematical Thought and the Origin of Algebra*. Mineola: Dover Publications.

Kline, M. 1980. *Mathematics, the Loss of Certainty*. Oxford: Oxford University Press.

Kojève, A. 1980. *Introduction to the Reading of Hegel*. Ithaca: Cornell University Press.

Latour, B. 1988. *Science in Action, How to Follow Scientists and Engineers Through Society*. Cambridge: Harvard University Press.

Latour, B. 2004. *Politics of Nature, How to Bring the Sciences into Democracy*. Cambridge: Harvard University Press.

Locke, J. 1988. *Two Treatises of Government*. Cambridge: Cambridge University Press.

Nelson, R. and Winter, S. 1982. *An Evolutionary Theory of Economic Change*. Cambridge: Harvard University Press.

Plato. 1968. *Republic*, translated by A. Bloom. New York: Basic Books.

Strauss, L. 1947. The Intention of Rousseau. *Social Research*, 14(4): 455–487.

Strauss, L. 1952. *Persecution and the Art of Writing*. Columbus: The Free Press.

Strauss, L. 1953. *Natural Right and History*. Chicago: The University of Chicago Press.

Weick, K. 1988. Enactment Sensemaking in Crisis Situations. *Journal of Management Studies*, 47(3): 551–580.

Weick, K. 1990. The Vulnerable System: An Analysis of the Tenerife Air Disaster. *Journal of Management*, (16)3: 571–593.

Weick, K. 1995. *Sensemaking in Organizations*. Thousand Oaks: SAGE Publications Inc.

Weick, K. 2010. Reflections on Enacted Sensemaking in the Bhopal Disaster. *Journal of Management Studies*, 47(3): 537–550.

Weick, K. and Roberts, K.H. 1993. Collective Mind in Organizations: Heedful Interrelating on Flight Decks. *Administrative Science Quarterly*, 38(3): 357–381.

2 How American Spiritual Capital Informs Business and Affects the Common Good

NICHOLAS CAPALDI

Introduction

The consensus from which we begin is: 1) that no one any longer seriously questions the superiority of free enterprise in meeting our material needs; (2) that free enterprise requires the transformation of political, legal, and cultural institutions; and (3) that there are legitimate concerns about whether that transformation on the whole is a good thing.

No one questions whether there are other goals besides making profitable products and services. What is at issue is: 1) What are these other goals? 2) How are these goals to be prioritized? 3) How are these other goals related to the goal of producing profitable products and services? Even in his much maligned essay, Milton Friedman makes clear that profit maximization presupposes a larger legal and ethical context. He does not explicate what it is, but he recognizes its existence.

In this chapter we address these concerns under the rubric of the 'common good'. Is there a larger and more coherent normative framework within which these individually legitimate concerns can be reconciled and addressed? We begin by pointing out that these concerns are not new. Rather there has been an ongoing debate between two clearly identifiable alternative narratives. Further, we specify the senses in which the Anglo–American business world reflects one of these narratives and the Continental (Western European) business community reflects the other. In our final section we discuss American Exceptionalism, that is, how a particular religious and cultural context informs business practice and achieves the common good.

The Two Narratives of Modernity

Historically speaking, two models or narratives have dominated modernity, the Lockean Liberty Narrative (Anglo–American) and the Rousseau/Marx Equality Narrative (Europe[1] and Japan).

---

1   Montesquieu, Constant, Tocqueville and Guizot in France, Kant and Humboldt in Germany, can be considered continental thinkers who would subscribe to what is here called Lockean.

The Lockean Liberty Narrative has three versions: Efficiency, freedom and religion. In the strict efficiency version, it is argued that human progress and human improvement go together. It is the pursuit of happiness that ought to be promoted, but fulfillment is left undefined. In the freedom version, it is argued that even if there were no net economic loss, there would be an end to freedom of speech and eventually freedom of thought and freedom of religion and the right to choose the government under which we live. We would see the triumph of mediocrity or a narrow public opinion imposing the same capricious and arbitrary standards on everything and everyone. These freedoms are considered good because they are instrumental to self-expression and personal autonomy, and the pursuit of happiness. For theorists like Tocqueville and Mill, freedom trumps efficiency and that is why they are often, incorrectly, identified with the egalitarian narrative. In other words, they argue that the defence of liberty requires more than the case for efficiency. We address the religious version below.

LOCKEAN LIBERTY NARRATIVE

The Lockean Liberty Narrative endorses the following:

'The Technological Project'

The Technological Project can be best described as a transformation of nature for human benefit. As described by Locke:

> *God, who has given the world to men in common, has also given them reason to make use of it to the best advantage of life, and convenience … it cannot be supposed He meant it should always remain common and uncultivated. He gave it to the use of the Industrious and Rational … not to the Fancy or Covetousness of the Quarrelsome and Contentious … for it is labor indeed that puts the difference of value on every thing … of the products of the earth useful to the life of man nine tenths are the effects of labor…*

(Locke 1691)

Advocacy of a free-market system wherein property rights are fundamental

The right to private property is a democratic right based on effort rather than aristocratic right of the few based on the accident of inheritance. Private property is not theft, and a government dedicated to the preservation of property is not an antidemocratic regime. Inequality of outcome is inevitable.

Limited government

Liberty is the limitation of government power on behalf of individual liberty. Recall Locke's endorsement of the right of revolution and his identification of the basic natural rights as life, liberty and property. Locke is most famous for his opposition to Robert Filmer's divine right of kings' justification of monarchical rule (Locke 1980). In *The Second Treatise* Locke maintains that legitimate government is grounded in the consent of the governed. Locke's case rests on the three pillars of liberty: Political liberty, economic liberty and cultural liberty. Embedded in this political liberty narrative is a connection with economic liberty and religious liberty.

Rule of law

Government is to be a representative form wherein the neutral rule of law replaces the biased rule of men. The rule of law is manifested both in the institutional arrangement of the separation of the branches of government and in the teaching of self-imposed limits on both the people and their chosen rulers as expressed in a doctrine of natural rights. In its Lockean formulation, these rights (such as life, liberty, property and so on) are absolute, do not conflict and are possessed only by individual human beings. Rights are morally absolute or fundamental because they are derived from human nature and God, and as such cannot be overridden; the role of these rights is to protect the human capacity to choose. Finally, such rights impose only duties of non-interference. The purpose of these rights is to limit government; the responsibility of government is to refrain from violating an individual's rights and prevent others from doing the same.

The rule of law encompasses what is sometimes called 'justice' or the 'common good.' The rule of law as common good consists of those procedural norms that permit individuals to pursue their private substantive goods. It exists only in a polity that is a civil association, that is, one that does not have a collective good. The thesis of this chapter is that understanding the common good as procedural requires a substantive underpinning; in the US, that underpinning consists of Judeo–Christian spiritual capital. Secular societies lack it. As presently expressed, Islamic cultures lack it.

A culture of personal autonomy

The dominant theme in Locke's work is that the best way of life is one in which the individual pursues happiness. He rejected the ancient view that one finds happiness by belonging or being with others.

In his essay *On Toleration*, Locke opposed a religious monopoly created and supported by the government. He envisions a connection between religious liberty and political liberty as manifested in the separation of church and state. Keep in mind that: 1) Locke wrote and distributed *The Second Treatise* anonymously a decade before he acknowledged authorship in 1691; 2) Locke went to Holland as a religious dissenter and returned to England only after the 1689 Bill of Rights secured a Protestant succession; and 3) Algernon Sidney had been executed in the seventeenth century for defending political liberty, religious liberty and economic liberty. By the end of the eighteenth century, Adam Smith and James Madison could openly defend the case for the three liberties.

Identification of a dysfunctional element in human society

Here, this is described as those elements that are considered 'quarrelsome and contentious'.

ROUSSEAUEAN EQUALITY NARRATIVE

Whereas in Locke, all negotiation begins with the status quo, in Rousseau the history of the status quo is one of force and fraud, and it taints all subsequent permutations of the economy. Whereas in Locke, once property rights are settled economic progress and growth for all commences, in Rousseau the very nature of a market leads inevitably to economic inequality. Whereas Locke offered three pillars of liberty, Rousseau will offer three pillars of equality: Political equality, economic equality and cultural equality. The Rousseauean Equality Narrative rejects the following:

The Technological Project

In the *Discourse on the Arts and Sciences*, Rousseau critiqued what we have called the Technological Project. Instead of satisfying genuine human needs, the arts and sciences are expressions of pride (promoting invidious self-comparison), and they have led to luxury as well as the loss of human liberty. This development is also the origin of inequality. This *First Discourse* emphasizes the huge costs to society in the development of the practical arts and sciences. Rousseau laments that the arts and sciences have promoted hypocrisy in dress, pretentiousness in manners, as well as absence of authenticity in demeanour. He makes the now famous case for the simple life of the noble savage.

The anti-technological project attitude survives in the contemporary ear as the environmental movement. Rather than a Lockean economy in which the technological project allows for infinite growth and wherein a rising tide raises all boats, we are offered a sustainable economy in which all are equal. The operative code word for equality is 'sustainability'.

A free-market economy

In the *Discourse on Inequality*, Rousseau offered a hypothetical historical reconstruction in which the division of labour is blamed for economic inequality. The result was a (Lockean) social contract in which the rich and powerful coerced the less fortunate into institutionalizing inequality. This *Second Discourse* carries his criticism of the Liberty Narrative one step further. Private property is theft, declares Rousseau in the opening paragraph of Part II (the theme of writers, like Proudhon, who were inspired by the Rousseauean dimensions of the first French Revolution and by subsequent defenders of the Equality Narrative). The inequality that emerges as a result of the arts and sciences is a product of that original theft where the few rich bamboozle the many, who are poor, into agreeing to a social contract that benefits only the few rich. The Liberty Narrative in Rousseau's estimation is no more than a fraud.

Limited government

Rousseau's own social contract is meant to displace this unhealthy hierarchy and inequality. History in general and the division of labour in particular lead to inequality. Whether it is physical, material or intellectual inequality, Rousseau takes the presence of the inequality of condition as the point of departure in the 'real' world of society. He questions whether the inequality can be justified, and his answer is that we cannot do so on the grounds provided by Locke.

In the *Discourse on Inequality*, Rousseau argued that the division of labour and the institution of private property are antagonistic to the perfection of human beings because, to anticipate the theory of justice propounded by John Rawls, not everyone enters the social contract 'naked' as it were or with a 'veil of ignorance'. The Lockean social contract, as seen from the Rousseau-through-Rawls lens in the twentieth century, is a fraud, if it ever actually took place at all. It is a fraud, first of all, because no such historical event ever took place. It is also a fraud because the few who were rich and powerful coerced – or forced – the less fortunate many into institutionalizing inequality. Anticipating John Rawls, again, everyone should enter civil society not knowing what is in store for them ahead of time. The notion that certain privileged folks have constructed a false narrative in order to pull a huge one over on the innocent and victimized many is central to the Equality Narrative.

In his book *Political Economy* Rousseau introduces the concept of the 'general will' – a concept central to the Equality Narrative. The concept becomes central in Rousseau's *Social Contract* where the general will becomes the standard by which all action is judged. Everyone gives up everything – especially private property – when leaving the state of nature in order to enter Rousseau's social contract. As a result, the atomistic individual is transformed into a communal citizen.

It is this attitude on the part of Rousseau and his followers that led Benjamin Constant (1988) to criticize them for reviving the ancient conception of liberty instead of embracing the modern conception of liberty. Rosseauean liberty, the liberty of the ancients, consists in 'exercising collectively, but directly, several parts of the complete sovereignty; in deliberating, in the public square ... compatible with this collective freedom [is] the complete subjection of the individual to the authority of the community ... No importance was given to individual independence, neither in relation to opinions, nor to labour, nor, above all, to religion' (Constant 1988: 311). There is thus a conception of liberty in the Rousseau Narrative but it is a 'liberty *to*' participate in collective decision making. Lockean Liberty, modern liberty in Constant's terms, is a 'liberty *from*'. The general will in the end embodies the ancient (and medieval) conception of a collective good, what Oakeshott (1991) describes as an enterprise association.

The individual is transformed into a willing citizen rather than into a Lockean calculating individual; the general will is reinforced and uplifted by a civil religion that favours communal orthodoxy over individual dissent.

Rule of law

But what are we to do with men having been born free and are everywhere in chains? Can something be done to transform this condition? At the heart of both the *Political Economy* and the *Social Contract* is the claim that the so-called Lockean Liberty Narrative is actually a narrative of contractual slavery for the vast bulk of the population.

The only way to have a just society is for everyone upon entering civil society to give up everything and retain nothing. They enter naked and innocent without the clothing of calculation and property. Thus the Rousseau 'correction' of Locke destroys the notion of unalienable rights because everyone alienates everything when leaving the state of nature. In its Rousseauean version rights are not ends in themselves; rights are means to the achievement of the ends. Rights are merely *prima facie*, may be overridden, and may be possessed by any entity, not just individual human beings. Such rights become welfare rights, in other words they may be such that others have a positive obligation to provide such goods, benefits or means.

The common good in the Rousseau Narrative is necessarily political, collective and secular (although it can invoke a civil religion).

Personal autonomy

Right and wrong for Rousseau are no longer to be found in an individual choosing to dissent against the actions of a tyrannical prince or overbearing majority. Instead, right and wrong are decided by the generalizing of the wills of individuals as they become citizens of a collective project. Moreover, the collective never errs. The general will for Rousseau is the foundation for political economy. Market conditions do not dictate government policy; government policy dictates economic policy.

The individual is transformed into a willing citizen rather than into a Lockean calculating individual. The transformation is reinforced by quasi-religious festivals on behalf of the secular good. The general economic and political will is reinforced and uplifted by a civil religion that favours communal orthodoxy over individual dissent.

Social dysfunction

Distinct from Locke, Rousseau maintained that this dysfunction is rooted in inequality; remove inequality and social dysfunction disappears; this is the origin of all victimization theses. There is no sentimental notion of equality in Marx; the workers would clearly not be equal to the planners, but it was assumed that this appearance of inequality would not be onerous or invidious in light of the collective good because the workers and the planners have a common bond. In one way or another, differences of function would not translate into differences of status in light of the collective good.

ADAM SMITH

Adam Smith restates the Lockean Liberty Narrative in the face of the Rousseauean challenge. In Book I of the *Wealth of Nations*, Smith espouses the technological project (Smith 1776). Echoing Locke, Smith argues that wealth and growth are the result of the labour that human beings put into nature. The division of labour leads to the invention of labour-saving devices, exemplified most notably in the pin factory (now represented on the present £10 note). Following Hume, who had written an essay 'On Commerce' to rebut Rousseau's charges that science and technology ruin society, Smith argues that technology and growth are on the whole better than living in a primitive agricultural society.

Like Locke, Smith endorses a competitive market as natural. Central to the production of wealth is the natural capacity of human beings to 'truck, barter, and exchange' with the butcher, baker and brewer for their daily beef, bread and beer (Smith 1759). Again, following Locke, Smith argues that the process of exchange is facilitated by the invention of money which properly understood is a medium of exchange rather than a substitute for wealth or the creation of value. Both Locke and Smith only introduce money into the discussion after they have talked about what is real in the process. Book IV contains Smith's famous discussion of the invisible hand (previously introduced in the *Theory of Moral Sentiments*, Smith 1759). This much discussed and controversial concept is at the very least an attempt to capture the dynamic and organic dimensions (unintended consequences) of a market economy.

With respect to the individual and the general culture, Smith puts forth a doctrine that Tocqueville would later call 'self interest rightly understood'. The exchange of surpluses among human beings is natural and this sociability, as he argued in the *Theory of Moral Sentiments*, is sown in human nature. This amounts to a sort of correction of Locke's understanding that sociability is more a calculation than instinctive. Moreover, Smith recognized the negative effects to the individual of a life defined solely by the division of labour. Smith also advocated religious liberty in the form of a market in religious sects.

The French Revolutionaries

There are similarities between the 1776 American *Declaration of Independence* and the 1789 French *Declaration of the Rights of Man and the Citizen*. But more important are the differences. The American Declaration announces that all 'Men are created equal' and proceeds to state that the purpose of government is to protect the individual right to the pursuit of life, liberty and happiness; the point of departure is natural equality and the goal is liberty. The French *Declaration* announces, in the fashion of Rousseau's *Social Contract*, that, 'Men are born free and equal in rights. Social distinctions may be based only on common utility'; the point of departure is liberty and the goal is equality. The French *Declaration* states, again in Rousseauean *Social Contract* fashion, that 'the law is the expression of the general will.' How 'sacred', then, are natural rights, if the 'general will' of the citizen becomes the voice of God?

Equally revealing are the differences between the American *Constitution* of 1788, as amended in 1791 with the addition of a *Bill of Rights*, with the three French Constitutions of 1791, 1793 and 1795. Title I of the 1791 French Constitution contains a fundamental tension between the liberty 'provisions guaranteed' by the Constitution and the 'guarantee' of the right to 'public relief' and the institutions of 'national festivals.' What are we to make of the word 'guarantee', a word that is absent from the American Constitution? The 1795 Constitution begins not with the legislative powers or a statement of purposes but the construction of executive power in the form of an Executive Directory. This move toward a Directory, and the later restrictions on intermediate institutions actually confirm the centrality of the Administrative State. It is, however, the 1793 Constitution that is the central contribution of the French Revolution to the Equality Narrative: 1) it repeats the tension between the 'sanctity of property' and the 'right to subsistence'; 2) it represents a direct democracy version of republicanism; and 3) it is a 'guarantee' of social and economic equality. We refer here to the Rousseau-inspired Jacobin, Maximillien Robespierre. In his justification of the Reign of Terror speech in February 1794, 'On the Principles of Morality' Robespierre says that the 'fundamental principle of the democratic or popular government ... is virtue which is nothing other than the love of country and ... the love of country necessarily includes the love of equality.' '[T]error is nothing other than justice...it is an emanation of virtue (Robespierre 1794).'

Nineteenth-century Socialism

Rousseau transforms the Lockean conception of rights from the rights of the individual to the rights of the community. Instead of the Lockean model wherein individuals retain rights upon entering society (and government is limited), in the Rousseau model each individual gives up each and all rights upon entering society; each person enters stripped of rights, and naked, abandons all attachment to a previous and stunted private self and acquires a new and grander public self. The general will replaces individual choice. Obedience becomes total rather than conditional. If you yearn for individual identity and personal autonomy, then it is the appropriate role of government 'to force you to be free'.

Rousseau's critique of modern society, especially the idea that private property was theft and that limited government is contrary to true and pure democracy and the general will, was adapted and broadened in the nineteenth century mainly by writers we now identify generically as 'socialist'. These writers, unlike Rousseau, were more willing to embrace technology, but they criticized the poverty, inequality, alienation and degradation, which they alleged, were consequences of what we have called the Technological Project. They focused on the unfairness – the inequality – of the distribution of the goods and services generated by the new technological world. They advocated the abolition of private property, which they asserted had unfairly concentrated power and wealth among a few, exacerbated inequality, and did not provide equal opportunities for everyone. But they sought not merely more equal opportunity; rather they defended more equality of outcome.

In many ways, the Equality Narrative should be called the 'inequality narrative'. What identifies someone as a proponent of the Rousseauean Narrative is: 1) a sense of being in an adversarial relation to what is taken to be the present system;[2] 2) a moral critique in which it is necessary to identify the 'bad guys'[3] and the 'victims'; 3) the advocacy of restructuring; and 4) the failure to provide an explicit account of how the new structure will function. They are voices of grievance (and hope) without an explicit plan!

Constant, Tocqueville and Mill

One of our main themes has been how the next generation understand themselves to be correcting or modifying the contribution of the earlier generations. Locke had offered both a natural rights and a utilitarian argument for liberty, the latter emphasizing the efficiency of the market. Hume and Smith had defended the efficiency of the market. But the efficiency argument on its own has been under attack as early as the nineteenth century, when Constant deplored the fact that so many intellectuals were mistakenly hostile to religion, taking what he considered the perversion of religion to be the essence of religion (Constant 1988). Constant opposed Rousseau's idea of a civic religion and advocated religious toleration. This not only checked centralized power but the truths individuals would find within religion, if not coerced, were essential both to true human fulfillment and to the preservation of liberal culture as a whole. A liberal state had to be both secular and tolerant; a liberal culture needed to be deeply religious. Similar arguments are to be found in the work of Daniel Bell, Irving Kristol, Peter Burger and even in Catholic social thought (Bell 1976, Kristol 1978, Burger 1988).

---

2   In the field of business ethics we are given an ethics 'for' not an ethics 'of.' The narrative is always reformist. If there is nothing to reform then there is nothing to say (Said 1996).

3   The original 'bad guys' in the 18th century were large feudal landowners and the victims were the small land owners and bourgeoisie; and in 19th century the bad guys were employers who owned factories and the victims were the workers. The narrative has been used by inhabitants of former colonies who were educated in the West, against former colonial powers, and now multinational corporations (Buruma and Margalit 2005). It has been used by blacks against whites, by immigrants against 'WASPS,' and by some feminists against perceived domination by white males.

The increasing calls in the nineteenth and twentieth centuries for an absolute equality, now understood as the call for the recognition of a collective good – equality and fraternity – that subsumed the individual good, raised the same alarm that it had in the eighteenth century. Tocqueville and Mill emphasized in their writings a conflict between equality and liberty. Tocqueville warned that modern man also had a great inclination to support the centralization of government which, given the history of the French Revolutions of 1789, 1830 and 1848, is the way to tyranny. This is what Hayek would later call *The Road to Serfdom* (Hayek 1994). Defenders of the Liberty Narrative justify removing or relaxing external constraints because they presume that there is some kind of basic internal psychological need for something like personal autonomy. They are reasserting in secular fashion the Christian doctrine of the dignity of the individual soul. This is what is behind J.S. Mill's defence of individuality. Individual liberty is the condition for the individual pursuit of happiness.

Mill realized that a 'correction' to Adam Smith was needed in that he had to 1) address the social question raised by the vast and growing socialist literature; and 2) restate the case for individual liberty on new and different intellectual grounds. Mill abandoned both natural right and the labour theory of value. He focused on both the increase in production and the control of population. He also provided a richer and deeper understanding of utilitarianism; some would argue that he transformed it, with an emphasis on personal autonomy that had a much greater impact on the subsequent development of the Liberty Narrative.

Mill distinguishes between the 'theory of dependence and protection', and the 'theory of self-dependence' when considering 'the probable futurity of the laboring poor'. Mill claims that the labouring poor will eventually love the taste of liberty that comes with the theory of self-dependence or self-reliance and will ultimately reject the government paternalism that comes with the theory of dependence. Moreover, labour and capital need not be locked in mortal combat and that through 'the co-operative principle' their mutual goals can be met. Present distribution is an historical accident and not a law of economics.

Mill's *Political Economy* (Mill 1848) anticipates both his *On Liberty* (Mill 2011) and *Subjection of Women* (Mill 1997). Mill sees a connection between the competition for goods and services with competition in the market place of ideas. His critique of the theory of the dependence of the poor on the rich mirrors his critique of the dependence of women on men. In *On the Subjection of Women*, Mill argues that competition and not custom should hold in the relationship between men and women. He is not asking for protective duties and bounties in favour of women; it is only asked that the present bounties and protective duties in favour of men should be recalled. In fact, the liberation of women is in part an economic argument linked to 'the theory of self-dependence' or what we have called the Liberty Narrative. Mill insists that the onus for presenting arguments for regulation has to be put on those who propose the regulation. Liberty is the default position.

For theorists like Mill, freedom trumps efficiency and that is why he is often, incorrectly, identified with the egalitarian narrative. Even if there were no net economic loss, there would be an end to freedom of speech and eventually freedom of thought and freedom of religion and the right to choose the government under which we live; we would witness the triumph of mediocrity or a narrow public opinion imposing the same capricious and arbitrary standards on everything and everyone. The defence of liberty requires more than the case for efficiency, but it does not require egalitarianism.

Marx, Engels and the Equality Narrative

Marx revised the Equality Narrative by borrowing from Locke, Smith, Ricardo and Malthus. The labour theory of value in the Liberty Narrative was a way of calling attention to the technological project and the promise of growth. Ironically, the labour theory of value, via Ricardo, becomes with Marx the new foundation and departure for the Equality Narrative. Despite his criticism of the Robinson Crusoe model as an illusory abstraction, Marx thought that Robinson (as he called Crusoe) represented the critical insight into the creation of use value over against the 'fetishism' of value in exchange. Malthus's 'dismal' message is that the optimism of classical liberalism is misplaced because the size of the population – will increase exponentially even though total production – will increase arithmetically. A second irony is that Malthus's turn towards the distribution of production within the community and away from the production of commodities for the improvement of well-being gave credence to the Equality Narrative of distribution over the Liberty Narrative of production.

In the *Manuscripts*, Marx speaks about the 'alienation' of labour from the end product and the process of production under a system of private property (Marx 1988). Here, he makes central what Smith made peripheral in his warning about the downside to the division of labor in Book V of *The Wealth of Nations* (Smith 1776). Marx also offers a glimpse of life without the division of labour in *The German Ideology* (Marx 1976): 'In communist society, where nobody has one exclusive sphere of activity but each can become accomplished in any branch he wishes, society regulates the general production and thus makes it possible for me to do one thing today and another tomorrow, to hunt in the morning, fish in the afternoon, rear cattle in the evening, criticize after dinner, just as I have a mind, without ever becoming hunter, fisherman, herdsman or critic.'

Marx accepts the distinction between use value and exchange value that we saw in both Smith and Mill, but he places a higher worth on use value than exchange value. Use value has true value because the commodities are produced to satisfy human needs. A pure labour theory of value denies that landlords and capitalists (entrepreneurs) contribute to the product any worth or value. This is a restatement of the argument that property is theft by another means. This Marxist argument has had a profound impact on workplace aspects of public policy and the strategy of trade unions in which so many disputes between management and labour turn on the length of the working day.

Instead of seeing the capacity to truck, barter and exchange as part of the natural way humans improve their condition, Marx considers exchange as the mechanism by which one set of humans – the owners – exploit those who have only their labour to sell on the market. Instead of seeing the natural course of the economy being toward growth on the one hand and the condition of the working class improving on the other hand, as do Locke, Smith and Mill, Marx predicts the ultimate collapse of capitalism and the decline of the condition of the working class.

With Marx, the Equality Narrative takes on a new and revolutionary tone. There is a strong dismissive tone to previous articulators of the Equality Narrative. There is no sentimental notion of equality in Marx. The workers would clearly not be equal to the planners, but it was assumed that this appearance of inequality would not be onerous or invidious in light of the collective good because the workers and the planners have a common bond. Differences of function would somehow not translate into differences of status in light of the collective good. The special status of intellectuals is preserved!

The proponents of the Equality Narrative yearn for a return to the collective identity of the ancient polis, what Oakeshott (1991) calls an enterprise association. The Equality Narrative depends on the case for the acceptance of strong government: A general will generates communal fraternity and this trumps an individual pursuit of happiness. Thus, regardless of whether the ideology is: 1) in the Marxist and strong socialist form of government ownership of the means of production; or 2) the softer socialism and progressive agenda of greater government regulation of the private sphere of life especially the relationship between capital and labour; or 3) planning for a more rational and fairer society, following Franklin. D. Roosevelt and the Great Society programmes, the Equality Narrative relies on government being the solution rather than the problem. The non-governmental sphere is the problem rather than the solution. The Equality Narrative contains a liberty component, namely, liberation from insecurity, fear, disease, hunger and misery, but this task will produce restraints on individual liberty.

EU versus the US[4]

Both defenders and critics of free-market economies largely ignore the historical–cultural context within which they operate (see however, McCloskey 2006, 2009, Fukuyama 1995). There are major cultural differences between Anglo–American models and the Continental model of the relation between commerce and the common good. There are significant differences between American (shareholder primacy) and Continental (stakeholder primacy) business practices. In the US and UK, 76 percent and 71 percent respectively of managers believe a corporation belongs to its shareholders; in Germany 82.7 percent, in France 78 percent, and in Japan 97 percent of managers believe a corporation belongs to all of it stakeholders. 90 percent of managers in the US and UK think dividends are more important than job security; in Germany and France large majorities believe the opposite (Allen and Gale 2000). Liability law in the US encourages risk-taking; in France and Italy there are civil and sometimes criminal liabilities for directors of failed corporations. Careers of top US managers can survive even several business failures; in many EU countries the CEO of a failed company ends his career (Macey 2008). These differences ultimately reflect the two narratives.

---

4   The Glorious Revolution in Britain and the US War of Independence were fundamentally different from the French Revolution. Anglo–American jurisprudence is fundamentally different from the Civilian tradition of France and the Continent. The US is a shareholder culture. In the US, family control of a business rarely lasts beyond the second generation; the majority of Americans are shareholders in equities. In Europe, until very recently, family estates and fortunes dominated the economy; most of the shares are still owned and voted by banks, insurance companies and other conglomerates. In common law countries, there is shareholder primacy; in civil law countries, shareholder wealth maximization is not the norm. In the Anglo–American world, the term 'capitalism' usually connotes a market economy; in the Continental world the term 'capitalism' connotes a social system as well as an economic system. Unlike the Brits and Continental Europeans, the US has never had a viable socialist tradition. As H.G. Wells pointed out close to 90 years ago, the United States not only lacked a viable socialist party, but also never developed a British or European-type Conservative or Tory party. Rather America has been dominated by pure bourgeois, middle-class individualistic values.

American Exceptionalism

THE AMERICAN FOUNDING AS A LOCKEAN AFFAIR

The Declaration of Independence reflects the continuity between the Founding and Locke: The emphasis on the natural right of the individual to life, liberty and the pursuit of happiness with (natural) equality as a point of departure rather than as a social outcome to be secured. By liberty the Declaration means: Economic liberty (the right to the fruits of one's labour in the form of private property); political liberty (the right to choose the form of government under which one shall live); and religious liberty (the right to worship God according to one's conscience).

James Madison, in *The Federalist No. 10* (Madison 1787), recognized the challenge of Rousseau's focus on inequality: 'The most common and durable sources of faction' are the 'various and unequal distribution of property'. Madison does not deny that the battle between the few who are rich and the many who are poor – the unequal distribution issue – is at the core of class war and factious politics, and thus the 'mortal disease' of every regime. He does, however, suggest that economic disagreements can be framed in terms of the more manageable differences of degree, or variety, of property ownership. It is better for free governments to tolerate the unequal distribution of income because it is a byproduct of a system of human improvement whose core value is individual liberty and the pursuit of happiness. By increasing the size of the pie, we can avoid the nasty politics of redistributing the slices of a fixed size pie. The improvement in the human condition, including the preservation of liberty, requires an increase in the wealth of the nation so that we can avoid the negative impact on liberty and justice of a zero sum game. Competition, not monopoly, is at the core of the Madison solution to the problems of faction that emerge in every civilized society. With competition comes the prosperity vital for the enhancement of political liberty. This is the origin of the ongoing debate on how to respond to poverty: Expand the economy (Lockean) or redistribute wealth (Rousseau).

Competition in the market becomes the model for politics. Politics is to be modeled on markets (Locke), rather than markets being modeled on politics (Rousseau). Democracy, understood, as majority rule, is a negative or blocking device for curtailing faction in the interest of individual freedom; it is not a positive device, as in Rousseau, for arriving at a collective general will. The separation of powers is an institutional auxiliary to aid regular elections in the effort to oblige the government to follow the rule of law and control itself. There is to be competition between the three branches of the federal government. 'Let ambition counteract ambition' in a system of 'opposite and rival interests'. Madison, like Adam Smith, favours competition facilitated by the extended orbit or extended market: It provides the infrastructure for the development of a multiplicity of religious sects which is the prerequisite for the preservation of religious liberty. Madison recognizes the interrelationship between political liberty, economic liberty and religious liberty. The US Constitution creates a commercial republic to protect the natural rights of individuals not to advance the collective interest of any majority.

HOW CRUCIAL IS RELIGIOUS FREEDOM?

Spiritual capital (Capaldi and Roosevelt Malloch 2012) is that aspect of social capital linked with religion and/or spirituality: 'The effects of spiritual and religious practices, beliefs, networks and institutions that have an impact on individuals, communities and societies', as noted by Wilhelm Röpke in *A Humane Economy* (1957), 'Self-discipline, a sense of justice, honesty, fairness, chivalry, moderation, public spirit, respect for human dignity, firm ethical norms – all of these are things which people must possess before they go to market and compete with each other. These are the indispensable supports which preserve both market and competition from degeneration. Family, church, genuine communities, and tradition are their sources.' The spiritual capital of the United States is rooted in the dissenting Protestantism of its original settlers, especially Puritans and Quakers. As Samuel Huntington claims in his book *Who Are We?* (2005), 'America was founded by British settlers who brought with them a distinctive culture … the English language, Protestant values, individualism, religious commitment, and respect for law. The waves of immigrants that later came to the United States gradually accepted these values and assimilated into America's Anglo–Protestant culture.'

We have identified the logic of modernity as comprising the following: Technological ProjectàFree Market EconomyàLimited Government→Rule of LawàCulture of Personal Autonomy→Technological Project

Each of these features is rooted in the Judeo–Christian God: The Technological Project occurs in the West because of a belief that the world was created with a special order hospitable to human flourishing. Recall Locke's claim about the industrious and the rational. With regard to the free-market economy, most of the practices we associate with capitalism were developed in medieval monasteries; limited government owes its origin in Augustine's doctrine of the Two Cities and the medieval confrontation between Church and State; the rule of law emerged out of the Christian conception of natural law; and the belief in individual autonomy harkens back to the Christian conception of the immortal individual soul.

To the extent that the logic of modernity is rooted in Judeo–Christian spiritual capital, America has been unique in preserving that connection. Americans identify themselves overwhelmingly with the Judeo–Christian spiritual heritage, long after it has disappeared as the cultural foundation of the EU (Western Europe). Recall the recent debate about conceptualizing the role of Christianity in the EU Constitution. To this day, most Americans subscribe to the Lockean Liberty Narrative, not the Equality Narrative that now dominates Europe; it is why America can combine a secular civil association with a religious culture instead of the Muslim belief in an enterprise theocracy; it is why America celebrates autonomy instead of the Asian belief in social conformity.

We characterize the early US by noting that it inherited the logic of modernity and all of its institutions: The technological röject (Bacon), economic (Smith), political (Locke) and legal (common law) institutions come from Great Britain. What distinguished the US from Britain was the lack of a feudal class structure which dominated Great Britain down into the twentieth century, an extensive virgin territory for applying it, and most especially the opportunity for a multitude of dissenting Protestant sects, Catholics and Jews to engage the new world with a religious fervour largely absent from the feudalistic Church of England.

By rejecting a hierarchical conception of the world, Protestants could accept that the political realm was no longer subordinate to the religious realm. At the same time, the political realm had to respect the independence of the traditional spiritual realm of Christianity. That realm as understood by Protestants meant the opportunity to do God's work by transforming the world economically. Equality before the law was an expression of Christian liberty and it came to mean that there should be no legal barriers to economic activity that did not apply equally to everyone. To place legal barriers in the economic realm was to thwart God's plan! The Protestant work ethic promoted the notions of the inner-directed individual, the emphasis on work or achievement, and differentiation based on achievement. A consequence of this conception of equality is meritocracy. Meritocracy is not just a reflection of personal merit but of divine preordination. It is God who inspires us and accounts for the differences in achievement. This higher status was accompanied by a sense of greater responsibility, not the privileges of self-indulgence. Whereas the medieval Catholic Church had sacralized the poor and institutionalized begging, Protestants such as Luther and Calvin viewed it as an abuse of public trust and a way of exploiting the more industrious members of society.

It is this foundation that accounts for the fact that the US is the most philanthropic country in the world, that private charity is a way of helping the poor, that privately funded non-profit foundations address social problems in imaginative ways that are incompatible with and incomprehensible to government bureaucracies. I remind the reader that the most prestigious universities and medical centres in the world are private US institutions. It is in this very special sense that American spiritual capital works for the common good.

As noted by Tocqueville, there is a vast network of private voluntary institutions that forms the social infrastructure of American life. Today there are 1.2 million public-serving not-for-profit organizations, 655,000 direct providers, 352,000 churches, 140,000 action agencies and 50,000 intermediary funding organizations. They employ 11 million paid workers or 7 percent of the American workforce. This is the epicentre of philanthropy and it is called on to help solve nearly all of America's problems.

Market economies have indeed transformed many if not all institutions. Millions of Americans and millions of people from around the world who came to America have made a successful adaptation to that challenge. But, many have not – hence the concern for so-called negative externalities. But if many have and many have not, then clearly it is not the externality that is the issue. If you believe that people are determined by their environment then you look to a potentially all-powerful institution, namely the State, to rectify the environment. If you accept the traditional Christian belief that individuals have free will and that they have the capacity to become autonomous and accept the responsibility of being free, then cultural assimilation and success depend on our consciously held beliefs. Instead of diagnosing externalities such as the culture of poverty in terms of the lack of resources, we can diagnose it as a state of mind. Specifically, I allude here to Michael Oakeshott's description of the pathology of the anti-individual:

> The emergence of this disposition to be an individual is the pre-eminent event in modern European history ... there were some people, by circumstance or by temperament, less ready than others to respond ... the counterpart of the ... entrepreneur of the sixteenth century was the displaced laborer ... the familiar anonymity of communal life was replaced by a personal identity which was burdensome ... it bred envy, jealousy and resentment ... a new morality ....not of 'liberty' and 'self-determination', but of 'equality' and 'solidarity' ... not ... the 'love of others' or 'charity' or ...'benevolence' ... but ... the love of 'the community' [common good] ... [the anti-individual or mass man] remains an unmistakably derivative character ... helpless, parasitic and able to survive only in opposition to individuality ... The desire of the 'masses' to enjoy the products of individuality has modified their destructive urge.

(Oakeshott 1991: 363–383)

Briefly, regarding Catholics in the US, let me state the following. The Catholic Counter-Reformation opted for a collective or enterprise association. This continued to influence the Papacy down to the early twentieth century. In 1885, Pope Leo XIII in his encyclical *Immortale Dei* insisted that Catholicism had to be the official state religion; in his 1895 encyclical directed to the US, *Longinqua oceani*, he criticized the American idea of the separation of Church and State and insisted that the Church should 'enjoy the favor of the laws and the patronage of public authority'. This view was rejected by the now-Protestantized American Catholics. In the last half of the twentieth century the American Catholic Church has been the tail that wagged the Vatican dog. When John Paul II in *Centesimus Annus* said that, 'The original source of all that is good is the very act of God, who created both the earth and humankind, and who gave the earth to humankind, so that we might have dominion over it by our work and enjoy its fruits' we hear echoes of Locke!

Critics of what I have said will rightly contest the impression that America is all about Lockean liberty. Is there not a counter-current of Rousseauean equality? The answer unequivocally is yes. This leads us to the phenomenon of the American Progressives, clearly not Marxists, but what Marx derisively calls 'the utopian socialists'. They believed that a regime dedicated to the preservation of property was an undemocratic regime because private property is only owned by the few. Progressives (such as John Dewey) were also influenced by the Hegelian quest for government under the guidance of technocrats, disinterested, or neutral leaders. They aimed to separate politics from administration and rely on the latter rather than the former. They thought that through cooperation, not competition, in the fields of both politics and economics, we could settle the disputes between labour and capital without having a revolution. By ridding politics of the influence of special interests, turning voluntary charity into 'the administration of things' we would all be well. We replace the world of unbridled self-interested competition with the world of detached public interest administrators, and thereby replace the old narrative of liberty with the new narrative of equality.

The New Deal and the Great Society programmes reflect this Progressive approach. It is not simply that the market economy is inefficient and not delivering food and shelter to the public, rather at the core is a concern with the fundamental fairness of life. The majority gets a raw deal (also known as the victimization thesis). The Liberty Narrative has failed the promise of democracy, and it is the duty of government to overcome this crisis. Religion has been secularized into crusades to eliminate domestic evils and appeal to the sense of social justice: In the name of equality and fraternity, the Progressives are morally outraged by the depressed and unfulfilled nature of the American regime. The upcoming 2012 election is in large part a clash between the two narratives.

Conclusion

There are three strands of the Lockean Narrative: One that emphasizes economic efficiency, one that emphasizes freedom and one that emphasizes the Judeo–Christian cultural context. I have focused on the latter because it specifically deals with the common good. Many European and some American scholars are themselves secular and sometimes dismissive of believers, gravitate to scientism and the mistaken belief that religious narratives will be intellectually superseded by secular scientific ones, and have a penchant for social scientific analysis that focuses on underlying structures rather than the influence of consciously held beliefs. I have emphasized how those consciously held beliefs make a considerable difference.

References

Allen, F. and Gale, D. 2000. *Comparing Financial Systems*. Cambridge: MIT Press.

Bell, D. 1976. *The Cultural Contradictions of Capitalism*. New York: Basic Books.

Burger, P. 1988. *The Capitalist Revolution*. New York: Basic Books.

Capaldi, N. and Roosevelt Malloch, T. 2012. *American Spiritual Capital*. South Bend: St. Augustine Press.

Constant, B. 1988. The liberty of the ancients compared with that of the moderns, in *Political Writings*, edited by B. Fontana. Cambridge: Cambridge University Press, 307–328.

Fukuyama, F. 1995. *Trust: The Social Virtues and the Creation of Prosperity*. New York: Free Press.

Hayek, F.A. 1944. *The Road to Serfdom*. Chicago: University of Chicago Press.

Huntington, S. 2004. *Who Are We?* New York: Simon & Schuster.

Kristol, I. 1978. *Two Cheers for Capitalism*. New York: Mentor.

Locke, J. 1980. *Second Treatise on Government*. Indianapolis: Hackett Publishing.

Macey, J. 2008. *Corporate Governance*. Princeton: Princeton University Press.

Madison, J. 1787. *The Federalist No. 10*. New York: J. & A. Maclean.

Marx, K. 1976. The German Ideology. New York: Prometheus Books.

Marx, K. 1988. Economic and Philosophic manuscripts of 1844. New York: Prometheus Books.

McCloskey, D. 2006. *The Bourgeois Virtues: Ethics for an Age of Commerce*. Chicago: University of Chicago Press.

McCloskey, D. 2009. *Bourgeois Dignity: Why Economics Can't Explain the Modern World*. Chicago: University of Chicago Press.

Mill, J.S. 1848. *Principles of Political Economy*. Indianapolis: Hackett Publishing.

Mill, J.S. 1997. *The Subjection of Women*. New York: Dover Publications.

Mill, J.S. 2011. On Liberty. Cambridge: Cambridge University Press.

Oakeshott, M. 1991. The Masses in Representative Democracy, in *Rationalism in Politics and Other Essays*, edited by T. Fuller. Indianapolis: Liberty Press, 363–383.

Robespierre, M. 1794. *Report on the Principles of Political Morality*. New York: Fordham University Modern History Sourcebook.

Röpke, W. 1957. *A Humane Economy: The Social Framework of the Free Market*. Wilmington: Intercollegiate Studies Institute.

Rousseau, J.J. 1987. *Rousseau's Political Writings: Discourse on Inequality, Discourse on Political Economy, On Social Contract*, translated by J.C. Bondanella. New York: W.W. Norton & Company.

Smith, A. 1759. *The Theory of Moral Sentiments*. London: A. Millar.

Smith, A. 1776. *Wealth of Nations*. London: W. Strahan and T. Cadell.

Smith, A. 1776. Nature and Causes of the Wealth of Nations. London: Strahan and Cadell.

PART II

Conceptualizing Global Leadership and Social Responsibility

3 Reconciling Domains: Corporate Social Responsibility and the Global Leadership Challenge

CIARA SUTTON AND LENA ZANDER

Introduction

There is great complexity in the responsibility of multinational firms when addressing global corporate social responsibility (CSR), as global companies exist in a web of institutional structures, organizational interests, and societal and cultural norms. A common theme in the growing CSR debate is the role of the firm in society and the extent of the firms' responsibilities to stakeholders beyond shareholders. Parallel to this discussion is the role of global leadership, what global leaders do, and how they take into consideration social and economic responsibilities while negotiating cultural paradoxes (Holt and Seki 2012).

Multinational enterprises (MNEs) face a complex matrix of ethical, economic and legal corporate social responsibilities (Carroll 2003), where business units and individuals hold different expectations as to how these should be prioritized and acted upon. To this we can add that such expectations also vary across country and culture borders complicating the matrix further. That such a paradox of requirements can paralyze an organization is unacceptable when there is a call for action and a decision to be made. Reconciling this matrix is the responsibility of global leaders and ultimately this is one of the key skills of a global leader. They must facilitate, reconcile and work through the oftentimes conflicting and overlapping contextual domains of CSR. But more than that, negotiating cultural paradoxes is an innate quality necessary for global leaders of today. By being people-oriented and focused, global leaders develop multicultural competencies that in turn help them to overcome cultural challenges (Holt and Seki 2012). Through doing so, global leaders are able to solicit support for CSR initiatives and secure implementation efforts. To acquire and develop these important qualities Butler, Zander, Mockaitis and Sutton (2012) propose that global leaders need to take on three roles: Boundary spanning, bridge making and blending. Boundary spanning has also been previously argued to be a critical role for initiating and implementing corporate global responsibility (D'Amato, Eckert, Ireland, Quinn and Van Velsor 2010).

In this chapter, we will first introduce the CSR concept before conceptually outlining how CSR domains in varying national and cultural contexts provide complexity. Following from this we will discuss how conflicting CSR prioritizations can be reconciled by global leaders who act as boundary spanners, bridge makers and blenders in their efforts to ensure employee and peer support for the global firm's CSR initiatives. We will address limitations and future research ideas, adding another layer of complexity, before discussing our concluding reflections.

Corporate Social Responsibility – The Domain

Developed from early ideas of firms' obligations to maximize profits within the boundaries of the law (Levitt 1958), the notion that a firm has extended obligations towards society is an increasingly relevant issue. National business environments are promoting CSR (Mohan 2006) and global guidelines have emerged intending to improve CSR (Waddock, Bodwell and Graves 2002).

CSR is a concept that is surrounded by definitional uncertainty, or at least there is an abundance of definitions that have been noted as biased towards specific interests (Van Marrewijk 2003). Structured attempts have been made to address the definitional challenges, for instance by Carroll (1999) who took a historical approach to tracing the development of CSR as a concept. More recent work by Dahlsrud (2006) goes some way to a reconciliation of definitional issues. In an analysis of 37 definitions of CSR and a review of frequency of use in both academic literature and practice, a set of five dimensions of CSR are identified. The dimensions of 'environmental', 'social', 'economic' and 'stakeholders' are considered necessary to understanding how CSR is defined, and in addition the 'voluntariness' dimension is added, referring to actions not prescribed by law. For example, a definition covering all five dimensions of CSR is provided by Van Marrewijk (2003): 'CSR refers to company activities – voluntary by definition – demonstrating the inclusion of social and environmental concerns in business operations and in interactions with stakeholders' (Van Marrewijk 2003:102).

Accepting that most CSR definitions are consistently referring to some or all of these five dimensions in some combination makes the lack of one universally accepted definition less problematic (Dahlsrud 2006), although of course the removal of one or more of the five elements in the definition means in practice that individuals and organizations can be referring to a very divergent set of practices under the CSR name. For instance, whether or not CSR consists of purely voluntary practices, or includes those required by law; or if CSR encompasses only activities that are aligned with and included within the business activities of the firm, or if philanthropic actions are also CSR. As this lack of consensus seems to be rooted in different institutional settings and cultural understandings (Matten and Moon 2005, 2008) we are unlikely to easily reconcile differences in the breadth of the construct. In fact, these definitional differences are an additional consideration for firms that operate across boundaries, as individuals and groups within the firm may define and view CSR differently. There are also continuing issues in a number of other areas, for instance CSR definitions do not provide guidance on how the dimensions of CSR should be balanced against each other in decision making (Matten and Moon 2005, 2008). There is also a lack of specific widely accepted theories that distinguish between global and local CSR (Husted and Allen 2006), and aspects of localization versus standardization in the CSR activities of the MNE have not received systematic attention. This means that determinants of CSR strategy outcomes (Muller 2006, Jamali 2010) are only recently discussed in the literature.

CORPORATE SOCIAL RESPONSIBILITY: LOCAL, GLOBAL AND HYPERNORMS

Some of the earliest discussions of the difference between local and global CSR focused on the idea of universal principals whereby religious, cultural and philosophical beliefs converge around certain core principles (Donaldson and Dunfee 1994). Local differences in norms are acknowledged and addressed to the extent that they may differ when not contradictory to these hypernorms. Hypernorms are therefore sets of principles about moral rights and obligations that are a standard to which all societies can be held (Husted and Allen 2006). The concept of hypernorms, or fundamental principles, assists in distinguishing between 'local' CSR, which deals with the firms' obligations based on the standards of a local community, and 'global' CSR, which is based on those standards to which all societies can be held and is therefore guided by hypernorms.

Global CSR issues, for example overarching concerns about human rights and environmental protection, are regulated and monitored by transnational agreements, governments and non-governmental organizations to ensure compliance to fundamental principles. Even so, it is considered that MNEs are uniquely situated to help solve these problems (Husted and Allen 2006) and reconcile across borders. Further, MNEs are considered by some as moral agents with responsibility for the spread of principles of human rights and sustainable development (Collier and Wanderlay 2005). With local CSR issues there is no global consensus of the firm's obligations, although it could be argued that obligations still may exist, depending on the specifics of the organization, the issue and the context.

THREE-DOMAIN CORPORATE SOCIAL RESPONSIBILITY 'PORTRAITS'

An early framework proposed to depict the social responsibility that business has with respect to global business and multiple stakeholders, was that by Carroll (2003, 2004). In the 'Pyramid of Global CSR' Carroll made limited adaptations to his original conceptual model of what he termed 'corporate social performance' (Carroll 1979) and the 'Pyramid of Corporate Social Responsibility' (Carroll 2001) to indicate requirements to global stakeholders. The suggestions were that the MNE needed to meet four levels of responsibility, being: Make a profit consistent with expectations for international business; obey the law of host countries as well as international law; be ethical in practices, taking host-country and global standards into consideration and; be a good corporate citizen, especially as defined by the host countries' expectations (Carroll 2004: 118).

The framework was intended to 'help managers think through in a systematic way the different stakeholder expectations placed on their organizations' (Carroll 2004: 118). The original pyramid framework received wide support, but also a number of criticisms, which were addressed by the development of a three-domain approach. The new approach was intended to address a number of conceptual flaws in the pyramid depiction. The three-domain model therefore incorporated the overlapping nature of CSR domains, the equivalence of all categories of corporate responsibilities rather than implying that there is a hierarchical relationship, and the debate on philanthropic activities as being either outside the duty of businesses, or subsumed by ethical responsibility (Schwartz and Carroll 2003). The three domains therefore consist of the 'economic' domain, being activities intended to have a direct or indirect positive economic impact on the corporation in question; the 'legal' domain, pertaining to the firm's responsiveness to legal expectations mandated and expected by society; and the 'ethical' domain, referring to the responsibilities of business as expected by the general population and relevant stakeholders (Schwartz and Carroll 2003: 508–510). The three-domain approach is, like the original pyramid model, not specifically addressing global corporate responsibility. However, the examples illustrating the multiple domains are in a number of cases those from MNEs operating in multiple contexts, thereby implying application to organizations operating internationally.

Carroll's (2003) idea that such domain specific portraits exist is supported by other studies, for example by van den Heuvel, Soeters and Gössling (2011) and Furrer et al. (2010) who found gender, generation and work position differences in ethical, legal and economical CSR orientations. Therefore, there is recent support that different functions and individuals within an organization will display diverse CSR 'portraits' based on their CSR prioritizations, with greater or lesser emphasis on each of the domains (see Figure 3.1).

Economic Orientation   Legal Orientation   Ethical Orientation

Figure 3.1   Corporate Social Responsibility Portraits

Source: Schwartz and Carroll (2003)

The context of international business offers a challenging setting for CSR, as there are many and diverse stakeholder relationships, and CSR practices and stakeholder expectations vary across countries (Mohan 2006). The three-domain approach suggests that an organizational action is ideal when there is a complete overlap of the three domains so that economic, legal and ethical responsibilities are simultaneously fulfilled (Carroll 2003). Some of these practices and expectations may converge around hypernorms, but not without active reconciliation, and in addition there are local needs that arise from specific communities and contexts within which the MNE is operating. While the framework of global CSR (Carroll 2004) provides a systematic way for managers to think about global CSR, it does not provide the solution. And while the three-domain approach recognizes the multiple domains affected by individual actions, it does not provide a way forward for global leaders when they face multiple 'three-domains' stemming not just from various functions and divisions, but also from multiple national and cultural contexts.

Differing domains could exist for all categories of stakeholders, including those external to the firm, for example suppliers and local communities, however our primary focus in this chapter is on those contained within the firm, across national and cultural borders, and thereby held by employees in international divisions and subsidiaries.

Corporate Social Responsibility and Leadership

What do we know about the overall role that global leaders play when it comes to initiating and implementing CSR initiatives? In the extant literature we learn that managerial decisions are critical to firm-level activities (Finkelstein and Hambrick 1996), that managerial values are used to guide decisions in general (Pant and Lachmann 1998), and CSR performance in particular (Agle, Mitchell and Sonnenfeld 1999). As for managerial motives for initiating CSR, Waldman, Siegal and Javidan (2006) introduce us to the literature on leaders' instrumental-based motives, for example promoting CSR for their own benefit (Friedman 1970) or for firm profitability (Russo and Fouts 1997). Personal interests and firm strategies may also overlap (McWilliams and Siegal 2001). Or as in the case of Vitell and Paolillo's (2004) study in Spain, Turkey, Great Britain and USA, managerial CSR decisions and the probability of implantation success was reliant on managers' individual ethical perspective as well as on organizational cultural values. CSR engagement may also be due to pure moral and ethical concerns leaving both self-interest and firm profits outside the decision-making process (Waldman and Siegal 2008). Yet, how leaders contribute to CSR implementation, or more specifically how they convince employees and peers to support and act on CSR initiatives has been given a limited treatment in the CSR literature (Waldman and Siegal 2008, Van Velsor 2009, Strand 2011). The leader's role in CSR initiatives and implementation and whether this differs across countries and cultures are questions that we will address in the subsequent section.

LEADERSHIP STYLES AND CSR

Studies seeking the connection between leadership styles (such as transformational, transactional, visionary and participative) and the successful rallying of CSR support and implementation of CSR initiatives are surprisingly rare (Van Velsor 2009, Strand 2011). But in order to better understand the role of leadership in CSR, or rather that of leader characteristics and behaviour as influencing employees in the firm to engage in CSR, we turn to the extant literature. Strand (2011) introduces us to some of the research in this area – for example Szekely and Knirsch (2005), who after studying German firms conclude that the most critical success factor for transforming a company into a socially responsible enterprise is true leadership. This involved securing the commitment at the top, and through the use of well-developed incentive systems reward managers at all levels as they realized sustainability practices throughout the organization. Here we can add that D'Amato, Eckert, Ireland, Quinn and Van Velsor (2010) reached a complementary conclusion after analyzing five in-depth case studies from Belgium, India, Norway, Poland and Spain, namely the importance of building a strong leadership culture that is supportive of CSR practices. By recognizing global responsibility as a process, not an outcome, firms should, according to D'Amato, Eckert, Ireland, Quinn and Van Velsor (2010), concurrently apply leadership practices that will develop and empower employees. This is also a reasoning advanced by Maclagen (1999) who argued that the way forward is to understand CSR as an employee participative process characterized by involvement and communication. For dedicated managers to have equally dedicated employees, Ketola (2006) suggests that for employees to trust their managers, and subsequently engage in CSR activities, managers need to be coherent, and consistent in their words and action. From this we understand that irrespective of whether CSR initiatives and implementation is viewed as a top-down or bottom-up process, contemporary global leaders are expected to transform CSR practices from ideals to reality through employee engagement and effort.

There are some studies that focus on transformational leadership as providing necessary leadership while inspiring employees. Shahin and Zairi (2007) found that transformational leadership in small and medium-sized Iranian firms was more effective for soliciting support for CSR practices, somewhat similar to the findings of Egri and Herman (2000), who could draw the conclusion that transformational leadership approaches were more successful in non-profit environmental, than in profit-earning organizations in the US and Canada. Waldman, Siegal and Javidan (2006) studied how transformational leadership, that is managers' charismatic leadership and intellectual stimulation of employees, is associated with the extent of CSR activities in US and Canadian firms. They found that intellectual stimulation was significantly related to strategic CSR, in other words to corporate business strategies, but surprisingly charismatic leadership was found to be unconnected to CSR presence. In other words, appealing to the brain (intellectual stimulation) was used to solicit support for strategic, business-connected CSR, but charismatic leadership was not found to be effective for the same purpose in the US and Canada. While these findings seem unexpected, perhaps ideas differentiating between 'explicit' and 'implicit' CSR (and their links to leadership styles) could provide us with some explanation.

The 'explicit and implicit duality' emerged from Matten and Moon's (2004, 2008) comparative work, where European firms exhibited implicit CSR and American firms demonstrated explicit CSR. They explain that implicit CSR is about values and norms that become mandatory, whereas explicit CSR is voluntary and implemented after strategic top management decisions. The voluntarily CSR actions, which may be the same as those exercised in firms with implicit CSR, are explicitly communicated to stakeholders to become a part of the business's image and goals. This duality between the externalized and the internalized CSR drivers was also supported in a review by Williams and Aguliera (2008), who especially point to British firms, which despite other Anglo–American similarities, were found to be closer to European firms, than to those in the USA.

In an in-depth study of a major Australian bank, highly rated on CSR indices, Angus-Leppan, Metcalf and Benn (2010) found that external CSR expressed in official documents (on and off the web) was related to 'autocratic leadership' defined as a reliance on formal position, policies and a reward versus punishment system. On the other hand, implicit CSR expressed by personal values and informal CSR discussions was found among those who exhibited 'emergent CSR leadership' (in other words, initiating CSR although not part of the job), or 'authentic leadership' (a close alignment between values and behaviour even when in conflict with organizational expectations). The co-existence of the explicit and implicit CSR when set outside the European–American divide suggests the need for more fine-grained cultural analysis where not only instrumental behaviour and leader motives are taken into account, to understand the drivers of leader decisions and actions (Waldman and Siegal 2008).

From earlier research we observe that leadership matters, that employees should be involved in the process, and that leadership styles used when soliciting support for and when implementing CSR practices vary across countries. This leads us to query whether manager and employee prioritization of CSR concerns vary across countries. In the subsequent section we turn to literature that provides a more detailed cultural analysis when examining the links between CSR and culture.

Cultural Value Orientation and Corporate Social Responsibility Prioritization

Culture's impact on CSR has remained largely unexplored (Egri and Ralston 2008). Yet as pointed out by Van den Heuvel, Soeters and Gössling (2010) the significance of cross-cultural differences has not gone unnoticed. Carroll's (1979) original four levels or categories of CSR responsibilities: Economic, legal, ethical and 'discretionary' (mainly social concerns such as contribution to the welfare of the community or nation) has been used to frame studies of CSR across countries and cultures. Crane and Matten (2007: 52) argue that 'whilst the four levels of responsibilities are still largely valid in a European context, they take on different nuance, and may be accorded different significance', a variation not only occurring within Europe but also in countries outside Europe whether Carroll's (1979) CSR typology or some other categorization is used in the study.

CEOs and other corporate leaders and managers vary across countries in how they value CSR in decision making and in their support towards CSR. For example Waldman, de Luque, Washburn, and Hous (2006) found that they could predict top management team members' CSR values, that is how much importance they think should be placed on different CSR concerns (shareholder/owner CSR, stakeholder CSR, and community state/welfare CSR), by using data on cultural dimensions from 15 countries across the world. High institutional collectivism was particularly associated with a CSR stakeholder orientation but also with community/state welfare concerns. This was expected according to Waldman, de Luque, Washburn, and House (2006) as in these cultures it is strongly encouraged to take into account the future, the better good of the community, and society at large, when deciding on management action. Power distance was also found to be a strong predictor of valuing CSR, especially stakeholder CSR, where more ethical concerns were predicted by low power distance. Waldman, de Luque, Washburn, and House (2006) point out that when less priority is placed on for example stakeholder CSR in a subsidiary, although in line with the national culture hosting the subsidiary, it will lead to conflicting policies and practices. The reason is a lack of alignment with, and could even be in direct opposition to, MNE headquarters' cultural predisposition. This is an example of the type of complication that can be expected in organizations spanning across cultures when trying to establish and implement a CSR policy worldwide.

Other evidence of a relationship between managers' CSR and cultural value orientations is provided by Williams and Aguilera (2008), who report the results of a large unpublished study by Egri and Ralston (2006). Here managers' values in 28 countries were directly related to the type of corporate responsibility they supported. For example in countries of a Roman Catholic heritage promoting communitarian norms, managers were supportive of social corporate responsibility, while those in ex-communist countries or Confucian-oriented countries were more likely to support economic corporate responsibility initiatives.

In contrast to the Egri and Ralston (2006) and Waldman, de Luque, Washburn, and House (2006) studies of managers' perceptions, Van den Heuvel, Soeters and Gössling (2011) surveyed employee CSR orientations. Building on Carroll's (1979) typology of economic, ethical, legal and discretionary (mainly social) CSR concerns, Van den Heuvel, Soeters and Gössling (2011) found that these concerns varied among employees across three culturally distinct country clusters. In Asia (Hong Kong, India and Singapore) and in the Anglo–American countries (USA and UK) legal regulations were in focus in contrast to the dominance of ethical concerns in Western Europe (Belgium, France, Germany, Luxembourg, Netherlands, Sweden and Switzerland). Discretionary CSR, that is social concerns, was ranked last in all three cultural clusters but differed significantly across them, with Western Europe placing more emphasis than the Asian and Anglo–American clusters on social concerns. Economic concerns on the other hand did not vary significantly across the clusters, but in ranking. In the South Asian and Anglo–American clusters economic concerns came second after legal, while in Western Europe both ethical and legal concerns were higher prioritized than economic concerns.

To explain these cross-cultural cluster differences, van den Heuvel, Soeters and Gössling (2010) draw on cultural theory, specifically using Schwartz (2006) cultural dimensions. For example, that Western Europe demonstrated a stronger orientation towards ethical CSR could be expected, stemming from an egalitarian cultural value orientation. Also, a hierarchical cultural orientation in the South Asian cluster could explain that more importance is placed on economic concerns, whereas the mastery cultural dimension is argued to lead to a smaller priority placed on social responsibilities in the Anglo–American cluster. In a similar manner cultural orientations are used to explain the other CSR results. Despite sample and CSR measure differences, we find that the Van den Heuvel, Soeters and Gössling (2011) findings largely echo those of both Egri and Ralston (2006) and Waldman, de Luque, Washburn, and House (2006).

Western European countries were found to diverge from other countries outside Europe in Egri and Ralston 2006) and van den Heuvel, Soeters and Gössling (2011) studies. In the Furrer et al. (2010) study of economic, environmental and social CSR, the participants from Western European countries were found to differ from those in the surveyed Central and East European countries in terms of less importance placed on economic CSR. As Crane and Matten (2007) suggested, CSR prioritizations even vary in significance within Europe. The results regarding social and environmental CSR also demonstrated differences in priority across the studied countries but not in line with a West versus Central and Eastern divide. In this study the findings are not explained by cultural dimension differences; instead Furrer et al. (2010) draw on cultural modernization institutional theory, arguing that in more industrially advanced countries environmental concerns are more favoured than in transitional or emerging economies.

CULTURALLY-BASED CORPORATE SOCIAL RESPONSIBILITY 'PORTRAITS'

In our literature review we have clearly identified that CSR concerns and prioritization vary across countries, and that these differences can be explained by culture theory. Following from this, we can depict the across-country differences in the 'weight' placed on the various studied CSR components as 'portraits' (Carroll 2003), however these CSR portraits differ across cultures, instead of functions or individuals as discussed earlier in this chapter.

These studies vary somewhat as to the type of CSR attitudes and orientations examined; these are not necessarily the 'economic, legal and social' triad as in Schwartz and Carroll's (2003) conceptualization. Although, van den Heuvel, Soeters and Gössling (2011) – in drawing on Carroll's 1979 typology – study economic, legal, ethical and 'discretionary' (mainly social or philanthropic concerns such as contribution to the welfare of the community or nation) CSR concerns, Furrer et al. (2010) decided to group together legal, ethical and discretionary into a 'social' concern category, add a new category labelled environmental, and keep the economic concerns category. These economic, social and environmental CSR categories were also in focus in the Egri and Ralston (2006) study. The potentially odd one out is Waldman, de Luque, Washburn, and House (2006) who differentiate between: 1) shareholder/owner CSR; 2) stakeholder CSR; and 3) community state/welfare CSR, but a closer look reveals that the first is mainly economic concerns such as firm profit, the second is about ethical aspects including employee welfare but also environmental types of concern, and the third category is about social concerns such as contribution to the welfare of the community or nation.

Hence the studies cut the CSR categories in slightly different ways but the evidence is clear that we can talk about culturally-based CSR portraits varying across countries. We could also see converging patterns illustrating which CSR priorities were placed in which countries across the different studies we reviewed. Further strengthening the support for the existence of culturally-based CSR portraits was the established connection between cultural orientations and CSR orientations. We have chosen to use results from the Egri and Ralston (2006) study to illustrate how the CSR portraits can vary across two different cultural contexts (see Figure 3.2).

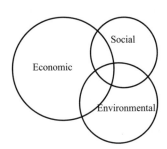

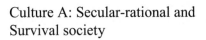

Culture A: Secular-rational and Survival society

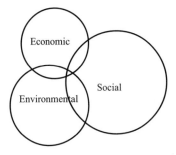

Culture B: Ethical idealism and Communitarian norms

Figure 3.2   Culture-based Corporate Social Responsibility Portraits

Source: Adapted from Egri and Ralston (2006)

Reconciling Domains and Managing Paradoxes

Global leaders, whether formally in charge or emerging as an advocate for CSR, face multiple motives, attitudes and values among employee and management when initiating and implementing CSR activities. First, as shown in the CSR literature and graphically depicted by the three-domain model (see Figure 3.1), individuals, for example on a functional basis, will differ in the weight that they give to the legalistic, economic and ethical concerns and responsibilities when making decisions regarding CSR. Second and similarly, the existence of distinct 'cultural CSR portraits' could be proposed (see Figure 3.2), based on the clear links between cultural orientation and CSR prioritization in the extant literature.

The global leader working across national and cultural and perhaps also functional borders, for example in top management teams, heading merger and acquisition integration teams or leading global virtual teams, will face differing and often conflicting CSR motives, attitudes and values, but is expected to deliver agreement by adhering to CSR hypernorms, to develop firm-specific alternatives, and to reconcile various local norms. We propose that to reconcile different CSR domains and manage across cultural paradoxes global leaders need to take on the roles of 'boundary spanners', 'bridge makers' and 'blenders'.

Boundary spanners, bridge makers and blenders have emerged as three roles, which although of value to any leader are critical to global leaders who work across multiple national and cultural contexts (Butler, Zander, Mockaitis and Sutton 2012). As such these three roles are also at the heart of leading global teams (Zander, Mockaitis and Butler, 2012). Global managers may have earlier relied on firm policies and practices for ensuring employee activities towards common goals but by being people-oriented and focused, they can develop multicultural competencies, which in turn will help them to overcome cultural challenges (Holt and Seki 2012) such as those posed by differing CSR attitudes or portraits. To acquire and develop such qualities Butler, Zander, Mockaitis and Sutton (2012) propose that global leaders need to take on these three roles. Zander, Mockaitis and Butler (2012) discovered that several studies indicated employee support for (and satisfaction with) team leaders who carry out boundary-spanning, bridge making and blending roles.

Acting as a boundary spanner involves spanning different groupings of people that differ in CSR values and attitudes, such as international subsidiaries, headquarters and other international organizational units in the MNE. The bridge-making role involves bridging cultural differences between team members within a team, for example in a top management team about to decide on company-wide CSR policies or practices, or in a regional management team where the individual country directors in the region have different CSR perceptions and prioritizations. Global leaders need not only span national and cultural boundaries across teams and make cultural bridges within a team, but they also need to blend groups of people together. This role is imperative, for example when various local CSR initiative teams are expected to become a regional or global team, and there is a need to work together as one. Another example is when units from a newly acquired firm need to be integrated with units in the acquiring firm, and the two units differ as to their CSR policies and practices. Reconciliation here is a delicate process, which a global leader can facilitate by acting as a blender.

While each leader will approach the reconciliation of the CSR domains and differing employee CSR priorities in a unique way, Figure 3.3 illustrates the generic process to a decision. Unlike the challenge of other global leader tasks, for instance leading multicultural teams with non-CSR-oriented tasks, the reconciliation of CSR is rarely intended as a synergistic outcome. Ultimately the objective is to overcome conflict in goals and resolve ambiguity for each action to be undertaken. A decision needs to be made that best serves the employees and divisions involved and is viewed as a satisfactory, if not ideal, outcome by all.

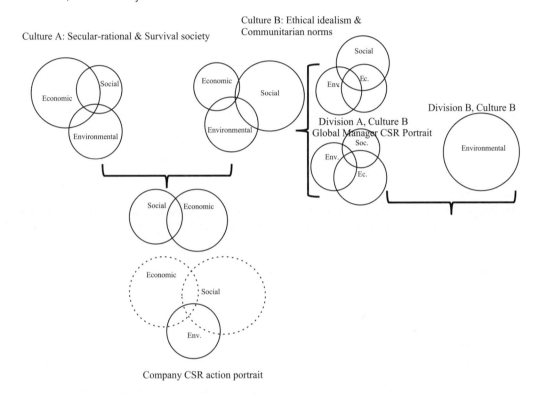

Figure 3.3   Boundary Spanning, Bridging and Blending: Culture-based CSR portraits

Our model, representing the reconciliation process, proposes that the leaders' held 'CSR portraits' influence the outcome but is not the only determinant. The global leader will meet a spectrum of functional and individual CSR portraits within the organization, and when their role specifically encompasses actions across borders their role of boundary spanning will in addition face differing cultural portraits, in themselves an integration of multiple individual level CSR preferences. The bridging role – bridging differing culturally-based preferences and expectations within groups such as the top management team, the regional directors' group or a post-acquisition or merger team – requires cultural code-switching, cultural intelligence and cultural competence. The blending role of the global leader will require the ability to switch frames from their own CSR portrait to the portrait of others, to find the nodes of commonality and bring together multiple CSR portraits to create a domain that encompasses the hypernorm, and providing cognitive closure to all employees.

The outcome of the reconciliation process may also depend on the strategy of the organization and the rigidity of the headquarters' stance towards CSR. This may also strongly influence the direction of the process as perspectives differ between organizations on whether MNEs should simulate centralized CSR strategies or whether they should be developed locally (Muller 2006). A strongly centralized CSR strategy with a universal approach to CSR internationally may require a stronger push by the global leader to blend towards the portrait held by headquarters. In this case the reconciliation process will be primarily top-down and would involve the global leader rallying support for a pre-determined CSR portrait and focusing heavily on finding local commonalities that can be drawn upon to match the headquarters' priorities. The global leader needs to find ways to create a sense of ownership and legitimacy of the CSR decision at the local level to ensure successful adherence to the directive (Jamali 2010). A more decentralized CSR strategy may allow the global leader to give greater prominence to the portraits of local divisions resulting in more fragmented, organizational-wide CSR outcome. A bottom-up reconciliation would likely involve the global manager selecting between proposals, suggestions and projects initiated at a local level based on local CSR portraits. The global leader supports the selection through funding allocation and by framing the initiative within the context of the global CSR stance (Jamali 2010). Whether a top-down or bottom-up process the global leader will need to boundary span, build bridges and blend, in order to reconcile conflicting demands and achieve a global CSR stance for the MNE.

Concluding Reflections

In this chapter we extend the stream of literature stemming from Carroll's early conceptions of CSR categories. We find evidence that these categories provide dilemmas and complexities for organizations that operate across cultural boarders. Differing priorities across MNE's international subsidiaries and other organization units can be viewed as culturally-based CSR-portraits. We have modeled a generic reconciliation process accounting for the global leader's own CSR concerns, international culturally-based CSR priorities and within-culture division-based CSR concerns. Rather than leaving this as a paradox, or at the level of macro forces, we have attempted to look more closely at the processes of reconciliation, highlighting the central role that global leaders play in organizational outcomes with respect to CSR. As they engage in boundary spanning, bridge making and blending they will be able to combine economic, legal, ethical, social and other aspects of CSR, which as concluded by van den Heuvel, Soeters and Gössling (2011), may be the best way for MNEs to address employees' culturally-based differing CSR demands.

To extend our thinking forward there are three additional considerations: The first is the influencing role and abilities of global leaders. For simplicity our model assumes static portraits of CSR preferences. If we assume that CSR portraits are not static, but may be subject to change through education, exposure and experience, and understanding of differing perspectives, then global leaders may also influence the portraits of stakeholders through an interactive process. This interactive process of influence could well be a source of authenticity for the global leader, whereby authenticity is seen as a positive leadership trait where the behaviours of the leader are true to him or herself (Luthens and Avolio 2003: 243) A global leader that only looks for commonalities and compromises may be perceived as weaker and less trustworthy in some cultural settings than a leader who uses their own CSR portrait as a statement of their position and intentions, and therefore tries to influence through the boundary-spanning process. Clearly in some instances the contradiction between finding commonalities between others and remaining authentic to oneself may be difficult to resolve. The global leader has a task duty to search out a solution to differing portraits; simultaneously, doing so may mean losing authenticity in the eyes of others within the organization. This balancing act is a further predicament to be resolved and how this is undertaken may be a further avenue to explore, to understand more fully both the role of global leaders and their associated required skills.

Secondly, the boundaries between the CSR domains are likely to differ between cultural contexts. Particularly returning to Carroll's (2003) original three-domain model, the system of law and the societal norms of ethics can differ between cultures. The extent of codification of ethics into law – for example as expressed by the cultural dimension of uncertainty avoidance (Hofstede 1980) – would suggest that the same action could be perceived by different societies as either a matter of law, or a matter of ethics, requiring additional reconciliation by the global leader. To what degree perceptions of boundaries differ and what actions more readily fall in an area of uncertainty would be a fruitful avenue for future research to more closely understand the most probable challenges facing future global leaders.

Thirdly, a natural extension of this model development would be to incorporate the influence of external stakeholders. This could include not only the portraits of the various external stakeholders, for instance suppliers and customers, but also how the interaction is managed and incorporated by the organization, and how differing portraits between the firm and external parties are reconciled. This may well be affected by the actions of global leaders, however it is likely that other organizational members will also play a harmonizing role in the process across the boundaries of the firm. Scholars may find Voegtlin, Patzer and Scherer's (2012) multi-level model of responsible leadership of interest as the proposed responsibilities do not stop at the individual employee or at firm level but also involves reaching out to external stakeholders outside the firm.

In developing a model extension in this chapter, our hope is that we move closer to understanding the skills and roles of global leaders as well as provide a more nuanced tool for leadership training. Our proposed model for reconciling conflicting CSR demands and associated paradoxes is also intended as a contribution to what has become known as 'responsible leadership' (Voegtlin, Patzer and Scherer 2012). As the most recent of leadership developments where leadership has moved from charismatic and visionary to ethical and authentic (including servant leadership), responsible leadership differs from these, yet encompasses them all. Responsible leadership has been proposed as the answer to 'who is responsible for what and toward whom in another connected business world' (Voegtlin, Patzer and Scherer 2012). Here we understand Voegtlin, Patzer and Scherer's (2012) view of responsible leadership as embedded in globalization processes, and that responsible leaders should think about the consequences of decisions for all affected parties, engage in an active dialogue, weigh and balance the differing interests. This elegantly sums up what we have tried to achieve with our CSR reconciliation model in this chapter.

When discussing responsible leadership at the firm level Davis, Whitman and Zald (2008) argue that globalization will continue to exert pressure for convergence of national standards into a more universal definition of global CSR. Yet quoting Martin Wolf they posit that 'the interests of a transnational company are not the same as those of the country from which it originates or of the workers it has historically employed'. It has become, to coin a phrase, a 'rootless cosmopolitan' (2004: 243–244) leading Davis, Whitman and Zald (2008) to argue that to talk about MNE's CSR obligations to their employees or communities is becoming meaningless. If MNEs are rootless, then in our view it will not lessen the need for global leaders to boundary span, bridge make or blend. On the contrary, we agree with Voegtlin, Patzer and Scherer (2012: 12) who posit that, 'As leadership is increasingly confronted with problems of cultural heterogeneity, moral dilemmas, and ethical conflicts, our understanding of responsible leadership places deliberative and discursive practices at the heart of leadership, thereby aiming for a legitimate and peaceful mode of conflict resolution.' The extended three-domain approach can be used in training and practice to incorporate reflections on individual leaders' CSR portraits as well as culturally diverging CSR portraits. It can also be used to frame discussions of differing typical portraits, as well as provide a deeper understanding of the process of reconciliation of differences in what we believe to be the future of MNEs, namely to become 'cosmopolitans with both roots and wings'.

References

Agle, B.R., Mitchell, R.K. and Sonnenfeld, J.A. 1999. Who Matters to CEOs: An Investigation of Stakeholder Attributes and Salience, Corporate Performance and CEO Values. *Academy of Management Journal*, 42(1): 507–525.

Angus-Leppan, T., Metcalf, L. and Benn, S. 2010. Leadership Styles and CSR Practice: An Examination of Sensemaking, Institutional Drivers, and CSR leadership. *Journal of Business Ethics*, 93: 189–213.

Butler, C.L., Zander, L., Mockaitis, A.I. and Sutton, C. 2012. Global leaders as Boundary Spanners, Bridge Makers, and Blenders. *Industrial Organizational Psychologists: Perspectives on Research and Practice*, 5(2), 246–249.

Carroll, A.B. 1979. A Three-dimensional Conceptual Model of Corporate Performance. *Academy of Management Review*, 4(4): 497–505.

Carroll, A.B. 1999. Corporate Social Responsibility: Evolution of a Definitional Construct. *Business & Society*, 38(3): 268–295.

Carroll, A.B. 2001. The Pyramid of Corporate Social Responsibility: Toward the Moral Management of Organizational Stakeholders. *Business Horizons*, July/August, 39–48.

Carroll, A.B. 2003. *Business and Society: Ethics and Stakeholder Management*. 5th Edition. Cincinnati: Thomson-South-Western.

Carroll, A. B. 2004. Managing Ethically with Global Stakeholders: A Present and Future Challenge. *Academy of Management Executive*, 18(2): 114–120.

Collier, J. and Wanderlay, L. 2005. Thinking for the Future: Global Corporate Responsibility in the Twenty-first Century. *Futures*, 37(2–3): 169–182.

Crane, A. and Matten, D. 2007 *Business Ethics: Managing Corporate Citizenship and Sustainability in the Age of Globalization*. Oxford: Oxford University Press.

Dahlsrud, A. 2006. How Corporate Social Responsibility is Defined: Analysis of 37 Definitions. *Corporate Social Responsibility and Environmental Management*, 15(1): 1–13.

D'Amato, A., Eckert, R., Ireland, J., Quinn, L. and Van Velsor, E. 2010 Leadership Practices for Corporate Global Responsibilities. *Journal of Global Responsibility*, 1(2): 225–249.

Davis, G., Whitman, M. and Zald, M. 2008 The Responsibility Paradox. *Stanford Social Innovation Review*, Winter: 31–37.

Donaldson, T. and Dunfee, R. (1994) Toward a Unified Conception of Business Ethics: Integrative Social Contracts Theory. *Academy of Management Review*, 19(2): 252–284.

Egri, C. and Herman, S. 2000. Leadership in the North American Environmental Sector: Values, Leadership Styles, and Contexts of Environmental Leaders and their Organizations. *Academy of Management Journal*, 32(4): 571–604.

Egri, C.P. and Ralston, D.A. 2008. Corporate Responsibility: A Review of International Management Research from 1998 to 2007. *Journal of International Management*, 14: 319–339.

Egri, C.P. and Ralston, D.A, 2006. *The Influence of Personal Values and National Contexts on Attitudes Towards Corporate Responsibilities*. Paper to the Third BC Organizational Behaviour Conference, Vancouver, Canada, 2006.

Finkelstein, S. and Hambrick, D.C. 1996. *Strategic Leadership: Top Executives and Their Effects on Organizations*. Minneapolis/St Paul: West Publishing.

Friedman, M. 1970. The Social Responsibility of Business is to Increase Its Profits. *New York Times*, 13 September.

Furrer, O., Egri, C.P., Ralston, D.A., Danis, W., Reynaud, E., Naoumova, I., Molteni, M., Starkus, A., León Darder, F., Dabic, M. and Furrer-Perrinjaquet, A. 2010. Attitudes toward corporate responsibilities in Western Europe and in Central and East Europe, *Management International Review*, 50(3): 379–398.

Hofstede, G. 1980. Culture's Consequences. Bevery Hills CA : SAGE Publications

Holt, K. and Seki, K. 2012 Global Leadership: A Developmental Shift for Everyone. *Industrial Organizational Psychologist: Perspectives on Research and Practice*, 5: 196–215.

Husted, B. and Allen, D. 2006. Corporate Social Responsibility in the Multinational Enterprise: Strategic and Institutional Approaches. *Journal of International Business Studies*, 37(6): 838–849.

Jamali, D. 2010. The CSR of MNC Subsidiaries in Developing Countries: Global, Local, Substantive or Diluted? *Journal of Business Ethics*, 93(Suppl. 1): 181–200.

Ketola, T. 2006. Do You Trust Your Boss? A Jungian Analysis of Leadership Reliability in CSR. *Electronic Journal of Business Ethics and Organization Studies*, 11(2): 6–14.

Levitt, T. 1958. The Dangers of Social Responsibility. *Harvard Business Review*, 34: 41–70.

Luthens, F. and Avolio, B. 2003. Authentic Leadership: A Positive Development Approach, in *Positive Organizational Scholarship: Foundations of a New Discipline*, edited by K.S. Cameron, J.E. Dutton and R.E. Quinn. San Francisco, CA: Berrett-Koehler, 241–261.

Maclagen, P. 1999. Corporate Social Responsibility as a Participating Process. *Business Ethics: A European Review*, 8(1): 43–49.

Matten D. and Moon, J. 2004. 'Implicit' and 'Explicit' CSR: A Conceptual Framework for Understanding CSR across Europe, in *CSR Across Europe*, edited by A. Habisch, J. Jonker, M. Wegner and R. Schmidpeter. Berlin: Springer-Verlag, 335–356.

Matten, D. and Moon, J. 2008. 'Implicit' and 'Explicit' CSR: A Conceptual Framework for a Comparative Understanding of Corporate Social Responsibility. *Academy of Management Review*, 33: 404–424.

McWilliams, A. and Siegal, D. 2001. Corporate Social Responsibility: A Theory of the Firm Perspective. *Academy of Management Review*, 26: 117–127.

Mohan, A. 2006. Global Corporate Social Responsibilities Management in MNCs. *Journal of Business Strategies*, 23(1): 9–32.

Muller, A. 2006. Global versus local CSR strategies. *European Management Journal*, 24(2–3): 189–198.

Pant, P.N. and Lachmann, R. 1998. Value Incongruity and Strategic Choice. *Journal of Management Studies*, 35(2): 195–212.

Russo, M. and Fouts, P. 1997. A Resource-based Perspective on Corporate Environmental Performance and Profitability. *Academy of Management Journal*, 40: 534–459.

Schwartz, S.H. 2006. A Theory of Cultural Value Orientation: Explication and Applications. *Comparative Sociology*, 5: 137–182.

Schwartz, M. and Carroll, A. 2003. Corporate Social Responsibility: A Three-Domain Approach. *Business Ethics Quarterly*, 13(4): 503–530.

Shahin, A. and Zairi, M. 2007. Corporate Governance as a Critical Element for Driving Excellence in Corporate Social Responsibility. *International Journal of Quality and Reliability Management*, 24(7): 753–770.

Strand, R. 2011. Exploring the Role of Leadership in Corporate Social Responsibility: A Review. *Journal of Leadership, Accountability and Ethics*, 8(4): 84–96.

Szekely, F. and Knirsch, M. 2005. Responsible Leadership and Corporate Social Responsibility: Metrics for Sustainable Performance. *European Management Journal*, 23(6): 628–647.

Van den Heuvel, G., Soeters, J. and Gössling, T. 2011. Global Business, Global Responsibilities: Corporate Social Responsibility Orientations within a Multinational Bank. *Business & Society*, 20(10): 1–36

Van Marrewijk, M. 2003. Concepts and Definitions of CSR and Corporate Sustainability: Between Agency and Communion. *Journal of Business Ethics*, 44(2/3), 95–105.

Van Velsor, E. 2009. Introduction: Leadership and Corporate Social Responsibility. *Corporate Governance*, 9(1): 3–6.

Vitell, S.J. and Paolillo, J.G. 2004. A Cross-cultural Study of the Antecedents of the Perceived Role of Ethics and Social Responsibility. *Business Ethics*, 13(2–3): 185–199.

Voegtlin, C., Patzer, M. and Scherer, A. 2012. Responsible Leadership in Global Business: A New Approach to Leadership and its Multi-level Outcomes. *Journal of Business Ethics*, 105: 1–16.

Waddock, S., Bodwell, C., and Graves, S. 2002. Responsibility: The New Business Imperative. *Academy of Management Executive*, 16: 132–148.

Waldman, D.A. and Siegal, D.S. 2008. Defining the socially responsible leader. *Leadership Quarterly*, 19: 117–131.

Waldman, D.A., Siegal, D.S. and Javidan, M. 2006. Components of CEO Transformational Leadership and Corporate Social Responsibility. *Journal of Management*, 43(8): 1703–1725.

Waldman, D.A., de Luque, M., Washburn, N., House, R. 2006. Cultural and Leadership Predictors of Corporate Social Responsibility Values of Top Management: A GLOBE Study of 15 Countries. *Journal of International Business Studies*, 37: 823–837.

Williams, C.A. and Aguilera, R.V. 2008. Corporate Social Responsibility in a Comparative Perspective, in *Oxford Handbook of Corporate Social Responsibility*, edited by A. Crane. Oxford: Oxford Press.

Wolf, M. 2004. *Why Globalization Works*. New Haven: Yale University Press.

Zander, L., Mockaitis, A.I. and Butler, C.L. 2012. Leading Global Teams. *Journal of World Business*, 47(4). 592-603.

4 Responsible Leadership: Business Myth or Corporate Reality?

CIARA HACKETT

Introduction

The financial crisis has highlighted some of the limitations of the global system. Enterprises previously thought to be too big to fail have learned the harsh realities of capitalism (Merill Lynch, Lehman Bros, Northern Rock), countries have been shaken considerably from the bankruptcy of Iceland to the near-collapse of the markets in Greece, Ireland and Italy. The current age of austerity has largely dominated supra-national and indeed global politics in the last few years. The extent of the crisis has illustrated that relationships between business, governments and society needs to be re-evaluated in light of shifts in the global market thereby recognizing that some countries have a more limited power of persuasion than some corporations.

This chapter is centered on an understanding of leadership. In defining leadership it looks at the literature on the area of the transnational capitalist class (TCC). By establishing this class as a leader in our global market – the chapter then explores how the TCC may in fact be more powerful than national governments. In assuming this power, questions need to be asked in relation to responsibilities that are aligned with an increase of power. This will be done through an analysis of how societal expectations of business enterprise have changed since the early twentieth century. The end of this discussion – which looks at national, federal and international trends – will then question the legitimacy of our expectations of business. Whether or not responsible leadership is a leadership committed to business maximization or in developing an embedded approach to sustainable business practice via corporate social responsibility(CSR)mechanisms will be explored. The chapter will proceed by analyzing the corporation's responsibility to shareholders and whether, by assuming a responsibility to wider society – which, as legislative advances seems to suggest is what they should be doing – they are acting beyond the scope of their role. A responsibility to wider society can be questioned and indeed may suggest that our understanding of 'company' and 'corporations' needs to be re-evaluated in light of global trends in the area. If it is believed that society is owed a responsibility by corporations, the regulation of this responsibility is also subject to discussion. It may be that corporations owe a responsibility to stakeholders but that, due to developmental failures on the national and international scale, the accountability mechanisms to ensure that corporations meet their responsibilities is decidedly absent or ineffective.

The Who's Who in Responsible Leadership Today

The governance structures of society are in a constant state of evolution. This section will address some of the discourse on the shifts in global governance and, by doing so will identify the parameters of leadership for the purposes of this chapter. Looking at the TCC as a means of addressing the scope of responsible leadership provides us with a conceptual toolkit which will facilitate a broader understanding of the area. Focused not only on the internal workings of the corporation, by addressing the wider power and control of corporations, the importance of external factors such as the importance of business leaders in society today – and especially responsible global leaders can be realized.

Numerous academics have, since the end of the last century discussed the demise of the nation state (Holton 1998, Strange 1996). Their reasoning behind this stems from the fact that states are constrained by jurisdictional boundaries. Robinson (2007) notes that 'capitalism has changed fundamentally' and calls for a new theory addressing capitalist expansion. The emergence of multinational corporations (MNCs), which can cross state and federal boundaries, does support the argument of the nation State's decline and by extension, national (and arguably federal) governments. To this end, Sklair (2001, 2006–2007) has identified what he terms as Transnational Practices (TNP).[1] Backer (2007–2008) takes a different route to Sklair, but ultimately arrives at the same conclusion. By focusing specifically on the role of regulations and their relationship with the MNC, he supposes a similar ideology to Sklair, in other words the notion that those individuals that govern the MNC have an emerging role on the global stage and as such, assumed responsibilities to society. Lozano et al. (2009) have recognized this when they speak about the ethical wealth of regions and countries. They believe that there is a need for a shared vision for the company and the nation and suggests that CSR is the vehicle by which this is understood. They go on to state that the knowledge society has forced us to rethink the network between the competitive advantage of nations and their ethical wealth. What this all suggests is that businesses are becoming increasingly as, if not more, powerful than States. That being the case, it seems as though academics in this area are suggesting that as their profits increase, so too does their social commitments to society. This does

---

1   Sklair (2001) describes this as follows:
   1. 'TCC based on the transnational corporation is emerging that is more or less in control of the processes of globalization.
   2. The TCC is beginning to act as a transnational dominant class in some spheres.
   3. The globalization of the capitalist system reproduces itself through the profit-driven culture ideology of consumerism.
   4. The TCC is working consciously to resolve two central crises, namely:
       (i) the simultaneous creation of increasing poverty and increasing wealth within and between communities and societies (class polarization crisis);
       (ii) the unsustainablity of the system (the ecological crisis)...'
   These are divided into three. First there is the economic aspect (which is the institutional form of the MNC), secondly the Political aspect (which he terms the transnational capitalist class) and finally the Cultural aspect (dubbed 'consumerism' by Sklair 2006–2007). Taken together, these transnational practices represent global capitalism. Although arguing that the global systems approach to globalization is not synonymous with global capitalism, the dominant forces in global capitalism are in fact the same forces prevalent in the global system (Sklair 2006–2007).

raise some issues which will be discussed later in the chapter relating primarily to the role of business and whether it is fair, just or reasonable to expect business responsibilities to change as it assumes more wealth and power.

Society has advanced considerably in recent decades, so much so that traditional global leaders (such as national and federal governments) have become disenfranchised from the global agenda as they can no longer be the main actors due to the boundary constraints mentioned above. This is an extension of Chimni's (2007) premise. In his work, he suggests that international law has disenfranchised third world countries from the first world. He argues that by removing them as main actors they are limited in the powers of enforcement. This chapter develops this idea by suggesting that the distinction between first world and third world has been obliterated by the entrance of the MNC into the global system. Extending dependency theories of the 1960s and 1970s (Dos Santos 1973, Frank 1967), today the actors in core-peripheral relationships have been altered considerably. Given the changing shape and scope of the global system today, the TCC is in fact the 'core' actor in the governance discourse, and States now operate a peripheral-type role (although some are more peripheral than others). This is a trend that has been noted in communications from international organizations, for example, the United Nations Norms on the responsibilities of transnational corporations and other business enterprises with regard to human rights. 'Taking note of global trends which have increased the influence of transnational corporations and other business enterprises on the economies of most countries and in international economic relations, and of the growing number of other business enterprises which operate across national boundaries in a variety of arrangements resulting in economic activities beyond the actual capacities of any one national state' suggests a recognition by such bodies that there is a new leadership hierarchy, and foremost in this hierarchy is transnational corporations. Interestingly, however, the discourse on the Norms and the ensuing United Nations Framework on Business and Human Rights would suggest that MNCs were vehemently opposed to it. Whether or not this is due to an encroachment on the standard voluntary approach to corporate responsibilities or whether it is simply due to committing global business to a responsible leadership on paper can be considered. Assuming the changing shape of leadership it is important to consider a new global leader – the perceived political faction in control of it: The TCC.

Sklair's (2001) work would suggest that the new global leaders are the TCC. This, he surmises, is comprised of corporate executives, bureaucrats, politicians, globalizing professionals and the media, and in defining transnational as 'forces, processes, and institutions that cross borders but do not derive their power and authority from the state' (2001) appears to differentiate transnational with international. Indeed Robinson (2007) notes this nationstate to interstate relationship as not going far enough. It may be that what Robinson and indeed Sklair and Chimni are positing is that society needs to be addressing inter-governance relations thereby removing the State-centric notions which have prevailed until this point. Sklair (2001) suggests that the term 'international' considers power and authority to be still derived from state or interstate relations. Transnational suggests that relationships transcend state relations, instead incorporating entites such as MNCs. In apparent agreement with this view, Chimni (2007) cites the TCC as 'constituted by the transnational fractions of the national capitalist classes'.

The purpose of such a class is to 'create ideal and local conditions not only for their own interests but also for the interests of the capitalist system as a whole' (Sklair 2001).

Under this ideology therefore, the TCC are making system-wide decisions suggesting some degree of uniformity. Chimni (2007) expands on this by claiming that the TCC seeks to unify the world market through the instrument of international law. The manner in which Sklair speaks of 'ideal and local conditions' indicates a recognition of country specific intracies but at the same time, ensuring a focus on the 'big picture' as opposed to national trends. Harvey (2003) recognizes the problems of this new type of governance. In his theory of new imperialism, he looks at leaders and analyzes how different backgrounds (political, economic and so on) impact on their understanding of their role in society. His theory opens with the notion that 'the fundamental point is to see the territorial and capitalist logic of power as distinct from each other … the relation between these two logics should be seen therefore as problematic and often contradictory rather than as functional or one side. This dialectical relation sets the stage for an analysis of capitalist imperialism in terms of the intersection of these two distinctive but intertwined logics of power' (Harvey 2003). What this seems to suggest is that governments and business leaders have different goals – it is in uniting these roles, or at least intertwining them, that capitalism can truly evolve to the advantage of not only these leaders but also society as a whole. Perhaps CSR then can act as the medium through which this is considered.

The system-wide nature of the TCC would bode well for the establishment of a global standard of social responsibility. The nature of capitalism has evolved from nationstate to interstate to inter-governance regions. Whereas this may limit State powers the potential for global realignment of standards is abundant. This seems to be recognized by the UN Framework on Business and Human Rights where they recognize the importance of tailoring the pillars of the framework to country specific conditions. This, together with the motivation of driving such a standard, will be considered later in this chapter. When looking at the business case for responsibility, the chapter will further develop the issues raised in this section.

The benefits of the TCC over traditional leaders (in particular national and even federal governments) lie in how the economic interests of its members are increasingly globally linked rather than exclusively local or even national in origin. Adding to this is the limitation of the regulatory power of the state. In failing to extend further than its boundaries, regulatory reach is severely constrained for state actors. This is particularly true for Europe at the moment where the impending treaties will ensure that federal policy can pose an additional constraint on national regulatory power in certain areas. Perhaps this is a point of note for future developments in this area.[2] The TCC are not subject to such jurisdictional constraints. These people, according to Sklair (2001) proclaim to be citizens of the world and the property, shares and corporation with which they work are increasingly globalized. Harvey (2003) speaks about 'territories', recognizing trading zones and social values as societal cohesion as opposed to official jurisdictional boundaries – an understanding which augments Sklair's comments. In short, the TCC are outward orientated and have global perspectives rather than the inward orientated and local perspectives advocated by the traditional leaders. The TCC in exerting economic control in the workplace, political control in international politics and cultural control in everyday life has cemented its position as a global leader: 'It is hardly a controversial proposition that global capitalism, driven by [M]NCs, organized politically through the TCC and fuelled by the culture ideology of consumerism, is the most potent force

---

2   The two treaties in question are the Fiscal Stability Treaty and the European Stability Mechanism Treaty.

for change in the world today' (Sklair 2007–2008). Indeed, with the rise of the TCC, there are some problems for governance structures, which shall frame some of the latter sections of this article. Padfield (2009–2010), for example, notes that 'corporations...are increasingly taking on roles as pseudo-governmental actors' – highlighting their rise in the global leadership stakes, but, off-setting this with the idea that they fail to '[incur] the accountability to the people generally associated with state action'. This also raises other questions in relation to democratic deficit, the definition of the corporation and the fact that corporations are generally non-elected (by the general public). Therefore, whether or not they have a mandate to engage with social issues remains a concern, as does accountability and the failure of accountability mechanisms to develop at the same rate as the size of the MNC. Again, this is discussed later in the chapter when considering the relationship between responsibility and accountability.

In considering the rise in dominance of the MNC, and indeed the force that controls this on a political scale (the TCC), this section accepts Sklair's proposition of the existence, and increasing power of the TCC. Shaped by national class structures, but based on a global level, members of this class have the ability and foresight to make 'global' decisions and disengage from some of the more fragmented policy directives shaped by nation states. The next section, in considering how to harness and shape this power, will consider how the new global leadership (the TCC), can theoretically advance a global CSR agenda. Indeed, this is something that Sklair (2007–2008) alludes to by acknowledging the need to focus on the globalization of human rights and responsibilities. He does not dwell on this point but, by mentioning it, emphasizes the ability of this new global leader, the TCC, to have responsibilities beyond the economic. The value of this statement in the light of the introduction of the UN Framework on Business and Human Rights may be called into question. The framework introduces three pillars; the second of which looks at the corporate responsibility to respect human rights. The initiation of this pillar suggests that there is a move toward TCCs having a recognized responsibility beyond economic even if it is soft law. However, the limitations of the UN Framework (the vagueness, lack of sanctions and so on), suggest that its role as an accountability mechanism is limited. Backer (2007–2008) does focus more on this issue than Sklair (2001), but only insofar as he considers the legal approaches to governance on a global level. In addressing the idea of hard law and how it is focused on human rights, in addition to developments that may touch on the activities of MNCs he makes some interesting observations. He is of the view that hard law as a means of regulating or driving MNC's agenda is too indirect as, to his mind, there seems to be continued opposition to the idea of a direct relationship between international law and economic collectives (Backer 2007–2008). Therefore, he contends that most of the law making in this area has been directed at States, a view which is agreed with by Lozano et al. (2009). This may be due to the failure of international law to develop at the pace of MNC's growth, a trend which is prevalent throughout this chapter and particularly in the final section.

The aim of this section was to define the parameters of leadership. In considering the development of MNCs, this section recognized the importance of including these entities within any definition of 'leadership' today. Traditionally, leaders were considered as governments of nationstates, federal regions and so on. but with the advance of globalization and the augmented role of business in driving economic agendas, business may now be considered as even more powerful than at least some nation states due to their ability to transcend national borders. Not being constrained by national boundaries ensures that their power and reach can, and in many cases has, surpassed the strength of nation States. Adding to this is the fact that most countries are dependent to some extent on capital generated by MNCs within their borders in order to enhance national growth figures and their role within the global system can be realized. In identifing multinationals and specifically the TCC as leaders, this section will facilitate the discussion around a 'responsible' leader in the next section of the chapter. This will address how our understanding of 'responsibility' and in turn 'responsible leadership' has changed over the years which hints at the need for flexibility in considering the scope of responsibility in an age of increasing globalization.

Business Case for Responsible Leadership

The previous section looked at defining leadership. This section, in accepting the definition of leadership outlined above, will consider the parameters of 'responsibility' and in so doing, 'responsible leadership'. It will explore the discourse on responsibility and then consider in the next section, within the confines of responsible leadership, to whom the TCC ought to be responsible. Whether or not the receivers of responsibility changes in tandem with the development of the corporation from a small business enterprise to a multinational entity will form the bulk of the discussion. First however, the term 'responsibility' will be addressed.

Responsibility in the context of this chapter refers to CSR. CSR has been subject to much definition over the years but for the most part it is the description of Elkington (1997) that remains true today, which is the view that CSR is the deliberate inclusion of public interest into decision making within corporations in a manner which is befitting the 'triple bottom line'-approach to business self-regulation (for example, People, Planet and Profits) or, perhaps on a wider interpretation to include the broader regulatory framework, a set of mechanisms for aligning corporate behaviour with the interests of society in reducing externalities and promoting a sustainable corporate sector. CSR, the fluidity of the concept and national divergence has meant that the interpretations and understanding of the paradigm differs depending on whether it is being addressed as a business or governance concept; the State through which it is being addressed and the governance model prevalent in said States. Despite this divergence, there are a number of key themes which are prevalent throughout the literature and indeed policies (where these are available).

The approach to CSR over the years has changed considerably which serves to enhance my concerns about the legitimacy of the expectations of responsibility which will be discussed later in this section. At the outset, large companies were encouraged to only have an economic role in society – in other words to maximize profit. This is reflected in judgments in the UK and US in the late nineteenth and early twentieth century respectively.[3] However, by the 1950s, the judiciary in the US begins to accept that business

---

3   UK company law case, *Hutton v. West Cork Railway Co* (1883) 23 Ch D 654 is the main example of this point. This case was concerned with whether or not directors of companies could use company funds to benefit non-shareholders. The court in this case held that it could not and some famous passages of the judgment are frequently used to this day in company law proceedings. In particular, Bowen LJ's judgment suggests that 'charity cannot sit at the boardroom table' and '[t]he law does not say there are to be no cakes and ale, but there are to be no cakes and ale except such as are required

enterprise could owe a duty to employees and other stakeholders in the organization.[4] Nonetheless, there remained some uneasiness about this approach with Friedman (1970) providing the famous mantra 'the business of business is business'. By the 1980s it would appear that Friedman's profit-centred approach to business had faded into the minority with the advent of Freeman's (1984) work on stakeholders. Freeman echoes the judgment in *A.P Smith v Barlow* suggesting that by engaging with non-shareholders, the business could increase profits in the long term. When the academic, judicial and business arenas accepted the premise of the stakeholder and indeed the assumption of 'responsibility', the literature expanded exponentially and with it the scope of the definition of 'stakeholder' and the extent of the 'responsibility' to said stakeholders. Perhaps the high water mark of this literature lies in the work of Mitchell, Argyle and Wood (1997) where, by defining the stakeholder as a group that influences, or is influenced by the MNC, the scope of the definition seems to include the environment and the unborn.

The responsibility of business – and if we assume that the TCC is now a global leader (thereby the need to consider the extent of 'responsible leadership') – is something which is increasingly becoming embedded in national legislation, regulations, policy approaches and so on.[5] In addition, at a more international level (and again the difference between

---

for the benefit of the company'. The relevance of this judgment today in the UK has been limited somewhat with the introduction of s.172 (1d) Companies Act 2006 but this will be discussed later in the chapter.

In the US, a similar decision was reached in *Dodge v Ford Motor Company* 204 Mich 459, 170 NW 668. (Mich. 1919). This case centred round the Model T car the success of which had meant that by 1916 the Ford Company had amassed a capital surplus of $60 million. During this time the price of the car had decreased and the wages of employers had increased. Ford wished to provide employees with special dividends with the view that some day they could afford one of these cars. He stated that,'My ambition is to employ still more men, to spread the benefits of this industrial system to the greatest possible number, to help them build their lives and their homes. To do this, we are putting the greatest shares of our people back in the business.' The Michigan Supreme Court did not accept this as a valid argument pointing out that a business corporation is organised for the profit of its shareholders and not for the benefit of non-shareholders (in this case employees).

4   *A.P. Smith Manufacturing Co v. Barlow*, 13 NJ 145, 98 A2d 581, (NJ 1953). This US case recognized that there was a legal connection between corporate philanthropy and goodwill. It also noted that an 'act that supports the public welfare can also be in the best interest of the corporation itself'. Of note also was the acknowledgment that increased profit maximization may be realized by the corporation in the long term for acting in a socially responsible manner. This theme will be addressed at the end of this section.

5   CSR is traditionally a product of the Anglo–American governance system. This includes the UK, US and Ireland. In the Scandinavian governance system, business was always required to take into consideration the impact of their decisions on non-shareholders – the structure of their governance system dictates the need to embed social responsibility considerations within business practice. In the two-tiered model of governance (typical of Germany and Japan), the inclusion of employees into corporate decision making seems to be an acknowledgment of the link between business and societal obligations. It may be the case therefore that the Anglo–American system, by requiring more from corporations based within their borders, is simply aligning the expectations from capital with developments in Scandinavia and elsewhere. In the US, there has been an introduction – at State level of constituency statutes. Dating from 1983 (Pennsylavania) these statutes broadly require directors of companies to consider the 'welfare of constituencies other than shareholders'. It seems as though the purpose of these statute was to prevent extreme short-termism and profit maximization corporate ventures. Post financial crisis it will be interesting to see any research that may emerge on the effectiveness of this legislation. There is however marked differences in the scope and requirements of the constituency statutes depending on the state. Keay (2010) looks at this in a good bit of detail but, for the purposes of this chapter it is sufficient to focus on the intention of moving the responsibilities of business (and in so doing the governing class, the TCC) from short-term to long-term goals.

This approach is also indicative of developments in the UK particularly with the enacting of s. 172 (1) Companies Act 2006. This provision states that:

(1) A director of a company must act in the way he considers, in good faith, would be most likely to promote the success of the company for the benefit of its members as a whole, and in doing so have regard (amongst other matters) to—

(a) the likely consequences of any decision in the long term,
(b) the interests of the company's employees,
(c) the need to foster the company's business relationships with suppliers, customers and others,

inter-national and trans-national is paramount here) there have been communications from the UN, the EU, the OECD and so on outlining the responsibilities that business owes (via its leadership) to not only its shareholders but also to stakeholders; the extent of this responsibility is of an ever-increasing value.[6]

From these developments it would seem as though governments, academics and indeed society at large have re-imagined the role of the corporation in society. It no longer appears sufficient to advance profit maximization as the goal of the company but instead the role of business seems to include a contribution to social development, the community in which it operates and to ensure that the broader group of stakeholders are considered when making business decisions. Yes corporations should behave responsibly and ethically and act with a 'moral' conscience, but, a number of problems arise that are not discussed in great detail in the literature to date. Whereas developments in the literature (and indeed the judiciary) do recognize the increased power of business and its ruling class (the TCC), no one appears to be asking the question as to whether it is fair, just or reasonable to make the TCC and the broader business community assume this mantle and the new responsibilities that this introduces to everyday business practice.

Much has been written on the business case for CSR and how, in an increasingly globalized market, goods that are 'brand marketed' as socially responsible can assist in carving out a competitive niche in the economy. This chapter does not intend to discredit this point of view but rather, is more concerned with a more fundamental question – why? Why should we, as society, expect business to take over some of the

---

(d) the impact of the company's operations on the community and the environment,

(e) the desirability of the company maintaining a reputation for high standards of business conduct, and

(f) the need to act fairly as between members of the company.

(2) Where or to the extent that the purposes of the company consist of or include purposes other than the benefit of its members, subsection I has effect as if the reference to promoting the success of the company for the benefit of its members were to achieving those purposes.

(3) The duty imposed by this section has effect subject to any enactment or rule of law requiring directors, in certain circumstances, to consider or act in the interests of creditors of the company.

The relevance of this legislation is the fact that national governments are now expecting corporations to extend their responsibilities beyond profit maximization to the point that they are now arguably encroaching increasingly on areas of governance traditionally held by national governments. From an Irish point of view also, there is a Companies Consolidated Bill passing through the Oireachtas at present, section 222 of which echoes in part s172 of Companies Act 2006 outlined above. What it indicates is a committed shift in expectation of the TCC. Whether or not this is a fair requirement remains to be seen.

6   The UN is increasingly interested in the role of business in society with publications such as the UN Global Compact. This communication espouses ten principles which outline a 'strategic policy initiative for businesses that are committed to aligning their operations and strategies with ten universally accepted principles in the areas of human rights, labour, environment and anti-corruption' (UN Global Compact). In addition, the recent introduction of the UN Framework for Business and Human Rights (Ruggie Principles) further illustrate the increasing interrelationship between business, government and society as understood by the organization. The Ruggie Principles consist of three pillars: the state's responsibility to protect human rights; the corporate responsibility to respect human rights and the right to remedy for those that have been affected.

At the level of the OECD, the most relevant communication is the OECD Guidelines for Multi-National Enterprise (updated 2011) which outlines 'recommendations for responsible business conduct that governments encourage enterprises to observe wherever they operate'. There have been criticisms of these guidelines especially round the fact that only 43 governments have signed up to the Guidelines meaning that more States have NOT signed up than ones that have.

Within the EU, there has been a number of communications on business responsibilities and obligations under CSR objectives dating from the 2001 White Paper on Promoting a European Framework for Corporate Social Responsibility. This communication recognised the voluntary nature of CSR but any procedures to improve the area had to be introduced on a national level. The current approach is outlined in the 2011–2014 Strategy on CSR which aims to strengthen global leadership on CSR in Europe with around 30 proposals for CSR commitments.

roles of government? As the first section outlined, business is, in many cases, more powerful than national governments and therefore more ideally placed to introduce social measures than governments (and without the fear of a backlash – leading to a failure of re-election and so on). Indeed the potential is for a global standard on CSR introduced by business which would in theory eliminate the varying standards and approaches. However, it could be contended that this is not a fair expectation to make of a business entity.

This section looked at responsibility and how approaches to CSR within corporations defines our understanding of responsible leadership. By quickly tracing the concept of CSR from its inception to the increased relevance in society today, this section looked at national approaches together with requirements from the international sphere. The last few paragraphs of this section question the rationale of our expectations of 'responsible leadership'. This question is fundamental to our understanding of leadership on a global scale and indeed the legitimacy of our expectations. This will be explored in the next section where the role of business is considered together with the limitations of the current system and how the global system requires reform before the utopia of responsible leadership can be effectively achieved.

Responsible Leadership: Legitimate Expectation?

Corporations are established for two purposes: To grow and to make profit. That is, and always has been, the nature of business. True, in recent years, expectation has risen in the requirements for 'responsible leadership' of business but, until quite recently, this responsibility has been largely voluntary in nature. Although recognizing the need to embed these voluntary ideals in legislation, regulation or policy approaches – at the same time, some concerns remain as to the legitimacy of this expectation. If a more concerted approach to 'responsible leadership' within the TCC is developed, the parameters of this responsibility need to be addressed. It is imperative that there is an advantage to business in being responsible, as, to persuade corporations to fill intracies in society beyond that which is advantageous to them (and requested simply because they are more powerful and in many cases wealthier than national governments). This section will look at whether it is fair, just or even reasonable to expect corporations to re-evaluate their purpose to include responsibilities to wider society (stakeholders). In addressing this point, the section will also consider whether governance structures have sufficiently advanced to ensure that responsibilities of corporations (CSR objectives) can be effectively regulated and if so, by whom.

By breaking down company obligations into different tiers, it becomes easier to address if and where the company obligations stop together with the interrelationship between the various obligations. There are three tiers of obligations:

1. The primary obligation of any corporation/company is to make profit for the owners (shareholders).
2. The secondary obligation of a corporation is to some stakeholders (particularly those connected to the firm: Employees, suppliers, consumers and so on).
3. The tertiary obligation then is to other stakeholders, the wider society and the environment.

In addition, it is perhaps useful to consider the primary and secondary obligations as 'negative' or 'bad'. Tertiary obligations can be considered (for now) as 'positive' or 'good'. When I speak about a 'negative' obligation, I mean that these are regulated for the most part by legal requirements: For example, a company must do X. Failure to comply with X will result in sanction Y. Not only is there a sanction, but the company will be considered 'bad' if it fails to comply. The tertiary obligation outlined above, is, for the most part a 'positive' expectation of society from business. Yes, we expect that they will do something 'good' in this area, but as yet it is not effectively regulated or mandated by legislation. It cannot be a rule, as there is no official sanction. Therefore, society would like a company to do X, but if they do not do so, or fail to comply with expectations, there can be no official sanction (although as consumers we can boycott goods and so on).

It is possible to use the interrelationships of aforementioned obligations to better address whether or not it is fair, just and reasonable to legitimately expect a company to act in the interests of stakeholders, and assume a general responsibility to society as new global leaders. When a company is being established, the main aim is to seek return to owners and shareholders – primary obligations. However, the primary obligations cannot reach their potential until a corporation undertakes its secondary responsibilities such as Health and Safety law, regulations and policies, employees' rights, sustainable supply chain management. So, the primary responsibility is dependent on the secondary responsibilities being fulfilled in order to become more successful. Company obligations are now delving into the tertiary tier. If we consider arguments of fairness, justice and reasonableness there are two approaches that can be considered.

First, supposing Mitchell, Agle and Wood's (1997) premise, there is the viewpoint that it is not fair, just and reasonable to expect that companies take into consideration those stakeholders that have not yet been. Whether or not there is a proximate relationship between stakeholders and the corporation first needs to be established. Increasingly, the literature, together with judicial decisions (such as the *AP Smith* case) and legislative provisions (for instance, The UK's 172 Companies Act 2006) would suggest that stakeholders are now a 'proximate group' that the corporation should be taking into consideration when making any decisions. Discourse arising from the OECD Guidelines and the UN Framework on Business and Human Rights would suggest that the corporation should avoid doing anything that may cause harm to stakeholders. Again this is more focused on not doing bad, than on doing good. Issues of foreseeability arise here and it is something that needs to be discussed in the future along with the questions that the next statement raises.

The corporation is a company set up to make profit. The primary objective of the ruling TCC therefore must be to ensure that profit is made. Social responsibilities can only ever be a secondary obligation. The developments on CSR seem to place social responsibilities on an almost equal footing with the primary obligation of profit raising the question as to whether a greater duty is owed to shareholders or to stakeholders. Arguably, as long as profit is made, the duty to the shareholder is fulfilled and the secondary duty to the stakeholder becomes relevant. Stakeholders however are a large and diverse group and, if you assume that they are those who are influenced by or can influence the corporation it seems as though the bigger the business the bigger the pool of stakeholders. Whether or not then it is 'fair, just and reasonable' to impose a duty on the TCC to assume responsible leadership via mandatory CSR mechanisms can be tied in with reasonable foreseeability (see above). This is something which is difficult on which to draw conclusions other than to suggest that the more powerful and wealthy a corporation is, the more capable they are of assuming the mantle of responsibility from national governments which would suggest that 'fair, just and reasonable' is subjectively focused on capacity of corporate reach. However, this does not negate the fact that social responsibilities are not within the traditional remit of business. To deem this as a 'fair' obligation of corporations and their ruling class may cause for a re-evaluation of global expectations of business in light of recent trends.

If the premise of responsible leadership is accepted, other issues need to be considered. Of paramount importance is the question as to whether the responsibility of the TCC can be regulated. The failure of current regulatory provisions to develop at the same rate as corporations suggests that even if the TCC has responsibility as a global leader to develop social provisions, there is no entity to hold them to account if they fail to do so. This leads to a crisis of not only accountability but responsibility.

There is another way to view this issue however, and, in doing so, avoids the argument of CSR as a public policy requirement which was considered above. If achieving better returns for primary stakeholders (shareholders) is influenced by effective responsibility to secondary stakeholders, can the argument be extended still further? What this is questioning is, whether or not bearing responsibilities to tertiary stakeholders can improve relations with secondary stakeholders which, in turn will theoretically provide for an optimum return for the primary stakeholder: The shareholder. Not only does it then become fair, just and reasonable to expect companies to assume this mantle of responsibility, but, if this is communicated effectively to the corporations, the gap in accountability mechanisms could be filled by the corporations themselves.

The challenge that then befalls legislators, regulators and policymakers is in embedding this effectively into national and international infrastructure to enable a transition to the 'global' when this becomes possible. This is relatively uncharted territory and provides those responsible for drafting with a balancing exercise. On the one hand, there is a need to ensure that a minimum standard of 'responsibility' by global leaders is met, but, on the other hand, not obstructing corporate innovation and the capacity for some corporations to exceed not only minimum requirements but maximum expectations given the power, wealth and reach of said corporate structures.

The recent, and arguably ongoing financial crisis, has highlighted the inadequacies of the global market system. Nation States are no longer the most powerful actors on the world stage. Corporations that transcend national boundaries have a much greater wealth and reach and are not bound by jurisdictional constraints in the same way as countries. Just as nation States are no longer as powerful, State government's capacity to advance socially responsible governance measures has also been undermined. Paramount in national government's concerns is the desire to attract and retain capital generated by MNCs. The change in leadership in the global stage from the State to the corporation suggests that corporations through the ruling TCC may have to assume the mantle of responsibility. Whether or not this is reasonable, fair or just in light of the ongoing crisis is questioned above, but its potential in light of limited accountability mechanisms is compromised.

Conclusions and Future Directions

As the hierarchy of leadership in the global system has changed, so too have our perceptions of what makes a global leader. In re-imagining the role of State, corporation and society, it is becoming increasingly clear that State relations have been undermined by the rise of the corporation. The class overseeing the activities of the corporation is the TCC and it is this class then that represents the new global leaders. In defining the TCC as leaders, the scope of their leadership can be addressed.

This chapter was concerned with 'responsible leadership'. In considering the responsibilities of the TCC to broader society, this chapter addressed conceptual developments with CSR. Noting the paradigm from early inceptions, it became increasingly clear that as corporations have grown in strength, power and wealth over the last century, so too have society's expectations of the corporation's responsibilities. This has advanced to the point that some jurisdictions today are enshrining CSR within mandatory legislation and on an international level, corporations are increasingly being encouraged to engage with norms and guidelines to ensure they are within the confines of 'responsible' behaviour. Noting the increasing power of the TCC has implications for the potential of a global standard on CSR. Whereas, this is/would be an excellent means of alleviating State dependency on global capital and indeed recognize that the main actors have shifted, there are some fundamental questions that need consideration. The final section of this chapter addresses some of the concerns of this new leadership role such as the purpose of the corporation and the fairness of responsibility requirements of the new global leaders.

There is undoubtedly a role for corporations and the TCC to play in advancing a social agenda. In assuming this role, there may need to be a re-evaluation of our decades-old definition of the purpose of the corporation – can we reasonably expect an equal, dual responsibility to both shareholders and stakeholders without re-evaluating our hitherto understanding? In establishing a global responsibility for which corporations should adhere, does international law need to evolve in order that responsibilities can be regulated and that there is a means of holding to account should responsibilities not be met? These are questions that can be addressed in the near future and in light of recent developments on the federal and international landscape (EU CSR Strategy 2011–2014 and the UN Framework on Business and Human Rights). In the interim, the right to responsibility may remain a hybrid of State duties and corporate responsibilities.

References

A.P. Smith Manufacturing Co v. Barlow. 1953. (13 NJ 145, 98 A2d 581), New Jersey.

Backer, L. 2007–2008. Multinational Corporations as Objects and Sources of Transnational regulation. *ILSA Journal of International and Comparative Law*, 14 (2): 499–525.

Chimni, B.S. (2007) 'The past, present and future of international law' *Melbourne Journal of International Law* 8:499 – 515.

Dodge v Ford Motor Company 204 Mich 459, 170 NW 668. (Mich. 1919).

Elkington, J. 1997. *Cannibals with Forks: The Triple Bottom Line of 21st Century Business.* Oxford: Capstone.

M. Friedman, 'The Social Responsibility of Business is to increase its Profits.' (1970) *New York Times Magazine.*

Freeman, R.E. 1984. *Strategic Management: A Stakeholder Approach.* Boston: Pitman.

Hale, K. 2003. Corporate Law and Stakeholders: Moving Beyond Stakeholder Statutes? *Arizona Law Review*, 45:823–828.

Harvey, D. (2003) *The New Imperialism*, Oxford University Press.

Holton, R.J. 1998. *Globalisation and the Nation State*. London: Macmillan Press Ltd.

Hutton v. West Cork Railway Co. 1883.(23 Ch D 654), United Kingdom.

Keay, A.R. 2011. Moving towards Stakeholderism? Constituency Statutes, Enlightened Shareholder Value and All That: Much Ado About Little? *European Business Law Review*, 22(1):1–49.

Lozano, J.M, Albareda, L. and Ysa, T. (2008) Governments and Corporate Social Responsibility. (Palgrave Macmillan).

Mitchell, R.K., Agle, B.R. and Wood, D.J. 1997. Toward a Theory of Stakeholder Identification and Salience: Defining the Principle of Who and What Really Counts. *Academy of Management Review*, 22(4):853–886.

OECD. 2011. *OECD Guidelines for Multi National Enterprise*. Paris: OECD Publishing.

Padfield, S.J. 2009–2010. Finding State Actions when Corporations Govern.*Temple Law Review* 82:703–736.

Robinson, W.I. (2007) 'Beyond the theory of imperialism: Global capitalism and the transnational state,' *Societies Without Borders* 2 (5): 12.

Sklair, L. 2001. *Transnational Capitalist Class*. Hoboken: Wiley-Blackwell.

Sklair, L. 2006–2007. Capitalist Globalisation: Fatal Flaws and Necessity for Alternatives. *Brown Journal of World Affairs*, 13(1):29–37.

Strange, S. 1996.*Retreat of the State: The Diffusion of Power in the World Economy*. Cambridge: Cambridge University Press.

United Nations Human Rights Council. 2003. *Norms on the Responsibilities of Transnational Corporations and Other Business Enterprises with Regard to Human Rights*, (UN Doc. E/CN.4/ Sub.2/2003/12/Rev.2). Geneva: United Nations Publications.

Vurro, C. The Evolutionary Path of the Concept of CSR, in *Developing CSR*, edited by F. Perrini, S. Pogutz, and A. Tencati. Cheltenham: Edward Elgar Publishing, 54–71.

REPORTS

A Renewed EU Strategy 2011-2014 for CSR http://eur-lex.europa.eu/LexUriServ/LexUriServ. do?uri=COM:2011:0681:FIN:EN:PDF Sourced on 12-10-2012.

Commission White Paper on CSR 2002 http://ew.eea.europa.eu/News/2002/7/1026911529/ Sourced on 12-10-2012.

Green Paper Promoting a European framework for CSR COM (2001) 366 http://europa.eu/legislation_ summaries/employment_and_social_policy/employment_rights_and_work_organisation/ n26039_en.htm Sourced on 12-10-2012.

5 *Leadership in Multi-identity Contexts: A Mediterranean Framework*

CELIA DE ANCA, SALVADOR ARAGÓN AND
CONCHITA GALDÓN

Introduction: No More Leaders, Please!

At a seminar on the new context in the Mediterranean region after the Arab spring, the main topic was the analysis of the characteristics needed for new leaders to guide the new societies in their transition periods. However, much to the moderator's surprise, the unanimous consensus from the audience was: 'No more leaders, please! The time for leaders is over – now it is up to us to lead our future!'

The revolutions that shaped the year 2011 had a clear message – whether in Egypt or Tunisia, individual leaders were nowhere to be seen. Although all of the movements were organized in terms of communication logistics or messages, no individual names appeared. For some, it was a sign of the Arab culture and its collectivistic tendencies, but the movements from Madrid to London and New York followed a similar paradigm in which no individual leaders emerged during the revolts.

Are we thus in a new era in which collective leadership is replacing the traditional individual leadership paradigm? If the traditional paradigm of leadership emphasized individual attributes and characteristics, the growing paradigm of collective leadership emphasizes the community and groups within which different leaders emerge for different tasks and then step back to leave the leadership role to others.

This chapter focuses on communities in organization and how the new forms of plurality that these new community-based identities create might also lead to new forms of organic leadership. First, we analyze the literature on leadership and ask the question: From individual leadership to collective leadership, is this a change of paradigm or a change in society? We proceed to identify a collective leadership paradigm, from communities of origin to communities of aspiration. Subsequently, we look at a case study of Morocco and Spain, investigating the multi-identity contexts in Mediterranean organizations. Finally, we conclude with implications for organic leadership in multi-identity organizations.

From Individual Leadership to Collective Leadership: A Change of Paradigm or a Change in Society?

THOUSANDS OF YEARS OF LEADERSHIP RESEARCH

What makes someone lead and others follow has been an area of interest since the beginning of thinking, as Plato's *Republic* explored (Avolio 2007: 26). The myth of the hero exists in the mythology of every culture, well before the famous ancient Greek heroes. Although much has been written about heroes and leaders throughout history, it is only in the twentieth century that systematic research on the matter began. The Victorian writer Carlyle, in his Great Man theory (1841), already defined a set of characteristics that distinguish effective leaders from ineffective ones. But probably the most influential work in the modern scientific literature on leadership is *The Theory of Social and Economic Organization* by the social scientist Max Weber (1947). Weber classified leaders into bureaucratic and charismatic categories, and argued that charismatic leaders could only emerge in the face of a social crisis.

These early studies have influenced the modern studies on leadership, most of which have focused on what differentiates leaders. The role that individual traits play in determining who emerges as a leader and how effective the person is in leadership positions has been subject of much research (refer to Bassand Avolio 1990, Chan and Drasgow 2001, Judge, Bono, Ilies and Gerhardt 2002). Avolio (2007), in his extensive literature review about leadership, quotes Den Hartog and Koopman (2001), Kirkpatrick and Locke (1991), Yukl (1998), and Bass (1985) to show that there are some universal traits leaders possess that are repeatedly associated with effective leadership, including persistence, tolerance for ambiguity, self-confidence, drive, honesty, integrity, internal locus of control, achievement motivation and cognitive ability.

In the mid-1970s, research about leadership moved beyond looking for the closed set of characteristics that made the perfect leader to considering that such a perfect leader might not exist. Instead, a leader might need to be entirely different depending on the circumstances in which he is leading (this idea was first presented in the contingency model developed by Fred Fiedler in the 1960s). Fiedler found that a leader's fit with the group and the task was more important in predicting outcomes than the leader's characteristics (Fiedler 1965). There are many different theories within the contingency paradigm. The most influential theory is path-goal theory (House and Mitchell 1974), which explains how leaders can affect the satisfaction of their followers. Other influential contingency theorists are Hersey and Blanchard (1982), proponents of the Life Cycle Theory, Fiedler and Garcia (1987), who developed the Cognitive Resource Theory,and Vroom and Yetton (1973), authors of the Decision Process Theory.

Leadership theory then took a more holistic approach,in which followers are regarded as influential and active elements of the leadership model. An example of such recognition of the role of followers is the deep interest generated by dual leadership styles proposed by Bass: transactional versus transformational leadership (Bass 1985, Bass and Avolio 1991). These styles are differentiated according to the reason why followers decide to follow the leader. Transactional leadership is based on a mutually beneficial exchange between leaders and followers in which leaders satisfy followers' needs. In return, followers comply with the demands of the leaders. By contrast, transformational leadership occurs when leaders are perceived as charismatic, visionary and inspirational by their followers.

Recent work by Avolio and his colleagues Gardner, Walumbwa, Luthans and May (2004) has attempted to take on the challenge of including all the core facets described above in explaining what constitutes 'authentic leadership development'. Their model of authentic leadership development includes elements of the leader, follower and context in explaining what actually improves or develops leadership. The new areas of research that examine networks, cross-cultural leadership or authentic leadership take a much more holistic approach than the traditional studies.

LEADERSHIP AND NETWORKS

An area of research that has attracted increasing interest is how the integration of leaders into networks impacts their leadership. The first research projects along these lines date of the 1950s and it proves how being central to a communication network influences the emergence of leaders and the effectiveness of the groups they lead (Bavelas 1950).In the 1970s, the proponents of the Leader–Member Exchange (LMX) Theory recovered the research about the relationships among leaders and followers. These theorists prescribed that a tight and mature dyadic relation of mutual obligation among leaders and followers is a good predictor of positive outcomes for the organization (Graen and Cashman 1975).

Later research has focused on the overall centrality of leaders in informal networks. Studies have shown that holding a central position in informal networks, especially in the case of friendship ties, is positively related to greater individual influence,and better leadership effectiveness. It also increases the attribution of having charisma by followers and improves the performance of the group (for example, Brass 1984, Brass and Burkhardt 1992, Pastor, Meindl, and Mayo 2002).

CROSS-CULTURAL LEADERSHIP

Cross-cultural leadership is particularly relevant for a more integrated approach that includes context specificity and relationships with followers across cultures. Initial research was conducted by Hunt, Boal and Sorenson (1990), who highlighted the fact that some countries have uniform and thus stronger cultures while others have weaker national cultures with multiple subcultures. This conditions the existence of more or less variance of individual super-ordinate prototypes. Individual super-ordinate prototypes condition the categories that are regarded as proper for a leader, and thus culture must be considered in leadership theories. Researchers have consistently found relevant implications of Hofstede's theoretical dimensions of culture (Hofstede 1980, 1991) on leadership (Jung, Bass and Sosik 1995).

House and Aditya (1997) noted that most of the studies conducted about leadership have focused on Western countries and Western cultures, more specifically American. According to their analysis, 98 percent of the evidence generated on the topic at the time was American in character (House and Aditya 1997). These concerns were overcome in the Globe Study. Focused on global leadership, this is a cross-cultural project developed in 60 different countries and implemented by 160 scholars around the globe. The project gathered data from 17,000 middle managers through questionnaires (House, Hanges, Javidan, Dorfman and Gupta 2004).

Contrary to a commonly held position that leadership relationships vary totally across cultures, Hartog, House, Hanges, Ruiz-Quintanilla, and Dorfman (1999), based on the evidence from the Globe Study, found that there are specific attributes of charismatic/ transformative leaders that are universally endorsed. They also find that some attributes are universally considered to be impediments to such leadership, and they find, in line with previous research, that some attributes of charismatic leadership are contingent on culture. Furthermore, empirical research in 12 countries has shown that different influence strategies that leaders use are perceived to be more or less effective depending on individual social beliefs. Also, cultural values can act as moderators of the impact that such individual social beliefs can have in the perceived effectiveness of influence strategies (Fu et al. 2004)

In summary, most work done in this discipline considers a leader as an individual influenced by the followers and the context but nonetheless an individual followed by other individuals or groups.

COLLECTIVE LEADERSHIP: THE NEW EMERGENCE OF AN OLD PARADIGM

Proponents envision collective leadership – a parallel approach to the leadership literature – as a kind of leadership that relies not on an individual but rather on a group of people. This way of understanding leadership has recently become a popular subject of study, which has been approached under different names: Shared leadership, distributed leadership, collective leadership,and, more recently, organic leadership. Following Avolio, Walumbwa and Weber (2009), we will refer to these terms interchangeably.

Although the interest in this view of leadership has peaked recently, traditional visions of collective leadership have existed for almost as long as the individual type of leadership. Classical literature gives us many examples. As early as 1610, the renowned Spanish author Lope de Vega wrote the play *Fuenteovejuna*, in which he told the story of the people of a town called Fuenteovejuna who stood against their cruel governor. Contrary to most plays, it is not the story of a hero who led the people of the town to stand up but is rather the story of a group of people who led themselves.

In management literature as early as 1924, Mary Parker Follet (Follet 1924) recognized the holistic nature of community and advanced the idea of 'reciprocal relationships' which conveyed the dynamic aspects of the individual in relationship to others. Follett was an advocate of what she called the 'integration' principle. This was based on non-coercive power sharing ruled by the notion of 'power with' rather than 'power over'.

Additionally, the Australian psychologist Gibb was the first one to talk about 'distributed leadership' in his *Handbook of Social Psychology* (1954). Gibb proposed yet another dual vision of leadership: Distributed leadership (shared across individuals in a group) versus focused leadership (borne by one individual).

Gronn (2002) explains that distributed leadership fits more realistically with the task-specialized workforce of the present times. He considers the distributed/focused dilemma as a continuum in which leaders and followers interchange roles for different tasks. In his view, distributed leadership has two characteristics: Interdependence and coordination. Within distributed leadership, he considers three different forms of joint action: Spontaneous collaboration (happens many times temporarily for a punctual task), intuitive working relations (based on reliance of co-leaders on each other), and institutionalized practices (formalized by design or by adaptation to existing informal structures).

In 2001, Hauschildt and Kirchmann identified the need for a team of promoters rather than a sole leader for effective innovation management in the face of increased complexity of innovation. According to their work, a project will require a power promoter, a technology promoter and a process promoter. Empirical results support their defence of the troika of shared leadership. Brown and Gioia also recommend the practice of distributed leadership as the most effective way to adapt to the changing environment of e-businesses (Brown and Gioia 2002).

In 2002, Pearce Manz and Sims defined shared leadership as follows: Shared leadership 'is a group process in which leadership is distributed among, and stems from, team members' (Pearce Manz and Sims 2002: 1). Shared leadership is becoming more and more common in an increasingly complex environment in which firms decide to rely not just on one head but rather on the coordinated effort of several people.

Spillane, Halverson and Diamond (2001: 27) refer to leadership practice or leadership activity, which they define with as follows: 'Leadership practice (both thinking and activity) emerges in and through the interaction of leaders, followers, and situation'. Under this paradigm,leadership emerges from social interactions and processes rather than from a pre-existing charisma of a meant-to-be leader (Crevani, Lindgren and Packendorff 2009). Researchers have made efforts to measure the effectiveness of shared leadership as compared to the more traditionally studied vertical leadership. The first to undertake this task were Avolio and colleagues, who found a positive correlation among shared leadership and perceived effectiveness in undergraduate teams (Avolio, Jung and Sivasubramaniam 1996). Pearce Manz and Simms (2002) found that shared leadership had a greater predictive power on team effectiveness than vertical leadership. The study by Carson, Tesluk and Marrone (2007) focused not only on the effectiveness of shared leadership but also on the necessary pre-existing conditions for it to emerge. They found that the emergence of shared leadership is more probable in the presence of an adequate internal environment, with a shared goal, social support,and where everybody's opinions are heard. Also, external coaching was a relevant predictor of the emergence of shared leadership. Arnone and Stumpf (2010) also moved beyond measuring effectiveness and focused on identifying specific success factors of shared leadership relations among co-CEOs. According to their findings, the success of such shared leadership relies on trust among the leaders, continued communication and respect among other elements.

Avery (2004) proposed the notion of organic leadership in his book *Understanding Leadership: Paradigms and Cases*. According to the proponents of this model, organic leadership incorporates many of the traits of shared, distributed or collective leadership but has a more holistic approach. These are the specific indicators that describe organic leadership:

- a self-governing team;
- high follower knowledge base (knowledge workers);
- group power via collaboration;
- high follower power;
- consensual decision making;
- distributed leadership;

- low on power distance inequality, uncertainty avoidance, individualism and masculinity;
- high diversity;
- adaptable to change;
- high self-accountability and self-responsibility, with commitment;
- network structure;
- suitability for complex and dynamic contexts.

As we have seen, when talking about individual leadership, three main areas tend to be analyzed:

1. the characteristics of the leader, including his personality and charisma;
2. the leader's relationship with followers and how different forms of leadership are more effective than others;
3. the context and how cultural differences effect the leadership process.

However, when talking about collective/organic leadership, the object to be analyzed is the group itself, relations among the members, and the identity links that make some groups more effective than others. This will be the subject of the next section.

Group Identity in a Collective Leadership Paradigm: From Communities of Origin to Communities of Aspiration

COLLECTIVE LEADERSHIP FOR A NEW COLLECTIVE SOCIETY?

Sociologists have tried to manage the social dimension of identities using a wide range of metaphors, as a basis for further theoretical developments. The metaphor has provided them with a representation that integrates both emotional and rational dimensions. According to Lakoff and Johnson (1980): 'Metaphors have entailments through which they highlight and make coherent certain aspects of our experience. Metaphors can create realities for us, especially social realities.' Figure 5.1 describes some of the principal metaphors to understand collective society.

Looking backwards, the first metaphor to appear was the tribal one, which extends from the classical sociology theory to the modern 'neo-tribalism'. The key concept that supported this approach was community. Later, the emergence of an increasingly connected society shifts the research agenda from the tribal to the network metaphor. Within this metaphor the research focus was oriented more deeply into the relationship itself than the group or community.

The tribe metaphor

In the field of the tribal metaphor, Michel Maffesoli (1988) was one of the first to name 'new way of being together' as neo-tribalism. At the end of the 1980s, he stated that the micro-groups that dominated the landscape of our societies were not residuals of former traditional social life but the key social fact of our experience in everyday living. These new organizations represent a new way of living everyday life based on a communal

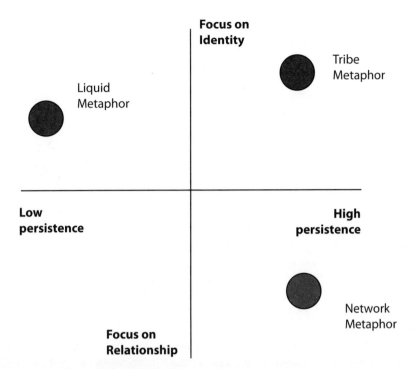

Figure 5.1   The Metaphorical Field of Collective Society

as opposed to an individual basis (Maffesoli 1988). The previous paradigm was based on the rational element and on the principle of individuation and separation; whereas the emerging one is based on the principle of empathy and is marked by the lack of differentiation, the 'loss' of oneself in a collective subject. A person in this new form of society can only find fulfillment in relation with others, with an emphasis on that which unites rather than that which separates. The community is characterized less by a project oriented towards the future than it is by this being together, the emotional warmth of companionship.

Maffesoli sees a movement in our society coming from the undifferentiated masses, characteristic of the former paradigm towards micro-tribes, where individuals seek to transcend their individualities by playing a role in open and free tribes that provide them with temporary identification. The phenomena that Maffesoli described at the end of the 1980s as just beginning in early chaotic stages, has fully exploded 20 years later, and now social groups are the DNA of our times. With the help of technology, they have defined the new structures within which our society is being transformed. Increasingly, these new forms of organization constitute not only forms of being together but also of working together, and are thus building emerging forms of organizations in which production and consumption are co-shared, co-organized and co-created.

The network metaphor

The network metaphor appears as a result of the emerging forms of relationships enabled by new information and communication technologies. Castell is the leading researcher in the use of it. According to Castell, networks allow a new kind of social relationship characterized by a collective behaviour, not a collective sense of belonging. Networks are neutral and do not have personal feelings – it is what people do in the networks that can lead to certain social processes.

In Castell's analysis, the power of identity in the new e-networks become the key driving force identities, the source of which lies in three patterns:

• Legitimizing identities: Those provided by institutions such as the State, political parties or unions, the Church, or a patriarchal State. Within the Network Society these forms of legitimized identity are weakening because they have lost their cohesive influence. As a result, two other forms of identity can be found in the Network Society.
• Resistance Identities: Top-down identities that are built around traditional values such as God, nation, family or territorial boundaries, or built around proactive social movements like feminism or environmentalism.
• Emergence of project identities: Where individuals link their personal projects together with others for a common good, this identity can be derived from certain resistance identities that have developed into identity forces.

The liquid metaphor

Bauman's (2008) idea of liquid modernity tries to resolve the tension between the social theory of modernity and some new social phenomena. According to his view, the undermining of familiar institutions and national and class-based identities has had important consequences for people's sense of identity. Similarly, Bauman notes that while the workplace was traditionally a very important source of personal identity, changes in the economy have rendered it far less reliable. Bauman proposes that the durable identities once associated with work have given way to looser and more provisional identities and conceptions of community that are subject to constant change and renegotiation. This set of provisional and always-traded identities is defined as liquid identity.

GROUP IDENTITY: FROM GROUPS OF ORIGIN TO GROUPS OF ASPIRATION

In the movement of society towards a greater communitarian affiliation, there is a clear movement of individuals from their groups of origin towards groups to which they aspire to belong and in which, without having to reject their identities of origin, they can also play out new identities of their choice.

The movement of communities of origin to communities of aspiration can be best described by the three Community metaphors described above. As Maffesoli (1988) indicates, those identities in the Tribe metaphor, unlike the identities of origin, are temporary. This new form of 'being together' is labelled 'sociality', in which the person (persona), instead of having a function, plays a role. In these new identities, individuals seek to transcend their individualities by playing a role in open and free tribes that provide them with temporary identification. In the Network metaphor, Manuel Castell (2004),describes the new forms of communal identity as projected identities. In the terminology of Bauman (2008), those new communities are liquid – they form and disappear as soon as the task is finished, to move into new forms of communities. In the three cases, it is now a question of individuals choosing identities that they consciously want to be a part of and contribute to, as well as being able to play with a multiplicity of identities and use them, as Maffesoli suggested, in as many different roles as their different affiliations allow.

We can belong to many communities at the same time, and this is what keeps us away from fundamentalism. In other words, our attention is shared with many different communities that may at times behave differently. Belonging to many, often opposite, worlds of course raises our level of stress, but it also keeps us healthy because life inevitably involves navigating on a sea of desires and compromises.

The fact that this new form of 'togetherness' is a product of decision and not of necessity is what makes it so rewarding to participate in. These communities of the 'network society', unlike those of the 1960s, are much more about sharing ideas than sharing feelings; in other words, feeling accepted is fine and desirable, but it is not the primary objective for joining.

GROUP IDENTITY IN MANAGEMENT LITERATURE

It is commonly assumed that there are two distinct processes of identification: One is self-identification or group identification, which is the process through which an individual decides to identify with a certain group; and the second is that of categorization, when the process is external to the individual and he or she has no choice in the matter. Social identity, and in particular group identification, has been widely studied in the management literature, being pioneered by Tajfel (1972). Social identification appears to derive from the concept of group identification (Tolman 1943) and could be defined as 'the perception of oneness with or belongingness to some human aggregate' (Ashford & Mael 1989).

A particular problem in this area is the frequent confusion between organizational identification and organizational commitment. In summary, the Social Identity Theory (SIT) conception of organizational identification as shared identity is new to the organizational behaviour literature. To date, the perception of identification has been confused with initialization of organizational goals and values, and with behaviour and affect. This is most clearly evident in research on organizational commitment. Unfortunately, this confusion has impeded application of the rich findings of SIT to organizations.

This led Turner (1984: 530) to propose the existence of a 'psychological group', which he defined as 'a collection of people who share the same social identification or define themselves in terms of the same social category membership'. A member of a psychological group does not need to interact with or like other members, or be liked and accepted by them. The individual seems to reify or credit the group with a psychological reality apart from his or her relationships with its members.

Also, although the SIT literature indicates that categorization is sufficient for identification to occur, the pervasiveness of formal and informal groups in organizations suggests that categorization is seldom the only factor in identification. Thus, the consequences of identification suggested by SIT, discussed below, may well be intensified in organizations.

Further, Brown and Williams (1984) suggested that individuals who regard their group identity as synonymous with their organizational identity are unlikely to view other groups negatively. Just as a strong group identity unifies group members, so too should a strong organizational identity unify organizational members. This is consistent with experimental research (Kramer and Brewer 1984) and the earlier discussion of holographic organizations. However, where the organizational identity is not strong and groups are clearly differentiated and bounded, the tendency toward biased intergroup comparisons suggests several effects.

Multi-identity Contexts in Mediterranean Organizations: A Moroccan–Spanish Research Study

For the past few years, at the Center for Diversity in Global Management of the IE Business School, we have been analyzing the accumulated expertise and knowledge of research initiatives and programme management in different regions throughout the world. We have been trying to capture what has worked well in past diversity policies and to integrate those elements into a more comprehensive model for managing plurality – the Multi-identity Context Model. This model has the potential to better tackle the management of multiple identities within an organization.

This new paradigm also recognizes the variety of identities that compose each individual. The many identities held by men and women can be grouped into identities of origin and identities of aspiration. At each given moment in time, identities of origin are those that are already incorporated within the person (being a man, disabled, Vietnamese, and so on), whereas identities of aspiration are, as the name indicates, aspiration-al (being part of the marketing department, belonging to the runners' club, being perceived as a member of the country of destination with all the rights it entails).

Our Multi-identity Context Model is currently being tested in a pilot project that the Center is developing with the support of the Bertlesman Foundation, the CDG Foundation in Morocco, and the IE Foundation. The project, Multi-identity Contexts in Mediterranean Organizations, builds on the work of a think tank on cultural diversity organized by the Moroccan ONA Foundation and the IE Foundation from 2005 to 2009.[1]

The objective of the think tank was to analyze Moroccan country perceptions and how the cultural perception of the country affected the product as well as the management relations of Moroccan businessmen towards Spanish businessmen and vice versa. The initial hypothesis was twofold: First,the cultural stereotypes and perceptions of a specific country subconsciously limit the development of business and trade since preconceived ideas filter a given product or a given behaviour, and secondly,without direct exposure to the real product or behaviour, self-fulfilling prophecies can occur, which in turn reinforce the stereotype.

The works of the think tank led to a fundamental understanding of how the lack of contexts constitute the basis for the creation of stereotypes. Perceptions are based on the direct experiences of some individuals that then become common perceptions. Direct experience had originally a concrete context, but when a description is separated from this direct experience, the result is a stereotype. When descriptions based on concrete experiences are converted into common perceptions and finally into stereotypes, a

---

1   The research was conducted by IE professors from the Center of Diversity in Global Management and professors from the ONA Foundation of Morocco between 2005 and 2008 using six structured focus groups containing a total of 90 managers in Morocco and Spain, following the methodology developed by the ONA and IE Foundations. The results of the focus groups were validated in a think tank of 20 international experts, which led to the design of a survey that was answered by 60 Spanish businessmen working in Morocco.

culture ends up being encaged with concrete and closed parameters, and ultimately even direct experience ends up confirming specific stereotypes.

As a typical example, a Spaniard who has never been to Morocco might ask friends for information, and probably someone would tell him something like: 'I have a friend who had a friend working in Morocco who told him that Moroccans spend hours drinking coffee and do business only for two minutes.' The person who had the first experience had a context – perhaps the business was not very clear and the Moroccan partner wanted to find out more information first, or the Moroccan partner was not very sure of where to go with the deal and may have been wanting to gain time. Whatever the reason, the fact is that there was a context for the story and now the context is lost, and the stereotype continues while lacking a context. Thus, the Spaniard who has received the information without a context will go to Morocco expecting that type of behaviour and will be blind to the real behaviour of the Moroccan business person.

At the other end, a Moroccan wanting to do business with a Spaniard might ask his friends whether anyone has ever had an experience, and someone might tell him something like: 'I had a friend who once had a friend who had some business with a Spaniard and found that he was really arrogant, only worried about short-term deals, and was not interested in the relationship.' Again, we have lost the context. Perhaps the Spaniard was not very fluent in French, and thus the distance was created by the language and not by the person; alternatively, the Spaniard might not have been too convinced of the business in particular and wanted to call the deal off. Whatever the reason, there was a context, but the context is now lost. Probably the Moroccan will see that type of behaviour in the Spanish business person whatever he or she does.

In both cases, no matter what the behaviour of the individual really is or how much each side's behaviour modifies the existing stereotype, it is likely that these changes will be ignored since the perception will be based on the stereotype – what is normally labelled 'change blindness' (Simons and Rensink 2005). Thus, self-fulfilling prophecies take place. Individuals would not have had a chance to be themselves but would have been perceived in a category, through the lens of prejudice, which would impede seeing the real individual.

Therefore, the first condition for an adequate cultural perception is to go back to the direct, personal experience in a concrete context, without depending of secondary descriptions lacking context. As such, one of the main outcomes of the cultural think tank was the creation of new contexts in which 'acquaintance reality' is essential – not really in order to describe things, but rather in order to know that descriptions depend on actual experiences (De Anca and El Hachami 2009: 98). A second conclusion was the fact that national culture is a very unreal concept in today's Morocco since we can still find a rural society based on traditional cultural models, which is in contrast to a highly developed, modern, dynamic society based on an international managerial culture. Therefore, the stereotyped perceptions of some of the traditional elements of Moroccan society – for example the common stereotype that Moroccan managers are 'fatalists' – is not valid as an instrument to define many of Morocco's modern enterprises.

The real fact is that many different identities co-exist in today's Moroccan organizations, and for that reason Moroccan organizations should be understood as formed by multi-identity cultural communities rather than by one homogeneous Moroccan culture. With country differences, some of the same results were given in the Spanish part of the think tank reflections, in which the hierarchical level, gender, education, travel experience or social status also define singular categories within the Spanish general cultural framework. These two basic ideas were added to the general conclusions of the think tank and helped to define the Multi-identity Context Model, as described in Figure 5.2 that will be tested in this pilot, which can help us to understand not only Moroccan organizations but also how identity influences different cultural contexts. The model thus intends to correlate the level that organizations have in diversity to their level of plurality. Plurality is defined by the multi-identity contexts existing in a given organization, while diversity is defined by the number of groups existing in the organization.

The Multi-Identity Context Model

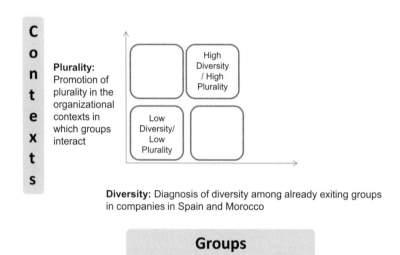

Diversity: Diagnosis of diversity among already exiting groups in companies in Spain and Morocco

Groups

Figure 5.2   The Multi-identity Context Model

The Multi-identity Context Model assumes the validity of the findings of Akerlof (Akerlof and Kranton 2000) on the value of identity for a better performance in organizations, and thus it intends to facilitate a better organizational identity link through contexts of multiple identities.

Akerlof's research on identity economics, following SIT (Akerlof and Kranton 2000) shows that the success of an organization depends on employees who share its goals; they are acting as part of a group, and this is what it means for workers to identify with their organizations. Therefore, if jobholders have only monetary rewards and only economic goals, they will 'game the system' to the extent that they can get away with it. But insofar as workers are insiders, with the same goals as their organizations, such a conflict of interest disappears. Akerlof and Kranton conclude that 'worker identification may therefore be a major factor, perhaps even the dominant factor, in the success or failure of organizations' (Akerlof and Kranton 2010: 90). One addition to this model is the fact that studies have found that workers typically identify with their immediate work group rather than with the organization as a whole.

The following three hypotheses are set for the research:

- Hypothesis 1: There are formal or informal contexts of multiple identities within an organization that give an indication of higher or lower plurality in the organization.

- Hypothesis 2:A higher degree of plurality, given also a higher degree of diversity in an organization will increase the possibility of the individual identifying with the organization through various communities of belonging.
- Hypothesis 3: A low degree of plurality given a low degree of diversity will also result in a high degree of identification with the organization by the members of the existing groups.

The research for multi-identity context in the organization consists of the following steps:

1. Mapping diversity: Diversity is here defined by the number of different groups in any given organization, which varies in different cultural contexts. Therefore, the first step in understanding plurality in a given organization is mapping the composition of the main identity groups of an organization, both origin groups (gender, culture) and other groups (by social class, status, profession and so on), both formal and informal, and both task-related and affinity-related.
2. Group mobility: After the mapping, the second part of the research involves a deeper analysis of each of the main groups in terms of:
   a) exit barriers;
   b) entry barriers;
   c) the level of internal identity cohesion;
   d) the level of identification with the organization that the group provides;
   e) the level of mobility among the different groups.
3. Plurality indicator: Analysis of group mobility will lead to analysis of the existence of contexts for multi-identity, which can provide the plurality indicator of the company.
4. Context development: After testing for its plurality indicator, the organization will understand the existence of or lack of formal or informal multi-identity contexts, as well as the capacity those contexts have to bring about a greater identification of its members with the organization. Thus, the organization will see the possibility of establishing those contexts, whether creating formal, multi-identity contexts for specific projects and tasks or allowing the formation of informal, multi-identity contexts where the need and capacity exist.

The study is being carried out in parallel in a sample of Moroccan and Spanish organizations, and after a series of focus groups (already conducted), the final phase of the research will be conducted in the following six months, with the final results to be provided in November. This first pilot analysis will help us to identify how companies can best build multi-identity contexts in different cultural frameworks.

Conclusions: Organic Leadership in Multi-identity Organizations

Paraphrasing Hanna Arendt, only among equals can an individual show his or her differences, (Arendt 1958). Following that line of thought, if organic leadership is emerging it will need contexts in which individuals can show their individual differences while being sure that those differences are appreciated in open, multi-identity contexts.

Traditionally, concrete leadership in organizations was understood as consisting of a charismatic person having personal qualities that enabled him or her to lead a group that performed and behaved in a homogenous manner. In other words, the personal differences were assumed to be left out of the equation, since efficiency was the key for organizational performance, and this efficiency was defined by a clear set of rules and procedures for all. This model was effective, but it limited the potential of many individuals who did not fit well in the given set of rules.

In the 1980s, transformational leadership emerged as a better-fitted leadership style for organizations, in which diversity was increasingly recognized, and people were encouraged to integrate into different networks in order to be among their own kind and thus work together in a better integration of their group of origin. In the new context of diversity, leaders emerge to help given communities move up in the organization. Developing emotional links with the leader was key for the success of the transformational leadership paradigm.

In the twenty-first century, complexity is the predominant characteristic of our organizations, and no one can tell anymore who is a minority and who is a majority. Mobility of groups is what best defines communities in the new organizations. In this fluid context, in Bauman's terminology, individuals can play out better than ever the multiplicity of their identities, joining some groups for a given purpose and identifying with others for other tasks. In this new multi-identity paradigm, organic leadership could be the most effective since the constant mobility of individuals among different groups requires constant change of leadership qualities. Thus, different leaders with only a short-term stay are emerging to complete short-term tasks.

The following figure (Figure 5.3) describes the change in the communities within organizations and the different types of leadership that are the most suitable in each paradigm.

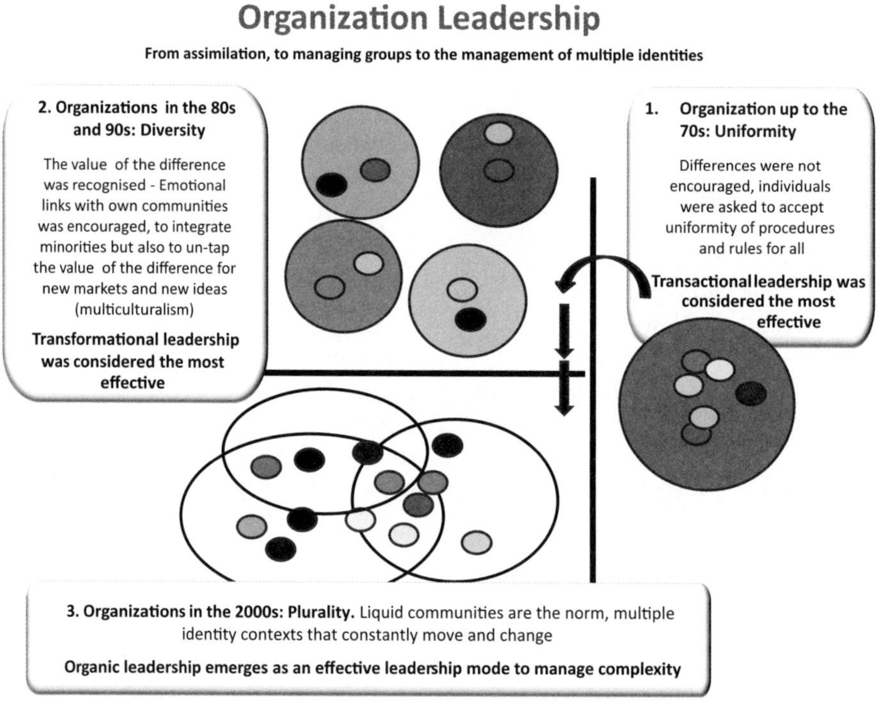

Organization Leadership

From assimilation, to managing groups to the management of multiple identities

2. Organizations in the 80s and 90s: Diversity

The value of the difference was recognised - Emotional links with own communities was encouraged, to integrate minorities but also to un-tap the value of the difference for new markets and new ideas (multiculturalism)

Transformational leadership was considered the most effective

1.   Organization up to the 70s: Uniformity

Differences were not encouraged, individuals were asked to accept uniformity of procedures and rules for all

Transactional leadership was considered the most effective

3. Organizations in the 2000s: Plurality. Liquid communities are the norm, multiple identity contexts that constantly move and change

Organic leadership emerges as an effective leadership mode to manage complexity

Figure 5.3   Organization Leadership in Multiple-context Identity

Managing multiple identities is an adapted model of the fluid and changing reality that characterizes our global society today. Traditional models require companies to first identify potential leaders and then train them; after being trained, leaders would go on to lead and achieve their groups' set objectives. In the new multi-identity paradigm, the focus is not on individuals but rather on the creation of a multi-identity context and then monitoring the free movement of individuals from their communities of origin to the communities in which they aspire to belong, while also eliminating the individual and collective barriers that prevent them from fully participating in their chosen communities.

Diversity is still the right word to express the world we live in, but it is a flexible plurality among individuals' multiple identities that can create the right environment for organic leadership to emerge and flourish in organizations on a level playing field so that we all can be different and bring our differences to bear on achieving a common goal.

References

Akerlof, G. and Kranton, R.E. 2000. Economics and Identity. *Quarterly Journal of Economics*, 115(3): 715–753.

Akerlof, G. and Kranton, R. 2010. *Identity Economics*. Princeton: Princeton University Press.

Arendt, H. 1998. *The Human Condition*. Chicago: University of Chicago Press.

Arnone, M. and Stumpf, S. (2010). Shared leadership: from rivals to co-CEOs. *Strategy & Leadership*, 38(2):15–21

Ashford, B. and Mael, F. 1989. Social Identity Theory and the Organization. *The Academy of Management Review*, 14:20–39.

Avery, G.C. 2004.*Understanding Leadership*. London: Sage Publications Ltd.

Avolio, B.J. 2007. Promoting More Integrative Strategies for Leadership Theory-building. *American Psychologist*, 62(1):25–33.

Avolio, B.J., Gardner, W.L., Walumbwa, F.O., Luthans, F. and May, R. 2004. Unlocking the Mask: A Look at the Process by Which Authentic Leaders Impact Follower Attitudes and Behaviors. *The Leadership Quarterly*, 15(6):801–823.

Avolio, B.J., Jung, D.I., and Sivasubramaniam, N. 1996. Building highly developed teams: Focusing on shared leadership processes, efficacy, trust, and performance. In M.M. Beyerlein and D.A. Johnson (Eds.), *Advances in Interdisciplinary Study of Work Teams: Team Leadership*,3:173–209. Greenwich, CT: JAI Press.

Avolio, B.J., Walumbwa, F.O. and Weber, T.J. 2009. Leadership Current Theories, Research and Future Directions. *Annual Review of Psychology*, 60:421–449.

Bass, B.M. 1985. *Leadership and Performance Beyond Expectations*. New York: Free Press.

Bass, B.M. and Avolio, B.J. 1990. *Manual: The Multifactor Leadership Questionnaire*. Palo Alto: Consulting Psychologists Press.

Bass, B.M. and Avolio, B.J. 1991. *The Transformational and Transactional Leadership Behavior of Management Women and Men as Described by the Men and Women who Directly Report to Them*. Report series 91-3, Center for Leadership Studies, State University of New York at Binghamton.

Bauman, Z. 2008. *Community: Seeking Safety in an Insecure World*. Cambridge: Polity Press.

Bavelas, A. 1950. Communication Patterns in Task-oriented Groups. *Acoustical Society of America*, 22:725-730.

Brass, D.J. 1984. Being in the Right Place: A Structural Analysis of Individual Influence in Organizations.*Administrative Science Quarterly*, 29:518–539.

Brass, D.J. and Burkhardt, M.E. 1992. Centrality and power in organizations. In *Networks and Organizations: Structure, Form and Action*, edited by N. Nohria and R. Eccles. Boston: Harvard Business School Press, 191–215.

Brown, M.E. and Gioia, D.A. 2002. Making Things click: Distributive Leadership in an Online Division of an Offline Organization. *The Leadership Quarterly*, 13(4):397–419.

Brown, R. and Williams, J. 1984. Group Identification: The Same Thing to All People? *Human Relations*, 37:547–564.

Carlyle, T. 1841. *On Heroes, Hero-Worship, and the Heroic in History*. London: James Fraser.

Carson, J.B., Tesluk, P.E. and Marrone, J.A. 2007. Shared Leadership in Teams. An Investigation of Antecendent Conditions and Performance.*Academy of Management Journal*, 50(5):1217–1234.

Castell, M. 2004. *The Power of Identity, the Information Age: Economy, Society and Culture*, (vol. II). Oxford: Blackwell (first ed. 1997).

Chan, K.Y. and Drasgow, F. 2001. Toward a Theory of Individual Differences and Leadership: Understanding the Motivation to Lead. *Journal of Applied Psychology*, 86(3):481–498.

Crevani, L., Lindgren, M. and Packendorff, J. (2009) 'We don't need another hero – Towards the study of leadership as everyday practices'. Paper for the 20th Nordic Academy of Management Conference, Aug 19-21, Åbo, Finland.

De Anca, C. and El Hachami, N. 2009. *Cultural Diversity in International Business: The Spanish-Moroccan Business Context*. Madrid: AECID.

Den Hartog, D.N. and Koopman, P.L. (2001). Leadership in organizations. In: Anderson, N., Ones, D.S., Kepir – Sinangil, H. and Viswesvaran, C. (eds.). *Handbook of Industrial, Work and Organizational Psychology, Volume 2*. London: Sage.

Fiedler, F.E. 1965. Engineer the Job to Fit the Manager. *Harvard Business Review*, 43(5):115–122.

Fiedler, F.E. and Garcia, J.E. 1987.*New Approaches to Effective Leadership: Cognitive Resources and Organizational Performance*. Oxford: John Wiley and Sons.

Follet, M.P. (1924). *Creative Experience*. New York: Logmans Green.

Fu, J.K., Tata, J., Yukl, G., Bond, M.H., Peng, T.K., Srinivas, E.S., Howell, J.P., Prieto, L., Koopman, P., Boonstra, J.J., Pasa, S., Lacassagne, M.F., Higashide, H. and Cheosakul, A. 2004. The Impact of Societal Cultural Values and Individual Social Beliefs on the Perceived Effectiveness of Managerial Influence Strategies: A MesoApproach. *Journal of International Business Studies*, 35(4):284–305.

Gibb, C.A. 1954. Leadership, in *Handbook of Social Psychology* (vol. 2), edited by G. Lindzey. Reading: Addison-Wesley, 877–917.

Graen, G.B. and Cashman, J.F. 1975. A Role-making Model of Leadership in Formal Organizations: A Development Approach, in *Leadership Frontiers*, edited by J.G. Hunt and L.L. Larson. Kent: Kent State University Press, 143–166.

Gronn, P. 2002. Distributed Leadership as a Unit of Analysis.*The Leadership Quarterly*,13:423–451.

Hauschildt, J. and Kirchmann, E. 2001. Teamwork for Innovation – the 'Troika' of Promoters. *R&D Management*, 31:41–49.

Hersey, P. and Blanchard, K. 1969. Life-cycle Theory of Leadership. *Training and Development Journal*, 23:26–34.

Hofstede, G. 1980.*Culture's Consequences: International Differences in Work Related Beliefs*. Beverly Hills: Sage.

Hofstede, G. 1991.*Cultures and Organizations: Software of the Mind*. London: MacGraw-Hill.

House, R.J. and Aditya, R.N. 1997. The Social Scientific Study of Leadership: Quo Vadis? *Journal of Management*, 23:409–473.

House, R.J. and Mitchell, T.R. 1974. Path-goal Theory of Leadership. *Journal of Contemporary Business*, 3:81–97.

House, R.J.,Hanges, P.J., Javidan, M., Dorfman, P. and Gupta, V. 2004.*Culture, Leadership and Organizations: The GLOBE Study of 62 Societies*. Thousand Oaks: Sage Publications.

Hunt, J.G., Boal, K.B. and Sorenson, R.L. 1990. Top Management Leadership: Inside the Black Box. *The Leadership Quarterly*,1(1):41–65.

Judge, T.A., Bono, J.E., Ilies, R. and Gerhardt, M.W. 2002. Personality and Leadership: A Qualitative and Quantitative Review. *Journal of Applied Psychology*, 87(4):765–780.

Jung, D.I., Bass, B.M. and Sosik, J.J. 1995. Bridging Leadership and Culture: A Theoretical Consideration of Transformational Leadership and Collectivistic Cultures.*Journal of Leadership and Organizational Studies*, 2(4):3–18.

Kirkpatrick, S.A. and Locke, E.A. 1991. Leadership: Do Traits Matter? *The Executive*, 5(2):48–60.

Kramer, R.M. and Brewer, M.B. 1984. Effects of Group Identity on Resource Use Decisions in a Simulated Comrnons Dilemma.*Journal of Personality and Social Psychology*, 46(5):1044–1057.

Lakoff, G. and Johnson, M. 1980. *Metaphors We Live By*. Chicago: University of Chicago Press.

Maffesoli, M. 1988.*Le Temps des Tribus: Le D*éclin de l'individualisme dans les Sociétés Postmodernes. Paris: Meridiens Klincksieck Editor.

Mehra, A., Dixon, A.L., Brass, D.J. and Robertson, B. 2006. The Social Network Ties of Group Leaders. *Organization Science*,17(1):64–79.

Pastor, J-C, Meindl, J.R. and Mayo, M.C. 2002. A networks effects model of charisma attributions. *Academy of Management Journal*, 45:410–420.

Pearce, C.L., Manz, C.C. and Sims, H.P. 2009. Where Do We Go From Here? Is Shared Leadership the Key to Team Success? *Organizational Dynamics*, 38(3):234–238.

Simons, D.J. and Rensink, R.A. 2005. Change Blindness: Past, Present, and Future. *Trends in Cognitive Sciences*, 9(1):16–20.

Tajfel, H. 1972. La Catégorisation Sociale, in *Introduction à la Psychologie Sociale*(vol. 1), edited by S. Moscovici. Paris: Larousse, 272–302.

Tolman, E.C. 1943. Identification and the Post-war World.*Journal of Abnormal and Social Psychology*, 38:141–148.

Spillane, Halverson, Diamond, (2001), Investigating School Leadership Practice: A Distributed Perspective, Educational Researcher, American Educational Research Association, Vol. 30, No. 3 pp. 23–28.

Turner, J.C. 1984. Social Identification and Psychological Group Formation, in *The Social Dimension: European Developments in Social Psychology* (vol. 2), edited by H. Tajfel. Cambridge: Cambridge University Press, 518–538.

Vroom, V.H. and Yetton, P.W. 1973. *Leadership and Decision-making*. Pittsburgh: University of Pittsburgh Press.

Weber, M. 1947. *The Theory of Social and Economic Organization* (translated by T. Parsons). New York: Free Press.

Yukl, G. 1998. *Leadership in Organizations*, 4th edition. Englewood Cliffs: Prentice Hall.

PART III

Cases of Global and Social Leadership

CHAPTER **6** *To Socially Responsible Leadership: Navigating the Pluralistic Complexities in a Global World*

VIPIN GUPTA

Introduction

In this chapter, we first identify two existing schools of socially responsible leadership: The individual, values-based model and the local stakeholder model. We identify the limitations of these existing models and propose a third, more global model, constructing a complete transcultural model that incorporates the two existing models. Finally, we present a leadership case study from India of Jaipur Rugs, and discuss how it has transposed transcultural dimensions of socially responsible leadership while navigating the pluralistic complexities in a global world.

The First School: A Values-based Model of Socially Responsible Leadership

The first and the earliest school of theorizing on responsible leadership was based on the individual-level theories of leadership that address ethical or moral challenges. This 'values-based' responsible leadership model focuses on the integrity of values espoused by the leader, and emphasizes three major characteristics: 1) concern for people; 2) members pursuing shared concerns; and 3) assuring accountability. The model is represented by several interrelated leadership theories: Ethical leadership (Brown and Trevino 2006), transformational leadership (Bass and Steidlmeier 1999); authentic leadership (Avolio and Gardner 2005), servant leadership (Greenleaf 1977, Liden, Wayne, Zhao and Henderson 2008), and virtuous leadership (Cameron 2011). Thus, Trevino, Brown and Hartman (2003: 14), in their study of ethical leadership, note: 'They care about people, respect people, develop their people, and treat people right.' If they need 'to downsize, they do it, but they do it with as much concern and interest for their people as possible'. They create and infuse values that the entire organizational team is expected to practice, and use rewards and punishments to hold people accountable to value standards (Trevino, Brown and Hartman 2003). Ketola (2006) reported that consistency and coherency as a component of integrity is an important component of a leader's successful promotion of corporate social responsibility (CSR) activities at the firm, because it creates trust between the leader and the followers. Ketola (2006: 13) concluded, 'It is useless for leaders to dream about the future, if noone trusts them.' Using GLOBE CEO data, Waldman, de Luque, Washburn and House (2006: 834) similarly found that, 'CEO leadership in the form of vision and integrity may be a driver in how subordinate managers view the importance of CSR in their decision-making.' In another study based on a European sample, Hind, Wilson and Lenssen (2009) found that acting with integrity and caring for people were the most important competencies for supporting responsible leadership.

Using the GLOBE study (House, Hanges, Javidan, Dorfman and Gupta 2004), one may identify cultural dimensions that are associated with the three characteristics of the values-based model as follows in Table 6.1:

Table 6.1   Values-based Model Characteristics and Associated Cultural Dimensions

Characteristics	Associated cultural dimensions
1. Concern for people	Humane orientation
2. Members pursing shared concerns	In-group collectivism
3. Assuring accountability	Performance orientation

The Second School: A Stakeholder Model of Socially Responsible Leadership

The second school on responsible leadership was the focus of a special issue of the *Journal of Business Ethics* in 2011 (Pless and Maak 2011). This 'stakeholder' model of responsible leadership focuses on integrating the efforts and interests of various stakeholders of an organization. In this model, responsible leadership is a cross between the individual-level, value-based approach and organizational-level CSR (Maak and Pless, 2006). Stakeholder focus and inclusion is seen as inherently good, sustainable and futuristic behaviour from an organizational standpoint (Avery and Bergsteiner 2011). Maak (2007: 340) observes how 'the responsible leader acts as a weaver of stakeholder relationships', thereby leveraging social capital for the organization. Stakeholder integration is values-based; in other words it is guided by 'a sense of justice, a sense of recognition, a sense of care, and a sense of accountability for a wide range of economic, ecological, social, political, and human responsibilities' (Pless 2007: 451).. Responsible leadership offers an equal opportunity to all stakeholders affected by a decision to participate and advocate their positions and critique other positions through the process of discursive dialogue, and with symmetric power relationships, and strives to achieve a consensus by weighing and balancing the different interests and advocating transcending the organizational point of view (Voegtlin 2011).

The distinctive characteristics of the stakeholder model, and the associated GLOBE cultural conditions, are identified below in Table 6.2:

Table 6.2   The Stakeholder Model and GLOBE Cultural Conditions

Characteristics	Associated cultural dimensions
Institutionalizing collective stakeholder interests	Institutional collectivism
Symmetric and inclusive power relationships	Low power distance
Futuristic sustainability	Future orientation

The stakeholder model may be approached from two perspectives: The traditional CSR perspective, and the contemporary sustainability perspective.

The traditional CSR perspective sees socially responsible leadership as a business obligation that entails three major types of decisions:

- Bearing near-term costs for maximizing eventual profits (self-serving strategy): The leaders seek to serve the interests of diverse stakeholders, in ways that enable maximizing the eventual returns for the stockholders. This view is at the heart of the principal–agent theory (Jensen and Meckling 1976), based on the model of a self-serving leader, a rational actor who seeks to maximize his or her individual utility by aligning it with that of the stockholders.
- Accepting lower profitability on an ongoing basis (satisficing strategy): The leaders are the stewards of the interests of diverse stakeholders, and must achieve a satisfactory trade-off between the returns expected by the stockholders and the interests of the other stakeholders. They do so by accepting decisions that do not necessarily maximize returns, but instead allow returns that are acceptable to the investors, and that also allow serving the interests of other stakeholders such as higher wages for the workers and lower prices for the customers. This view is exemplified by the satisficing theory of decision making (Simon 1957).
- Investing a share of profits in socially responsible domains (surfacing strategy): The formalized systems of strategic decision making in organizations are based on the analysis of private benefits and costs, but the social, cultural, political and psychological processes at work may give rise to a realized strategy that is different from the espoused strategy (Bowman and Johnson 1992). The realized strategy may exploit several public goods and may impose several public costs; the socially responsible leaders are committed to surface such externalities. In order to sustain these public goods and to optimize organizational returns, socially responsible leaders seek to share a part of the profits with the public as compensation. Thus, Crouch (2006: 1534) interprets CSR as a 'behaviour by firms that voluntarily takes account of the externalities produced by their market behaviour', and Vogel (2008) identifies CSR as a form of self-regulation to govern the market through non-prescriptive regulation. Examples of surfacing strategy behaviour include charity and other philanthropic activities that bridge social gaps between those that the organization chooses to

include in its value chain, and those that are excluded. It works in the near term by allowing organizations to secure tax credits and other government incentives.

In the context of traditional CSR obligations, the stakeholder-based socially responsible leadership has the capacity to deliver strong financial performance, endure difficult economic and social conditions, and help the organization maintain a leadership position (Kantabutra and Avery 2011). However, given the costs associated with the obligatory concept of CSR, some scholars have asserted that the only socially responsible behaviour is to serve the interests of the stockholders by maximizing profitability, and that attempts to serve the interests of any other type of stakeholders is in fact socially irresponsible (Friedman 1970, Siegel 2009).

The contemporary sustainability perspective offers an alternative view of socially responsible leadership as a business opportunity. The leadership model using a sustaining strategy strengthens relationships with all the stakeholders (for instance by creating an organizational and social culture of responsibility), and thus helps organizations lower costs, increase revenue, accelerate growth, decrease variability in future cash flows, enhance legitimacy, strengthen reputation, and improve conditions within the firm and in the business environment. This results in a positive contribution to bottom-line results (Sethi 1979, Aguilera, Rupp, Williams and Ganapathi 2007, Jensen 2002, Barnett 2007).

The four strategies implied by the Stakeholder model are summarized below in Table 6.3:

Table 6.3   Stakeholder Model Strategies

	Near-term approach	**Ongoing approach**
Maximizing returns criteria	Self-serving	Sustaining
Optimizing returns criteria	Surfacing	Satisficing

Limitations of Existing Models of Socially Responsible Leadership

To understand the limitations of the existing models of socially responsible leadership and to identify a way forward, it will be useful to recognize how over the course of history, the general understanding of socially responsible leadership has evolved and shifted.

TRADITIONALISM AND NATURAL THEORY

In ancient Greece and Rome, as well as in the Christian medieval age, a 'natural theory' of culture for socially responsible leadership was espoused. Since the general concepts of ethics, politics and knowledge were a function of the immutable laws and first principles of the cosmos, a socially responsible leader was expected to lead with the 'natural disposition of human beings', in other words according to the laws that have a universal cosmological foundation (González, Moskowitz and Casto-Gómez 2001). This is a narrow perspective of the transcultural model, which identifies socially responsible leadership with core values.

MODERNISM AND RELATIVIST THEORY

In the eighteenth and nineteenth centuries, human life began to be perceived as a dynamic process ruled by laws created by human beings themselves, rather than a simple derivative of the general laws of the universe. That led to the emergence of a traditional relativist theory of culture, identified as the process through which humanity humanizes itself, in other words constituting itself gradually in time and in history, allowing for the development of the spirit of human freedom. In the traditional theory of culture, such as that of Hegel (1953), human freedom is identified with the gradual release from the tyranny or constraints of laws of nature. Thus, those cultural systems that seek harmony with nature are seen as inferior to those that seek mastery over nature. Similarly, those 'high' cultures that rely on rationalized and referential hermeneutics (musical codification, secularized art, literature, philosophy, historiography) are seen as superior to 'popular' cultures that rely on lived experiences. The society or the organization was seen as the true carrier of the culture, since only through them did the people become aware of their identity, values and destiny as members. The society and the organization reflect the general will, or what Hegel (1953) referred to as Volksgeist, of the people, and only as their members do people experience true freedom. Thus, identification was presumed between the values of the people, the organization and society, and it became possible for a socially responsible leader to be guided by a set of core, essential values, and to bring about consensus among a set of stakeholders through a process of open dialogue and rational discourse. In the traditional theory of culture, the organization or the society is seen as an escape from the chaos of the nature, into the habitat of organizational or social civility and order, and the socially responsible leader is an architect of this habitat. This is a broad perspective of the transcultural model, which identifies socially responsible leadership with the process of defining the general will of all stakeholders, through open dialogue and consensus building. This perspective is based on the genealogy of the visible and the short-term microstructures of power-relationships (Foucault 2006) between the stockholders and other stakeholders.

POSTMODERNISM AND RELATIONAL THEORY

In the contemporary postmodern world, people, organizations and society may not have isomorphic values that are a transparent extension of human conscience and free will. Instead, these values tend to be heteronomous, contingent on the working relationships people have among themselves and with organization and society. The critical or relational theory of culture suggests that the relationship between people and work culture cannot be presumed to be of harmony and order, as it has a socio-political character that may be disruptive if not appropriately directed. It expands the challenges for socially responsible leadership by adding the genealogy of the invisible, embedded, enduring and long-term macrostructures of power (Wallerstein 1994). One major perspective based on the critical theory of culture is the 'world-system' (Wallerstein 1994). The world-system is a network of interdependencies with people, organizations and societies around the world, the differences among whom are not necessarily due to their varying levels of cultural development, but rather to their functional position. Some people, organizations and societies, and the values propagated by them, occupy the central, hegemonic function, while others are relegated to the peripheral, marginal function. The causative force is not the differential transcendental competencies of the humans, but the socially constructed power relations that are both global in character and subject to complex historical transformations. In critical theory, culture is the 'battleground where the control of meaning is decided' (González, Moskowitz and Casto-Gómez 2001: 147). In this battleground, the leader may be pushed to assume hierarchical differences among people, and to assign them place in the social division of labour based on these differences.

Thus, a stakeholder-oriented socially responsible leadership is susceptible to push forward the hegemony of married, male, literate, heterosexual and white organization and societal citizenry, while relegating the interests of the minorities, immigrants, foreigners and women to the background. This is so because it is concerned with the homogenization of the differences among different stakeholders, by promoting a consensus organization-focused value system. The relational theory, on the other hand, calls for learning how to create a space where the heterogeneous values and behaviours may co-exist for the sake of the entire world-system. Based on this, we next propose a third school of socially responsible leadership.

—

Towards the Third School: A Transcultural Model of Socially Responsible Leadership

The stakeholder model of socially responsible leadership holds corporate leaders responsible for not only economic activities, but also for social responsibilities by creating enduring links between the two and by addressing conflicting issues. Thus, it can potentially help an organization respond to the social and economic crisis. However, it faces constraints in creating continuity and meaning to address the needs of the world that is constantly evolving from transcultural contact and globalization. In a contemporary interconnected global society, socially responsible leaders cannot afford to serve the interests of only a finite and defined set of organizational stakeholders. Instead, organizations and their leaders are being called upon to address the needs of a wider audience that includes 80 percent of the world's population living on less than two dollars per day. Further, in a pluralistic global context, socially responsible leaders cannot afford to be rigid about their values. An open mindset is essential for the socially responsible global leaders to facilitate learning from the diversity of cultural values, across social boundaries. Lipman-Blumen (2000: 45) observes that we have entered the 'Connective Era', where 'only those leaders with the capacity to harness the tensions spawned by interdependence and diversity will gain the connective edge' and be able to meet the ever-changing demands of this new reality.

Therefore, we propose a third 'transcultural' school of socially responsible leadership, focused on the well-being and progressive development of communities across cultures. In a pluralistic global environment, the leaders interact not only with the followers and the stakeholders, but also with communities having diverse cultural endowments. In many such communities, a majority of the members are silent and invisible spectators, who might perceive or actually have little stake in an organization. In the transcultural model, socially responsible leadership is about offering a democratized and culturally-sensitive space where diverse members across different communities are able to productively engage with the organization. For instance, recognition by men of the male-centered masculine codes, and the inclusion of women by embracing gender-sensitive practices, is an example of transcultural socially responsible leadership (Simons, Vázquez, and Harris 1993). Simons, Vázquez and Harris (1993: 245) note that transcultural leadership is about being 'rounded in one's own culture but having the culture-general and culture-specific skills to be able to live, interact and work effectively in a multicultural environment'.

The transcultural perspective enhances the stakeholder leadership model by incorporating societal-level diversity and cultural plurality. Socially responsible leadership is not bound by the dominant, finite, visible, and aggressive groups and members of stakeholders in an embedded context, but demonstrates sensitivity to the broader, infinite, invisible, diverse and pluralistic community landscape in a transcendental context. Thus, it shows the capacity and ability to pierce through the institutionalized forces, powers and pressures, in order to be able to grow and develop the stakeholder base and enrich the value base and other culturally-sensitive endowments through transnational exchange.

One must not, however, overestimate the opportunity value of working with peripheral and invisible resources. Mobilizing such resources is subject to significant institutional resistance, and the costs involved in qualifying such resources by educating, training and credentialing can be substantial (Karnani 2007). A transcultural model of socially responsible leadership deploys multiple lenses to address the limitations of the stakeholder-oriented model, and to mitigate its own potential limitations. Thus, the relational cultural theory is complemented with critical lenses offered by technical, political and postmodern theories (Butin 2005), to promote transformative learning and democratizing the social relationships among different stakeholders, and with the organization and the society. These lenses are as follows:

1. Cultural lens: As noted earlier, this lens calls for an enlightened sense of identity – providing a humbling experience to those occupying hierarchically privileged positions, and an empowering and emancipating consciousness to those at the bottom of the pyramid.
2. Technical lens: This lens views socially responsible leadership as one among several leadership strategies. The transcultural model's transformative impact lies in mobilizing broader-based resource endowments and innovative synergies between the invisible and the visible resources, for strengthened competitive advantage of the organization.
3. Political lens: This lens requires the transcultural model to be implemented through a context of critical leadership influence and critical self-reflection, which alerts people to the dominant values and positions, promotes transformation of power relationships, and thereby produces a level playing field of mutual appreciation and exchange among all members.
4. Postmodern lens: This lens calls upon a leader to enact the transcultural model by helping to disrupt and reconstruct the boundaries and the norms by which the organization and various audiences make sense of themselves and the world. For instance, societies that are seen as markets may get reconstructed as co-producers, and the groups that are seen as recipients of knowledge may get reconstructed as contributors to knowledge.

The four lenses for implementing the Transcultural model are summarized below in Table 6.4:

Table 6.4   Transcultural Model Lenses

	Tactics in relation to the invisible groups	Tactics in relation to the dominant groups
Within group tactics	Empower (cultural lens)	Transform (political lens)
Across group tactics	Connect (technical lens)	Disrupt and reconstruct (postmodern lens)

From a transcultural perspective, socially responsible leadership has three additional characteristics: 1) inter-cultural consciousness and competence; 2) diversity consciousness and competence; and 3) equipoise consciousness and competence. Karim (2003: 35) defines inter-cultural consciousness as 'a synergistic combination of essential cognitive, emotional and behavioral knowledge and skills for inter-cultural competence and a commitment to consistent, caring, and ethical application of those skills and knowledge'. This is likely to be supported by the cultural dimension of assertiveness, which is associated with interpersonal and cross-cultural communication effectiveness and cultural competence. The concept diversity consciousness refers to the knowledge, skills and commitment to the inclusion of under-represented and invisible members, such as women, minorities, specially-abled and foreign nationals. This is likely to be supported by the cultural dimension of gender egalitarianism, which is associated with the opportunities accessible and realized by women. The third concept of equipoise consciousness refers to recognition that the transcultural encounters are wonderful opportunities to bring higher order stability, order, continuity, balance and emotional resilience through organizational learning, transformative development and technological exchange. This is likely to be supported by the cultural dimension of uncertainty avoidance, which is associated with an emphasis on order and continuity. In summary, Table 6.5 shows the distinctive characteristics of the transcultural model, and the GLOBE-based cultural dimensions that are likely to be associated with them.

1. Emphasis on inter-cultural consciousness: The focus of the stakeholder-oriented socially responsible leadership – as of the relativist theory of culture – is on large events, social aggregates, and representative or influential individuals (Steinberg 1996). In contrast, the relational theory of culture calls for a socially responsible leader to take a more generous view of the values and stakeholder interests, in other words to develop inter-cultural consciousness and competence. The transcultural leader should pay more attention to stories that would have been and are often dismissed as trivial or irrelevant, and to the experiences and voices of individuals and groups of people on the margins (Steinberg 1996). The leader must question the commonly held assumptions of what is significant and what is trivial. The leader must not be captivated by the big narrative and overly broad generalizations about trends and stakeholder ideologies, but be attentive to uncovering the small alternative narratives, particular voices and concerns, and stories and perspectives of the forgotten subjects

Table 6.5   Transcultural Model Characteristics and Associated GLOBE-based Cultural Dimensions

Characteristics	Associated cultural dimensions
1. Inter-cultural consciousness	Assertiveness
2. Diversity consciousness	Gender egalitarianism
3. Equipoise consciousness	Uncertainty avoidance

   – the disenfranchised, the women, the bottom of the pyramid and the dissenters of all sorts (Steinberg 1996). Thus, transcultural leadership requires sensitivity about cultural intelligence, more so than the ability to communicate with and convince the stakeholders about the value of common organizational interests. It also produces a 'heightened awareness of the presence of fractured meaning, paradox, ambivalence, and contradiction in people's experiences and voices' (Steinberg 1996: 353), or what Gorham (1996) refers to as the 'discursive ambiguities' 'perversions' and 'collective heteroglossia'.

2. Emphasis on diversity consciousness: The stakeholder model of socially responsible leadership conceals social inequities inherent across and within different groups of stakeholders. In the relational theory of culture, critical discourse acts to change the process of leadership to one of cultivating people's 'ability to question, deconstruct, and then reconstruct knowledge in the interest of emancipation' (Leonardo 2004: 12). A transcultural leader engages in a language of transcendence, feeding a capacity to imagine an alternative reality and a hope for the entire world-system (Giroux 1983), by promoting transformative learning in which 'the interests of all [people] should be identified and accepted' (Dant 2003: 159). While promoting transformative learning, the Transcultural Model of Socially Responsible Leadership is sensitive to the diverse cultural systems and their distinct models of learning.

3. Emphasis on equipoise consciousness: As in the relativist theory of culture, the stakeholder-oriented socially responsible leadership assumes a loosely materialist view of leader consciousness and behaviour (Steinberg 1996). The imperative for socially responsible leadership behaviours is material conditions and changes, in other words emergence of the new structures of power in organizational and societal life around stakeholders beyond the stockholders. This transcultural leadership, however, is not an agency of the organization for advocating the interests of its core group of stakeholders, and for dominating and exploiting those who are not empowered as stakeholders (Boateng 2003). Instead, such leadership is a catalyst of awareness, conversations, dialogue and exchange encompassing all members of the world-system. The success of the transcultural leadership is anchored less on the basis of its effectiveness as a vehicle for furthering the teleological interests of the organization, and more on the basis of how well it responds to the aspirations and well-being of its broader democratized audience. In this Transcultural Model of Socially Responsible Leadership, a generous view of the targeted audience becomes the mechanism for furthering the interests, vibrancy and sustainability of an organization.

Summary: Concentric Mapping of the Complete Transcultural Model of Socially Responsible Leadership

In sum, the Transcultural Model of Socially Responsible Leadership demonstrates commitment to consistent, caring and ethical application of those skills and knowledge that mobilize inter-cultural and diverse endowments to bring equipoise through organizational learning, transformative development and technological exchange. Thus, it ensures continuity in times of change, perseveres in the face of challenges, and positively impacts the triple bottom line – People, Planet and Profits. The transcultural model (see Figure 6.1) is able to deal with the dynamic and constantly evolving challenges in a complex, pluralistic and globalized world. It is a multi-level construct, which includes values-based leadership at the individual/intra-organizational level, stakeholder-oriented leadership at the local/organizational level, and transculturally sensitive leadership at the global/societal level.

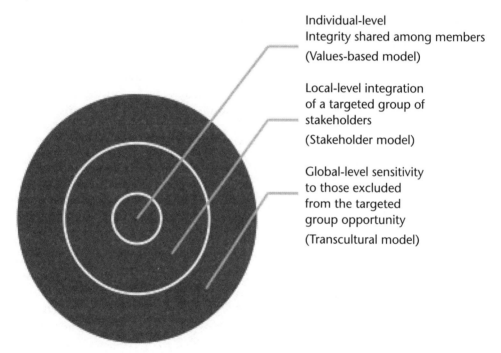

Individual-level
Integrity shared among members
(Values-based model)

Local-level integration
of a targeted group of
stakeholders
(Stakeholder model)

Global-level sensitivity
to those excluded
from the targeted
group opportunity
(Transcultural model)

Figure 6.1   Mapping the Transcultural Model of Socially Responsible Leadership

Since this transcultural model is grounded in both individual as well as organizational level models of socially responsible leadership, its implementation needs to be sensitive to the local context. This may be seen in Ntseane's (2011) discussion of the socially responsible leadership approach appropriate to the Afrocentric model of transformative learning. Here, a leader is expected to present and preserve the diverse intellectual and philosophical traditions of the African culture. These expectations constitute the core values of socially responsible leadership, the integrating principle for various stakeholders in the organization's community, and the transcultural bridge of distinction and exchange with the rest of the world.

In Africa, traditionally, knowledge is produced and communally owned as attested by the proverb 'Kgosi ke thothobolo e lathelwa matlakala'.[1] Thus, learning activity in Africa is seen as a collective knowledge production platform, rather than being leader dominated. Another proverb 'mmua lebe o búa la gagwe',[2] calls for the leader to support the open space system of communication, and to arrive at conclusions through consensus. These culturally-based knowledge acquisition and production systems are complemented with dissemination to the entire community through songs, plays, poems, dance, theatre and storytelling. This process of learning is defined and influenced by the people's connectedness to the earth and all its inhabitants as well as ancestral spirits, and their systematic self-consciousness of the need to assume fully one's place in the world (Ntseane 2011). Thus, instead of using dominant research and learning methods, the community should be given the power to influence and shape the method – to define collective problems and the solutions. Further, the method and the knowledge generated both must reflect the primacy of the spirituality – the connectedness with all things and with the spiritual. In addition, the knowledge generated ought to be emancipatory – freeing and empowering people, such as helping them open their 'pelo ya bobedi'[3] by recognizing their purpose on earth, such as being useful and giving back to the community (Ntseane 2011). Finally, gender and female voice plays an important role in the transformative learning through the process of collective empowerment and responsibility, rather than individually. For instance, the national anthem of Botswana acknowledges, 'emang basadi a re tshwaraganeng go direla Lefatshe la rona'[4] (Ntseane 2011).

Overview of a Leadership Case Study from India: Jaipur Rugs

We present a leadership case of how invisible members were connected with global value chains, and how that became the basis for defining organizational interests and goals, and contributed to organizational success as well as broader community development.

Table 6.6 presents GLOBE cultural data on societal cultural practices in India. The data are presented in the form of Practices Index, computed as percentage of the difference between India's score and the lowest score, divided by the range on that practice:

First, Indian societal culture is characterized by a high concern for people, group and performance accountability. These conditions are likely to be conducive for the values-based model of socially responsible leadership. Second, India's societal culture is also characterized by a high concern for institutional collective interests and for the long term, but the power relationships tend to be strongly asymmetric and non-inclusive. These conditions are likely to hinder the emergence of a stakeholder model of socially responsible leadership, which hinges upon a discursive dialogue among stakeholders sharing symmetric power relationships. Finally, India's social culture is characterized by low assertiveness and gender egalitarianism, and only moderate uncertainty avoidance. These conditions are likely to make the transcultural model of socially responsible leadership rather uncommon in India.

---

1   'A leader is an information/knowledge dumping site and thus has to be a good listener and analyst.'

2   'Every voice must be heard.'

3   'Second heart.'

4   'Women standup and together with men let us collectively develop our nation.'

Table 6.6   Indian Societal/Cultural Practices According to GLOBE Characteristics

Characteristics	Associated cultural dimensions	Practices Index: India
1. Concern for people	Humane orientation	68
2. Members pursing shared concerns	In-group collectivism	84
3. Assuring accountability	Performance orientation	60
4. Institutionalizing collective stakeholder interests	Institutional collectivism	57
5. Symmetric and inclusive power relationships	Power distance (low)	83
6. Futuristic sustainability	Future orientation	60
7. Inter-cultural consciousness	Assertiveness	23
8. Diversity consciousness	Gender egalitarianism	25
9. Equipoise consciousness	Uncertainty avoidance	51

A relevant research enquiry is how can a transcultural model of socially responsible leadership be implemented in a values-based context, that practices neither symmetric power relationships (as required under the stakeholder model) nor much of boundary-crossing consciousness (as required by the cultural lens to transcultural model)? We hypothesize that it is possible to implement transcultural leadership in such a context, if socially responsible leadership is interpreted as transforming the context in ways that bring power symmetry and promote boundary-crossing exchanges.

To investigate this hypothesis, we look at the case of the Chaudhry family who are the owners and the leaders of Jaipur Rugs based in the city of Jaipur, India. N.K. Chaudhry founded Jaipur Rugs as a small family business in the 1970s, and started exporting in 1986. By 2008, Jaipur Rugs was the largest manufacturer and exporter of Indian hand knotted rugs, and also produced tuft and flat woven styles. Below we analyze the Chaudhry family in terms of the nine major characteristics of the transcultural model of socially responsible leadership. These materials were gathered by the author based on three field visits, and extensive interactions with the Chaudhry family, employees, and artisans, over 2008–2011:

1. Concern for people: The Chaudhry leadership was guided by a deep concern for the welfare of the weavers. The traditional, unorganized rug industry in India, as in many other low-income nations, was characterized by the use of similar traditional designs and materials. The firms faced significant competition, selling primarily in the local market, and commanding low prices. To remain viable, the use of low-cost child labour and women labour was rampant, while men were deployed to instruct, supervise and control this illiterate and impoverished labour.

2. Members pursing shared concerns: The Chaudhry leadership began by removing the males from their middlemen and supervisory roles, and provided looms directly to

the women weavers, organized into small groups, who worked together weaving a rug on their loom. More experienced women weavers were designated as leaders, who worked as weavers but also offered instructions to fellow less experienced weavers, who worked on the different part of the rug alongside. This was possible because, depending on the size and design complexity, a rug might require several women to work simultaneously for up to one year. Former experienced weaver supervisors, who had a deep appreciation of the weaving techniques associated with different designs, were retrained as designers. Since they were all illiterate, they were trained to work in a computer-based design centre using customized visually-based design software. The latest international design books were provided for inspiration, enabling creation of fusion contemporary designs, which commanded strong interest by wholesale rug buyers in the international markets – particularly the US, the initial country of focus. Those who had some education were appointed to the different managerial positions in the company.

3. Assuring accountability: The Chaudhry leadership empowered women weavers by concentrating on the development of human capability and skill at the grassroots level through training and leadership opportunities. The weavers were paid per piece (depending on the size, complexity of design, and quality of finished product in terms of defects and amount of rework required). Thus, rewards and punishments were built in the payment system. While most women weavers earned only the legal minimum wages when translated into daily wages, many chose to work for fewer than eight hours. The looms were situated in the villages at or near their homes, in order to provide a more humane working environment. That allowed women to take time off to take care of their household chores and children. Significantly, Jaipur Rugs was competitive and was able to scale up its model and its international demand, without the need to cut down on the wages or to hire child labour or to use exploitative methods. Further, women weavers were assured year-round consistent work because of the international demand, in an industry traditionally characterized by cycles of work and idling.

4. Institutionalizing collective stakeholder interests: The Chaudhry leadership is committed to serving the interests of its diverse stakeholders – including its family members, employees, weavers and other artisans, as well as its customers. In order to build greater global demand, the two eldest daughters in the Chaudhry family decided to pursue higher education in the US, and open a marketing subsidiary of the company in the country. Since many of the women weavers chose to reduce the number of hours worked in response to their increased and consistent wages, the Chaudhry family needed to identify new villages, often in far flung areas and in neighbouring states, and train and qualify new women weavers in order to assure timely order fulfillment. Therefore, the eldest son decided to leave his higher education in the US unfinished, and return to Jaipur to lend a helping hand to Mr. Chaudhry. As the scale of operations grew, the family began to face greater pressures from the overseas wholesale buyers for timely delivery. Under the leadership of the eldest son, the Chaudhury family decided to introduce information technology for better tracking of its weaving and other processes, and for providing up-to-date information on the status to the buyers. During the 2008–2010 global financial crisis, the family faced additional pressures from the buyers on the pricing front, putting the company into red. The youngest daughter of the family was entrusted with the responsibility of

developing a strategy for reaching out directly to the overseas retailers, bypassing the wholesale buyers, in order to support brand building and realize higher prices. She formed relationships with the leading designers in the world, and launched new lines of rugs that carried the name of the designer and of Jaipur Rugs, along with the brand names of the retail chains that sold those lines. Previously, all the rugs had carried the names of the wholesale buyers. The new approach yielded significantly higher price realizations, which were used for nearly doubling the weaver compensation, hiring professionally trained managers (to work alongside the grassroots promoted managers), and introduce enterprise resource planning system SAP for monitoring each of the 84 processes involved from shearing the wool to packing in rug business.

5. Symmetric and inclusive power relationships: In order to transform the traditionally asymmetric power relationships with the weavers, the Chaudhry family formed the Jaipur Rugs Foundation, and hired professionally trained managers. The Foundation seeks to develop its women weavers into entrepreneurs owning their independent looms, instead of working on the Jaipur Rugs-owned looms. The Chaudhry family believes that this will create stronger work ethic and commitment among the women. The Foundation also runs adult education classes for its women weavers, imparting knowledge about hygiene and ecology, numeracy and literacy, so that they may not be exploited, such as by the shopkeepers, for not knowing what price is written on something they wish to buy, and so that they learn to keep their surroundings clean. In some cases, Jaipur Rugs has directly benefitted from these offerings, for example through a hygienic environment that prevents integration of dust into rugs, thus enhancing the rug life. By the end of 2011, more than 750 women had completed 300 hours of classes, covering first and second grade content, with a goal of educating a total of 5,000 women by 2015. Most of the former graduates have shown an interest in attending school as adult students. The Foundation is also creating a curriculum to train selected women weavers to get employed by Jaipur Rugs, and to have a career advancing them to managerial positions. All these initiatives are also having a positive impact on the children of the women weavers, who are showing greater commitment to education and learning.

6. Futuristic sustainability: The Chaudhry family has faced several challenges in the near term, but has remained committed to protecting the interests of its weavers, its employees and its customers. In terms of its approach to traditional CSR, the Chaudhry family pursues a satisficing strategy – accepting low, reasonable returns, and sharing the lion's share of the rewards with the weavers, in the form of higher wages, carpet weaving training programmes, livelihood projects and rural development such as safer drinking options. At the same time, the family is focused on ensuring profitable growth in order to scale up and to serve even more weavers. Therefore, it is constantly looking for opportunities for strengthening relationships with various stakeholders and innovations that help enhance legitimacy, strengthen reputation and improve conditions within the firm and in the business environment. As an illustration, the company has launched a village factory model, wherein several looms are put in a central place in a village, rather than being dispersed across homes in that village or neighbouring villages. The model is attractive for some women weavers, who are able to devote dedicated time without being distracted by routine chores and are thus able to work full time, helping to reduce cycle time and allowing Jaipur Rugs to take on more lucrative orders with shorter delivery times.

7. Inter-cultural consciousness: Traditionally, the rug companies and the customers have focused on providing attractive designs and a good product. The Chaudhry family is host to several student groups from the US. In 2011, one of the visiting student groups suggested including the names and the stories of women weavers with each rug, to build a direct connection between the weaver and the end customer, and allowing Jaipur Rugs to sell directly to the customers, in the process forging a more sustainable connection with the international retailers. Another student group from the same university suggested categorizing the competencies of rug weaving, classifying women weavers on these competencies, and then assigning work and introducing a mentorship programme based on those competencies. The student group also offered funding to pilot design and dance competitions among the rural communities where the company operates, as a way to recognize, promote, preserve and reinterpret indigenous and traditional knowledge and creativity at the grassroots. The company piloted these competitions in March 2012, with huge success and involvement of 500 members of the rural community including the artisans, their children and other members of the community. It has also hired a public relations company in the US and established a communication department in Jaipur. That has immediately brought in social investors interested in supporting Jaipur Rugs.

8. Diversity consciousness: The Chaudhry family is also striving to leverage the complex interplay of diversity with other factors, such as experience, in order to establish a greater system-wide confidence in the creativity of the grassroots. In one of the remarkable recent experiments, a few of the most experienced women weavers have been given total freedom to weave a rug using their own creativity, and not according to the designs given by Jaipur Rugs. Since these women weavers had been exposed to a range of traditional and contemporary designs over their working lifetime, their very first attempt turned out to be a unique design that commanded a price five times more than normal. On the basis of the strong interest by a prestigious retain chain in India, Jaipur Rugs has transcribed this unique design into a drawn design for other women weavers to make, and has shared the rewards with the creators.

9. Equipoise consciousness: The Chaudhry family's leadership has been a catalyst of awareness, conversations, dialogue and exchange encompassing an expanding group of members of the world-system. The late C.K. Prahalad (2010) used the Jaipur Rugs case study in the fifth edition of his influential book, *Fortune at the Bottom of the Pyramid*, as an example of how a successful business connects the grassroots with the global supply chains. The Planning Commission of India has approached the Chaudhry family seeking its assistance in using the Jaipur Rugs model as a basis for developing a natural programme for empowering weavers. The governments of neighbouring nations in South Asia have also requested assistance in replicating similar models in their own nations, in order to grow out of the image of the rug industry as minefield for exploiting children and women.

In summary, our analysis indicates how the Chaudhry family has evidenced all major characteristics of socially responsible leadership, as reflected in the transcultural model. Though the early formation and growth of Jaipur Rugs was based on the vision and the values of empowering women weavers and offering them sustainable livelihoods, significant innovative efforts and creative strategies and dedicated partnerships were required in order to move towards a landscape where women weavers could be meaningful participants, voicing their interests as critical stakeholders. The family started off with an idealistic cultural lens of empowerment. Over time, it has used additional lenses to actualize and further this goal. At the start of 2012, Jaipur Rugs served more than 40,000 weavers and hand spinners, and had a goal of serving more than 100,000 artisans in India. From a technical lens, it has used several techniques to strengthen the connection of the weavers with the end customers. From a political lens, it has begun to create an interest among the dominant voices in the power of the previously silenced groups. Additionally, from a postmodern lens, it has begun to blur the boundaries between the grassroots and the glasshouses.

Conclusions

In conclusion, this chapter builds on the emergent discourse on the socially responsible models of leadership. It identifies the cultural conditions associated with the two existing models – values-based and stakeholder-oriented. Four strategies associated with the stakeholder-oriented model are also identified. It then furthers this discourse by identifying limitations of these two models, and proposes a transcultural model. The characteristics of this model and the need for using multiple lenses for implementing it are discussed. A complete transcultural model is mapped using a concentric approach. Finally, a case study is presented from the Indian context, which shows how a family is exercising a complete transcultural model of socially responsible leadership.

References

Aguilera, R.V., Rupp, D.E., Williams, C.A. and Ganapathi, J. 2007. Putting the S Back in Corporate Social Responsibility: A Multilevel Theory of Social Change in Organizations. *Academy of Management Review*, 32(3): 836–863.

Avery, G.C. and Bergsteiner, H. 2011. Sustainable Leadership Practices for Enhancing Business Resilience and Performance. *Strategy and Leadership*, 39(3): 5–15.

Avolio, B.J. and Gardner, W.L. 2005. Authentic Leadership Development: Getting to the Root of Positive Forms of Leadership. *Leadership Quarterly*, 16(3): 315–338.

Barnett, M.L. 2007. Stakeholder Influence Capacity and the Variability of Financial Returns to Corporate Social Responsibility. *Academy of Management Review*, 32(3): 794–816.

Bass, B.M. and Steidlmeier, P. 1999. Ethics, Character, and Authentic Transformational Leadership Behavior. *Leadership Quarterly*, 10(2): 181–217.

Boateng, K. 2003. *Radio in Accra: A Confluence of National and Traditional Representations*. Paper to the International Communication Association Annual Meeting, San Diego, CA, 23–27 May 2003.

Bowman, C. and Johnson, G. 1992. Surfacing Competitive Strategies. *European Management Journal*, 10(2): 210–218.

Brown, M.E. and Trevino, L.K. 2006. Ethical Leadership: A Review and Future Directions. *Leadership Quarterly*, 17(6): 595–616.

Butin, D. 2005. *Service-learning in Higher Education: Critical Issues and Directions*. New York: Palgrave Macmillan.

Cameron, K. 2011. Responsible Leadership as Virtuous Leadership. *Journal of Business Ethics*, 98(1): 25–35.

Crouch, C. 2006. Modelling the Firm in its Market and Organizational Environment: Methodologies for Studying Corporate Social Responsibility. *Organization Studies*, 27(10): 1533–1551.

Dant, T. 2003. *Critical Social Theory: Culture, Society and Critique*. Thousand Oaks: Sage Publications.

Foucault, M. 2006. *History of Madness*. New York: Routledge.

Friedman, M. 1970. The Social Responsibility of Business is to Increase Its Profits, *New York Times Magazine*, September 13.

Giroux, H. 1983. *Theory and Resistance: A Pedagogy for the Opposition*. Westport: Bergin and Garvey.

González, F., Moskowitz, A. and Castro-Gómez, S. 2001. Traditional vs. Critical Cultural Theory. *Cultural Critique: Critical Theory in Latin America*, 49: 139–154.

Gorham, M.S. 1996. Tongue-tied Writers: The Rabsel'kor Movement and the Voice of the 'New Intelligentsia' in Early Soviet Russia. *Russian Review*, 55(3): 412–429.

Greenleaf, R.K. 1977. *Servant Leadership*. New York: Paulist Press.

Habermas, J. 2001. *The Inclusion of the Other: Studies in Political Theory*. Cambridge: MIT Press.

Hegel, W.F. 1953. *Reason in History: A General Introduction to the Philosophy of History* (vol. 1–3) (translated by R.S. Hartman). Arlington: Liberal Arts Press.

Hind, P., Wilson, A. and Lenssen, G. 2009. Developing Leaders for Sustainable Business. *Corporate Governance*, 9(1): 7–20.

House, R.J., Hanges, P.W., Javidan, M., Dorfman, P. and Gupta V. 2004. *Culture, Leadership, and Organizations: The GLOBE Study of 62 Societies*. Thousand Oaks: Sage Publications.

Jensen, M.C. 2002. Value Maximization, Stakeholder Theory and the Corporate Objective Function. *Business Ethics Quarterly*, 12(2): 235–256.

Jensen, M.C. and Meckling, W.H. 1976. Theory of the Firm: Managerial Behavior, Agency Costs and Ownership Structure. *Journal of Financial Economics*, 3(4): 305–360.

Kantabutra, S. and Avery, G. 2011. Sustainable Leadership at Siam Cement Group. *Journal of Business Strategy*, 32(4): 32–41.

Karim, A.U. 2003. A Developmental Progression Model for Intercultural Consciousness: A Leadership Imperative. *Journal of Education for Business*, 79(1): 34–39.

Karnani, A.G. 2007. The Mirage of Marketing to the Bottom of the Pyramid. *California Management Review*, 49(4): 90–112.

Ketola, T. 2006. Do You Trust Your Boss? A Jungian Analysis of Leadership Reliability in CSR. *Electronic Journal of Business Ethics and Organization Studies*, 11(2): 6–14.

Leonardo, Z. 2004. Critical Social Theory and Transformative Knowledge: The Functions of Criticism in Quality Education. *Educational Researcher*, 33(6): 11–18.

Liden, R.C., Wayne, S.J., Zhao, H. and Henderson, D. 2008. Servant Leadership: Development of a Multidimensional Measure and Multi-level Assessment. *Leadership Quarterly*, 19(2): 161–177.

Lipman-Blumen, J. 2000. *Connective Leadership: Managing in a Changing World*. New York: Oxford University Press.

Maak, T. 2007. Responsible Leadership, Stakeholder Engagement and the Emergence of Social Capital. *Journal of Business Ethics*, 74(4): 329–343.

Maak, T. and Pless, N.M. 2006. Responsible Leadership in a Stakeholder Society – A Relational Perspective. *Journal of Business Ethics*, 66: 99–115.

Ntseane, P.G. 2011. Culturally Sensitive Transformational Learning: Incorporating the Afrocentric Paradigm and African Feminism. *Adult Education Quarterly*, 61(4): 307–323.

Pless, N.M. 2007. Understanding Responsible Leadership: Roles Identity and Motivational Drivers. *Journal of Business Ethics*, 74(4): 437–456.

Pless, N.M. and Maak, T. 2011. Responsible Leadership: Pathways to the future. *Journal of Business Ethics*, 98(Suppl. 1): 3–13.

Prahalad, C.K. 2010. *The Fortune at the Bottom of the Pyramid: Eradicating Poverty Through Profits*, 5th edition. Upper Saddle River: Wharton School Publishing.

Sethi, S.P. 1979. A Conceptual Framework for Environmental Analysis of Social Issues and Evaluation of Business Response Patterns. *Academy of Management Review*, 4(1): 63–74.

Siegel, D.S. 2009. Green Management Matters Only if it Yields More Green: An Economic/Strategic Perspective. *Academy of Management Perspectives*, 23(3): 5–16.

Simon, H.A. 1957. *Models of Man, Social and Rational: Mathematical Essays on Rational Human Behavior*. New York: Wiley.

Simons, G.F., Vázquez, C. and Harris, P.R. 1993. *Transcultural Leadership: Empowering the Diverse Workforce*. Boston: Gulf Publishing.

Steinberg, M.D. 1996. Stories and Voices: History and Theory. *The Russian Review*, 55(3): 347–354.

Trevino, L.K., Brown, M. and Hartman, L.P. 2003. A Qualitative Investigation of Perceived Executive Ethical Leadership: Perceptions from Inside and Outside the Executive Suite. *Human Relations*, 56(1): 5–37.

Voegtlin, C. 2011. Development of a Scale Measuring Discursive Responsible Leadership. *Journal of Business Ethics*, 98(Suppl. 1): 57–73.

Vogel, D. 2008. Private Global Business Regulation. *Annual Review of Political Science*, 11: 261–282.

Waldman, D., de Luque, S., Washburn, N. and House, R. 2006. Cultural and Leadership Predictors of Corporate Social Responsibility Values of Top Management: A GLOBE Study of 15 Countries. *Journal of International Business Studies*, 37(6): 823–837.

Wallerstein, I. 1994. *Geopolitics and Geoculture: Essays on the Changing World-System*. London: Cambridge University Press.

7 *The Global Team Leader Dilemma: Diversity and Inclusion*

JUNKO TAKAGI AND HAE-JUNG HONG

Introduction

Globalization has brought the issue of cultural diversity to the forefront of management issues in today's organizations (Kwak 2003, Merrill-Sands, Holvino and Cumming 2000) such that the issues at a global level and the juxtaposition of cultural differences is now considered by many academics and practitioners as a strategic issue for multinational corporations (MNCs) and essential for their competitive success (Bartlett and Ghoshal 1989, Nohria and Ghoshal 1997, Maxwell, Blair and McDougall 2001). The globalization of markets, products, firms and even individuals has influenced the way work is organized. With the increasing popularization of a global mindset, the concept of global teams has become a standard for all MNCs. Much of the decision-making processes and operational implementation of global strategies is carried out in teams in MNCs and global teams are thus particularly critical for enhanced organizational performance. Global teams have also been identified as ideal training environments for developing global leadership competencies (DiStefano and Maznevski 2000).

In this chapter, we focus on the challenges faced by global team leaders, and the roles they play in successfully managing global teams. The main challenge in managing diversity generally is the fine balance between maintaining heterogeneity and promoting inclusion. On the one hand, the diversity literature emphasizes the positive value created by diversity in teams. Diversity in teams encourages creativity, innovation and learning. On the other hand, the underlying assumption of organizations to improve efficiency and performance towards a common goal based on the Weberian notion of bureaucracy more often than not leads to structures and practices that work better when there are fewer differences between collaborators.

The global teamleaders' particular position juxtaposes these two potentially opposing tendencies in which global diversity needs to be managed within teams in an efficient manner in order to maximize performance. In other words, their role is to bring out the differences that exist in their teams, and to bring these differences together in an efficient and optimal manner so as to generate new ideas and new learning opportunities for the firm within a limited time frame. Not only are they expected to cultivate cultural differences within their teams, but it is essential that they simultaneously create common understandings within the team in order for the team to be able to propose coherent innovation. Thus, their role consists of maintaining divergence and creating convergence within their teams. We call this the global team leader dilemma. The role played by team leaders in this situation is critical for firms in their globalization strategies. In this chapter, we present a qualitative study of global team managers in a French MNC in order to investigate the global team leader dilemma. We analyze how global team leaders perceive their teams, their role as team leaders, and issues related to team performance. We propose a tentative model to understand the role of global team leaders in different types of global teams. First, we present a discussion of the literature on global teams. We particularly focus on definitions of global teams, and the attention that is paid in the literature on the difficulties and weaknesses of global teams. This leads us to our study of the global team leader dilemma based on interview data with global team leaders in a French MNC. Based on our analysis, we propose a model of the global team leader dilemma.

Global Teams

DiStefano and Maznevski (2000) define global teams as 'teams of managers from different parts of a multinational organization working together to achieve a team-specific mandate that is global in its scope' (DiStefano and Maznevski 2000: 196). At the same time, they note that the phenomenon of global teams is very similar to multicultural teams that deal with regional mandates. According to Adler (1997), a multicultural team is one where two or more cultures are represented among its members. While global team members may be distributed geographically, research on virtual global teams for example indicate that face-to-face team interactions are essential at key points in team interaction (Jarvenpaa and Leidner 1998, Maznevski and Chudoba 2000, Townsend, DeMarie and Hendrickson 1998). These definitions have in common the notion that people who are from potentially different cultures work together on a common, collective task or mandate. At the same time, whether or not these people need to continually share the same geographical space is not specifically determined as in the case of virtual teams. The definitions do not specify the frequency or nature of team interactions. Since the literature remains general regarding the distinction between global and multicultural teams, we will treat them as similar phenomena in our discussion of the literature.

Multicultural teams are often used to improve organizational effectiveness in the global business environment (Cox 1993, Galbraith 2000, Kirkman and Shapiro 2001, Kirchmeyer and McLellan 1991, Tung 1993). It is argued that, given the increasingly complex environment, culturally diverse teams are better adapted to this complexity and are able to contribute different perspectives which may enhance adaptability, problem solving, creativity, innovation and subsequently performance (DiStefano and Maznevski 2000). Culturally diverse teams are also expected to have a greater variety of social networks, and thus richer sources of information (Cox 1993, Cox and Blake 1991, Milliken and Martins 1996, Hitt, Hoskisson and Kim 1997, O'Reilly, Williams and Barsade 1998, DiStefano and Maznevski 2000). Thus, MNCs implement multicultural teams in order to encourage flexibility, responsiveness and improved resource allocation and utilization to meet the dynamic demands of an increasingly global business environment and to exploit the potential of foreign markets (Mowshowitz 1997, Snow, Snell, Davison and

Hambrick 1996). Multicultural teams have proliferated in the workplace, and this trend is likely to continue in the future (Adler 1997, Hambrick, Scott, Snell and Show 1998).

At the same time, it has been observed that organizational processes tend to systematically reduce rather than exploit the variety of perspectives that different people can bring (Brunsson 1982). Studies tend to show that team members encourage conformity and ignore differences (George and Bettenhausen 1990). So although diversity may be useful for generating new ideas, it is frequently suggested that diversity hinders rather than helps organizational performance due to low consensus, negative political dynamics, and lack of coherence and consensus needed for action (for example, Cox 1993).

In addition, the literature on teams also highlights the tendencies for individuals to prefer others who are like themselves in social interaction (Bettenhausen and Murnighan 1991, Earley 1993, Zander 1997) such that members tend to interact most comfortably and extensively with similar others (Lincoln and Miller 1979, Marsden 1988, Tsui and O'Reilly 1989). Due to such ingroup preferences, multicultural teams are likely to have structured gaps and faultlines between cultural groups (Lau and Murnighan 1998, 2005, Li and Hambrick 2005). Consequently, studies find that multicultural team members often face challenges in cooperative decision making (Anderson 1983, Fiedler 1966, Kirchmeyer and Cohen 1992, Watson, Kumar and Michaelsen 1993), with negative consequences for cultivating trust and effective communication (Govindarajan and Gupta 2001). According to this line of reasoning, the business case for diversity may be compelling in theory but is not necessarily supported in practice.

Thus, although differences in cultural backgrounds provide the possibility for multicultural teams to perform well (for example, Ling 1990, McLeod and Lobel 1992, Watson, Kumar and Michaelsen 1993), unless these differences are managed so as not to generate conformity, they may be a source of liability for team performance. In a study reconciling conflicting perspectives and past results regarding the role of cultural diversity on team processes and outcomes, Stahl, Maznevski, Voigt and Jonsen (2010) carried out a meta-analysis of 108 empirical studies and concluded that while culturally diverse teams experienced more conflict and less social integration of its members, they were more creative. This study indicates that the benefits of global teams are generally manifested in an increased level of creativity. At the same time, considering the difficulties with the integration of team members and the higher levels of conflict, these teams were perhaps not performing at their full potential. It leaves room for improvement on other measures such as increased adaptability to new environments, problem solving and capitalizing on wider social networks. Other cultural challenges for multicultural teams cited in the literature include: 1) dealing with coordination and control issues; 2) maintaining communication richness; and 3) developing and maintaining team cohesiveness (Joshi, Labianca and Caligiuri 2002; Marquardt and Horvath 2001). The Stahl, Maznevski, Voigt and Jonsen (2010) study and others indicate that the most critical and practical challenge for multicultural teams is managing conflicts and encouraging coherence across the cultural boundaries of its members (Joshi, Labianca and Caligiuri 2002, Marquardt and Horvath 2001, Matveez and Nelson 2004).

The literature on global teams thus highlights the potential for the business case but focuses on the challenges of cultural integration and the consequences on team performance. There is general agreement that in order for global teams to fulfill their potential, it is essential to manage conflicts between and cultivate cohesion across cultural boundaries. We also need to take into account different possible configurations of global teams. Teams may be face to face or mostly virtual, and in the same geographical location or not. Under these conditions, the role of coordination in encouraging and sustaining communication and coherence within the team becomes essential and we see the importance of the global team leader in undertaking this role.

The Global Team Leader Dilemma

The role of the global team leader is to effectively manage the team and its different elements so as to optimize team performance. Taking into account the potential difficulties tied to working in global teams, the leader needs to particularly manage cultural differences so as to reduce the negative effects of cultural conflicts and to generate synergies based on cultural differences. The global team leader manages the fine balance between too little cultural integration which may exacerbate conflicts and too much integration which may significantly dilute the diversity of ideas generated and exchanged in order to exploit the potential of the team by encouraging creativity. The global team leader occupies a frontier role of encouraging two potentially conflicting processes: Encouraging the expression of differences and generating integration and shared meanings.

In order to investigate global team leader's perceptions of global team challenges and how they deal with them, we interviewed 20 team leaders who manage global teams in a French MNC. Our sample of team leaders worked in the marketing function in three different divisions within the firm. The interviews were open ended, and team leaders were asked about their experiences with teams, the global elements in teams they had worked with, the interactions and contributions of their team members, and what aspects were important in teamwork and team performance. We found that a pattern emerged from the interview data based on two themes: 1) team leaders' definitions of a global team; and 2) team leaders' perceptions of challenges working with global teams depending on their definitions. In this section, we first present the overall perceptions of global teams that leaders have. This is followed by their definitions of what constitute global teams, and their perceived challenges in managing these teams.

TEAM LEADER'S OVERALL PERCEPTIONS

In all our interviews with global team leaders, there is agreement that cultural diversity is important for team performance. The following quotes are examples of this common perception:

If you work with globalized vision, it has to integrate many different cultures, nationality, backgrounds, very important.

We observe that globalization naturally encompasses working with cultural diversity and increased creativity in the minds of global team leaders. Cultural or international diversity is mentioned quite often by team leaders, and some also talked about cultural diversity as something that required a continual adaptation and that this was a key competency in managing diversity in teams. Some also mentioned the role of diversity in the process of confrontation of ideas, generating more creativity.

For leaders in our sample, global team leadership requires working with cultural diversity and functional diversities, with the objective of creating new products for marketing managers. Global teams are taken for granted as essential in meeting this objective, and while leaders perceive challenges, they underscore the importance of this diversity for their activities and also for the stimulation generated by this diversity.

They also stress the importance of communication and circulation of information so that all the available information is shared among team members and there is transparency. At the same time, leaders perceive that this is also difficult to achieve. The following quotes show these tensions between the need for shared information and difficulties due to communication problems:

Team leaders perceive that their role in managing the complexity of issues, processes and cultures is one of coordination where they place themselves in the centre of action, and they need to bring the divergent elements of the team together so as to facilitate information flow, exchange of ideas and creation of value. In these general impressions of global team leaders in our study, we already observe the emergence of the global team leader dilemma: the importance and necessity for cultural diversity to deal with globalization of business on the one hand, and the problem of coordination of a culturally diverse team on the other. This is a recurring theme in global team leaders' perceptions and reflects existing discussions in the literature.

WHAT CONSTITUTES A GLOBAL TEAM?

We came across concrete examples of different types of global teams in our field work. We found that team leaders' day-to-day experiences with teams differed as did their perceptions of what constitutes a global team leader. Based on our analysis, we present a typology of global teams in Table 7.1.

For some team leaders, their role consists in managing multiple local regional teams. These teams are dispersed across geographical regions, and the cultural diversity exists across teams with interaction between these teams being mediated by the team leader at

Table 7.1   Typology of Global Teams

Type of global team	Characteristics and work contexts
Multiple regional teams	Regional teams Role of team leader to work with regional teams separately and collectively Organize meetings between teams Recruitment of locals/expats Creating new markets, understanding market needs, developing markets and local HR
Multinational teams	Team with physical proximity of members from different countries Global team leader works to bring different team members together Often the choice of team leaders to have multicultural mix, determining who they want in terms of nationality Team objective to come up with new ideas, new products, strategy for new product and so on

headquarters. These managers deal with cultural diversity on a daily basis through their interactions with different regional teams. Also, they organize meetings between teams on a regular basis to create face-to-face team interactions and exchange. These leaders travel extensively to work closely with their regional teams, and bring together all or some part of their teams together regularly. This type of global team reflects DiStefano and Maznevski's (2000) definition of global teams and multicultural teams dealing with regional mandates. We label these teams 'multiple regional teams'.

Leaders of such teams emphasize the importance of coordination within regional teams and also between regional teams. Their work consists of working on a daily basis with multiple regional teams and from time to time bringing these teams together to discuss, exchange and make common decisions regarding products for the whole region. In order to create and stay in touch with their teams, these managers travel extensively. It is common for these managers to be on the road continually, and in different directions.

Other means used by these managers in particular to enhance team work within and between their regional teams are new technologies, such as video conferencing.

For these managers, finding efficient and effective means to stay in regular contact and to maintain communication flow with their regional teams is essential. The constitution of their regional teams is important and team leaders also report that they work on understanding local human resources in order to recruit and maintain talent.

For other team leaders in our sample, they work with their teams made up of members from different countries with diverse cultural backgrounds in the office on a day-to-day basis. Thus there is a certain amount of regular, face-to-face interaction between people from different cultural backgrounds. Their teams consist of members who are in the same location with regular interaction between members whose cultural characteristics are diverse. The interaction between team members is frequent and the team leader is confronted with managing these interactions in real-time. We label these teams as 'multinational teams' but recognize the similarity of this type of team to Adler's (1997) definition of multicultural teams.

We came across another sub-type of global teams in both cases. This sub-type consists of multinational and multiple regional teams in which the team members themselves were also multicultural (in other words, internalizing two or more cultures) such that the cultural complexity of the team was increased. In all cases, the team leader is accountable for a mandate that is multinational in scope.

Our analysis highlights the different daily realities of global team leaders in terms of where they encounter cultural diversity in their work with global teams. In multiple regional teams, the experience of cultural diversity resides in the role of the team leader since there is limited regular interaction between regional teams. Team members generally work within a single cultural context with team members who are culturally similar. The cultural encounters between regional teams are organized by the team leader punctually to discuss and make decisions collectively. In multinational teams, there is constant face-to-face interaction between global team members who work together in the same location so that the team members themselves have to deal regularly with cultural diversity. In both cases, team leaders need to manage cultural diversity, but the diversity management practices differ according to where the diversity is located – within the team as in the case of multinational teams, or within the role of the team leader as in the case of multiple regional teams.

GLOBAL TEAM LEADERS' PERCEPTIONS OF CHALLENGES IN GLOBAL TEAMS

In our analysis, we found that team leaders' perceptions of challenges regarding team management is directly related to the type of global team with which they work. Leaders' perceptions of diversity and how they manage it differs depending on whether it is integrating diversity within a team or whether it is dealing with regional teams.

In multiple regional teams, leaders identified a need to understand local cultures. The leaders working with these teams emphasized the importance of their own cultural adaptation in order to better understand the characteristics of the regional markets and also the labour force of the region so as to develop the best teams (in comparison with competitors) in their respected regions. The perceived effort therefore lies primarily in the team leader to adapt to regional values and meanings and not necessarily to impose their own or firm's cultural values.

For the multiple regional team leaders in our study, this is not always comfortable. Sometimes, they endeavour to have an impact on local practices, but they understand that this can only be achieved by a thorough understanding of the status quo in their regions. At the same time, leaders also cited the dangers of adapting too much to local culture and thereby bypassing the opportunity to develop managerial processes. For some of these managers, global team leadership is not about being irreplaceable, but achieving sustainable team performance in a global environment.

For leaders working with multinational teams, the key challenge is related to the integration of different cultural elements in a team. They are particularly attentive when introducing new elements to the team. Coaching team members is perceived to be important and there is general agreement that the process involves first integrating the diverse elements and then leveraging differences to benefit from the diversity.

The functional prerogative for multicultural team leaders is to put different perspectives together to develop new ideas, products and strategies. In order to achieve this efficiently, leaders describe a two-step acculturation process within their teams. First, there is a need to inculcate new team members with a common language, work method and a shared understanding of issues. Team leaders give examples of difficulties some team members face at this stage due to cultural and/or individual limitations. Leaders emphasize the importance of team members' acculturation with the main culture (either main national culture or organizational culture or both) and only once this fit is established is it possible to effectively communicate differences within the team. There is a shared belief that once this initial cultural integration is achieved, then the second stage of sharing differences and benefiting from the cultural diversity becomes possible. At this second stage, team leaders place an emphasis on bringing cultural differences together through mutual exchange and the development of an understanding of differences. We see that in contrast to the multiple regional groups, the cultural adaptation in this case is a requirement placed on team members as well as the team leader and team members are expected to develop their cultural intelligence and to adapt to the culture of the firm headquarters. Team leaders need to understand the cultural background of team members.

A summary of our analysis of global team leaders' perceptions of challenges is presented in Table 7.2.

Our study indicates that different types of global teams present team leaders with different challenges and call for different approaches on these leaders. We found that

Table 7.2 Global Team Leaders' Perceptions of Team Challenges

	Perceived team challenges	Team leader role
Multiple regional teams	To understand regional characteristics and needs Create best regional teams	Leader's personal cultural adaptation to regional cultures Manage between HQ and regional team Coordination across regional teams
Multinational teams	Team members' acculturation to the main team culture Establishment of common language, shared understanding	Inculcate team with common values and processes Management of cultural conflicts through integration process Understanding cultural differences in order to generate exchange of cultural differences as added value

the global team leader dilemma that was referred to at the beginning of the chapter is experienced more frequently by leaders of multinational teams than multiple regional groups. However, team leaders for both types of teams are faced with issues of acculturation and integration. The issue of cultural fit at the individual level exists for both team models. Whereas the need for acculturation resides most prominently in the team leader for multiple regional teams, it is also sought in team members for multinational teams. We argue that the global team leader dilemma is less visible in multiple regional teams since the tension between integration and diversity is found within the team leader role and less between team members. The challenge lies in the degree to which team leaders are able to acculturate to and understand and integrate cultural differences of their regional teams, while at the same time embedding their actions in corporate processes so as not to adapt completely to local regional cultures. Multinational team leaders clearly state that they need to deal with both cultural integration and exchange of differences within their teams. Our study shows that team leaders deal with this dilemma by identifying a process first of acculturation of diverse team members, then of cultural exchange which is facilitated by their own cultural intelligence. Thus, rather than continuously juxtaposing two potentially conflicting processes, there is a segmentation of team processes to create a favourable environment for cultural exchange.

Conclusion

In our study, global team leaders are fully aware of and have developed ways of dealing with the global team leader dilemma. Under conditions where the global diversity of teams is perceived to be necessary and enriching to the work process, team leaders try to find ways to maximally exploit this diversity through inclusion and differentiation strategies.

In this study, two forms of global teams emerged based on the experiences of managers whom we interviewed. The means for managing global diversity in order to increase the effectiveness of these teams differed according to the team typology. Our analysis shows that global diversity may be managed internally within the team leader by developing his/her cultural intelligence as in the case of multiple regional teams. It may also be managed through a collective team effort on the part of the team leader and team members by the development of a common language and understanding of issues and methods as in the case of multinational teams. In both cases, the dilemma is dealt with directly by the team leader through a process of integration either internally within the team leaders' understanding of differences, or within the team through a two-step process.

The model of global team challenges presented in this chapter indicates the importance of understanding the type of global team and where the global diversity resides within the team in order to identify potential challenges and to determine appropriate strategies to deal with the global team leader dilemma. Our findings also suggest possibilities for future investigation of global teams, team member composition and their interactions, and global team leader training and competencies.

References

Adler, N. (1997). *International Dimensions of Organizational Behavior*, 3rd edition. Cincinnati: South-Western.

Anderson, L.P. (1983) Managing of the Mixed-cultural Work Group. *Organizational Behavior and Human Performances*, 31(3): 303–330.

Bartlett, C. and Ghoshal, S. (1989). *Managing Across Borders: The Transnational Solution*. Boston: Harvard Business School Press.

Bettenhausen, K.L. and Murnighan, J.K. (1991). The Development of an Intragroup Norm and the Effects of Interpersonal and Structural Challenges. *Administrative Science Quarterly*, 36: 20–35.

Brunsson, H. 1982. The irrationality of action and action rationality: Decisions, ideologies, and organizational actions. *The Journal of Management Studies*. 19, 29–43.

Cox, T. (1993). *Cultural Diversity in Organizations: Theory, Research, and Practice*. San Francisco: Berrett-Koehler.

Cox, T. and Blake, S. (1991). Managing Cultural Diversity: Implications for Organizational Competitiveness. *The Academy of Management Executive*, 5(3): 45–56.

DiStefano, J.J. and Maznevski, M.L. (2000). Creating Value in Diverse Teams in Global Management. *Organizational Dynamics*, 29(1): 45–63.

Earley, P. C. (1993). East Meets West Meets Mideast: Further Explorations of Collectivistic and Individualistic Work Groups. *Academy of Management Journal,* 36(2): 319–348.

Fiedler, F.E. (1966). The Effect of Leadership and Cultural Heterogeneity on Group Performance: A Test of the Contingency Model. *Journal of Experimental Social Psychology*, 2(2): 237–264.

Galbraith, J.R. (2000). *Designing the Global Corporation*. San Francisco: Jossey-Bass.

George, J.M. and Bettenhausen, K. (1990). Understanding Prosocial Behavior, Sales Performance, and Turnover: A Group-level Analysis in a Service Context. *Journal of Applied Psychology*, 75: 698–709.

Govindarajan, V. and Gupta, A.K. (2001). Building an Effective Global Business Team. *MIT Sloan Management Review* Summer, 63–71.

Hambrick, D.C., Scott, C.D., Snell, A. and Snow, C.C. (1998). When Groups Consist of Multiple Nationalities: Toward a New Understanding of the Implications. *Organizational Studies* 19: 181–205.

Hitt, M.A., Hoskisson, R.E., and Kim, H. (1997). International Diversification: Effects on Innovation and Firm Performance in Product-diversified Firms. *Academy of Management Journal*, 40, 767–777.

Jarvenpaa, S.L. and Leidner, D.E. (1998). Communication and Trust in Global Virtual Teams. *Journal of Computer-Mediated Communication*, 3(4), 791–815.

Joshi, A., Labianca, G. and Caligiuri, P.M. (2002). Getting Along Long Distance: Understanding Conflict in a Multinational Team through Network Analysis. *Journal of World Business*, 37: 277–284.

Kirchmeyer, C. and Cohen, A. (1992). Multicultural Groups: Their Performance and Reactions with Constructive Conflict. *Group and Organization Management*, 17(2): 153–170.

Kirchmeyer, C. and McLellan, J. (1991). Capitalizing on Ethnic Diversity: An Approach to Managing the Diverse Work Groups on the 1990s. *Canadian Journal of Administrative Sciences*, 8(2): 7–9.

Kirkman, B.L. and Shapiro, D.L. (2001). The Impact of Cultural Values on Job Satisfaction and Organizational Commitment in Self-managing Work Teams: The Mediating Role of Employee Resistance. *Academy of Management Journal*, 44: 557–569.

Kwak, M. (2003). The Paradoxical Effects of Diversity. *MIT Sloan Management Review*, 44(3): 7–8.

Lau, D.C. and Murnigham, J.K. (1998). Demographic Diversity and Faultlines: The Compositional Dynamics of Organizational Groups. *Academy of Management Review*, 23(2): 325–340.

Lau, D.C. and Murnigham, J.K. (2005). Interactions within Groups and Subgroups: The Effects of Demographic Faultlines. *Academy of Managing Journal*, 48(4): 645–659.

Li, J. and Hambrick, D.C. (2005). Factional Groups: A New Vantage on Demographic Faultlines, Conflict, and Disintegration in Work Teams. *Academy of Management Journal*, 48(5): 794–813.

Lincoln, J.R. and Miller, J. (1979). Work and Friendship Ties in Organizations: A Comparative Analysis of Relational Networks. *Administrative Science Quarterly*, 24(2): 181–199.

Ling, S.C. (1990). The Effects of Group Cultural Composition and Cultural Attitudes on Performance, unpublished doctoral dissertation. University of Western Ontario, Canada.

Marquardt, M.J. and Horvath, L. (2001). *Global Teams: How Top Multinational Span Boundaries and Cultures with High-Speed Teamwork*. Palo Alto, CA: Davis-Black.

Marsden, P. V. (1988). Homogeneity in Confiding Relations. *Social Networks*, 10(1): 57–76.

Mateev, A.V. and Nelson, P.E. (2004). Cross Cultural Communication Competence and Multicultural Team Performance: Perceptions of American and Russian Managers. *International Journal of Cross Cultural Management*, 4(2): 253–270.

Maxwell, G.A., Blair, S. and McDougall, M. (2001). Edging towards Managing Diversity in Practice. *Employee Relations*, 23(5): 468–482.

Maznevski, M. and Chudoba, C. (2000). Bridging Space over Time: Global Virtual Team Dynamics and Effectiveness. *Organization Science*, 11(5): 473–492.

McLeod, P. L. and Lobel, S.A. (1992). The Effect of Ethnic Diversity on Idea Generation in Small Groups. In: *Proceedings of the Academy of Management Annual Meeting Best Papers*, 227–231.

Merrill-Sands, D., Holvino, E. and Cumming, J. (2000). Working with Diversity: A Framework for Action. *CGIAR Gender and Diversity Working Paper, No. 24*. Nairobi, Kenya: Consultative Group for International Agricultural Research, Gender and Diversity Program.

Milliken, F.J. and Martins, L.L. (1996). Searching for Common Threads: Understanding the Multiple Effects of Diversity in Organizational Groups. *Academy of Management Review*, 21(2): 402–403.

Mowshowitz, A. (1997). Virtual Organization. *Communications of the ACM*, 40(9): 30–37.

Nohria, N. and Ghoshal, S. (1997). *The Differentiated Network: Organizing Multinational Corporations for Value Creation.* San Francisco: Jossey-Bass.

O'Reilly, C.A., III, Williams, K.Y. and Barsade, W. (1998). Group Demography and Innovation: Does Diversity Help? In *Research on Managing Groups and Teams*, Vol.1., edited by D. Gruenfeld. St. Louis: Elsevier.

Snow, C.C., Snell, S.A., Davison, S.C. and Hambrick, D.C. (1996). Use Transnational Teams to Globalize Your Company. *Organizational Dynamics*, 32(4): 20–32.

Stahl, G.K., Maznevski, M.L., Voigt, A. and Jonsen, K. (2010). Unraveling the Effects of Cultural Diversity in Teams: A Meta-analysis of Research on Multicultural Work Groups. *Journal of International Business Studies*, 41(4): 690–709.

Townsend, A.M, DeMarie, S.M. and Hendrickson, A.R. (1998). Virtual Teams: Technology and the Workplace of the Future. *Academy of Management Executive*, 12(3): 17–29.

Tsui, A.S. and O'Reilly, C.A. (1989). Beyond Simple Demographic Effects: The Importance of Relational Demography in Superior Subordinate Dyads. *Academy of Management Journal*, 32(2): 377–401.

Tung, R.L. (1993). Managing Cross-national and Intra-national Diversity. *Human Resource Management*, 32(4): 461–477.

Watson, W.E., Kumar, K. and Michaelsen, L.K. (1993). Cultural Diversity's Impact on Interaction Process and Performance: Comparing Homogeneous and Diverse Task Groups. *Academy of Management Journal*, 36(3): 590–602.

Zander, L. (1997) *The License to Lead: An 18 Country Study of the Relationship between Employees' Preferences Regarding Interpersonal Leadership and National Culture.* Stockholm: Institute of International Business, Stockholm School of Economics.

PART IV

Stakeholders of Corporate Leadership

8 *The New Requirement for Social Leadership: Healing*

GREGORY A. NORRIS

Context

THE GROWING NEED TO BECOME AN AGENT OF GOOD

Social responsibility expectations on companies are escalating. Leading companies are now called upon to demonstrate not just 'responsibility' but global leadership in relation to the impacts of the company on society and on outcomes that diverse sets of stakeholders are concerned about. It could be said that just being socially responsible is no longer seen as socially responsible. Thought leadership, multi-stakeholder leadership (not just engagement), and most of all performance leadership on societal impacts are becoming imperatives for any company that would be perceived as an ethical corporation with a correspondingly strong brand reputation.

This higher standard for companies may be linked to a higher standard to which we are holding ourselves as individuals. Studies of the millennial generation in particular (people born generally between the early 1980s and 2000) show them desiring to do good at a personal and societal level, and holding themselves accountable to be activists for social justice. A recent study of 7,000 youth around the world found that justice (defined there as 'to do what's right, to be an activist') was consistently cited among the top three motivators (pulled from a list of 16) by youth from around the world (McCann Group 2011). The other two motivators consistently among the top ten were needs for authenticity and for connection/relationship/community.

In a study led by the organization TakingITGlobal, youth in regions across the world consistently ranked 'activist' among the top six important roles for youth, from among more than 20 possible roles (Corriero 2004). In Africa and Asia 'activist' was ranked second behind 'student'.

For decades, consumers have chosen to not buy from companies because they disagree with the social or political values of the company; this practice is called boycotting. But among younger consumers in the US, a recent study found a dramatic rise in what is called 'buycotting' – choosing to buy from companies because they agree with the social or political values of the company (Pew Research Center 2010). For the millennial generation, buycotting was as prevalent as boycotting. And the younger the generation, the higher the importance of buycotting.

From this we can infer that the future is a place where leadership on corporate social responsibility (CSR) is becoming more about leadership than about responsibility; more about inspiration than avoiding to offend; more about healing than avoiding harm. Of course, CSR has long been about 'beyond compliance', but up to the present time, this still tends to mean going beyond the required levels and metrics in reducing risks or damages or externalities. And this is largely because we are endowed with increasingly sophisticated and expansive tools for tracking and reporting negative impacts, while we lack a calculus and even a clear concept of how we might measure beneficial impacts.

In conversations with the chairman of one of the world's leading corporate sustainability think tanks, Geoff Lye told me recently of the growing evidence of a shift by the most progressive corporations in how they are framing their sustainability strategies. This involves going beyond minimizing the negative impacts or risks which they impose on society to delivering positive environmental and social value – rooted in a commitment to truly making the world a better place. The challenge that they face is the lack of tools or even a framework from which to do this sort of assessment, especially in a comprehensive way.

A SUPPRESSED AWARENESS THAT WE ARE ALL DOING BAD

We have learned during the past decades that every product, and therefore also every day in the life of every citizen in industrialized countries, has a 'footprint'. In brief, the footprint of a product is the sum total of all the negative impacts of pollution released and resources consumed over the entire supply chain and life cycle of the product. Footprints can have multiple dimensions. We increasingly speak not only of carbon footprints (WRI/WBCSD 2009) but also water footprints (Hoekstra, Chapagain, Aldaya and Mekonnen 2011), toxic footprints (Liroff 2009), biodiversity footprints, (JNCC 2009), poverty footprints (Oxfam 2010), slavery footprints (slaveryfootprint.org), and the list continues to grow.

For any impact category, a person's total annual footprint is the sum of the footprints of all the products which the person buys or uses in the course of a year. A research project at the Norwegian University of Science and Technology uses economic input/output methods of life cycle assessment (LCA) to calculate the carbon footprint of each country, in absolute and per-capita terms (Hertwich and Peters 2009). Organizations such as companies have footprints as well. As reviewed briefly in the next section, standards recently released for calculating the carbon footprints of organizations draw heavily on LCA methods and databases, and indeed even reference the ISO standards for LCA.

The footprint of every person and every organization is, by definition, unavoidably negative – in the sense of being bad news for the planet and its people. For several years in a row, at the end of a semester-long course at Harvard on LCA, I ask participants whether they feel the planet would have been better off had they never been born. With only rare exceptions, nearly all of them sheepishly acknowledge that yes, they guess so.

THE NEED FOR AN ACCOUNTING THAT GUIDES ACHIEVEMENT OF NET GOOD

But how can this be? What are the implications of this informal finding indicating that many of today's people believe we are a burden on the planet? Or, more positively, how can we make it *not* the case, how can we empower consumers and companies to become forces for positive net impact? Individuals have the desire, and companies are starting to discover the economic potential, of fulfilling this promise. How do we achieve it?

The quick answer at the individual level is that in addition to consuming goods and services, we can also do positive things that actually reduce pollution. By analogy to the term footprint, I have coined the term 'handprint' to refer to the beneficial environmental and social impacts that we can achieve. We can, as people and as organizations, have a net-positive impact within a particular impact category such as climate change, if the good that we do, the positive changes we purposefully bring about in relation to that impact category, are greater than our footprints for the same category.

Most people would like to live in such a way, and most organizations would benefit from operating in such a way, that the net planetary impact of one year of their activity were positive. But we are only recently gaining the ability to understand or measure our footprints, and we seem to even lack the concept of a handprint. To live net-positive lives, and to operate net-positive companies, we need simple-to-use, meaningful and informative methods for estimating our footprints and handprints. The remainder of this chapter makes a first attempt to fill this need. The methods, tools, data and results of LCA are a great place to start, for both footprinting and handprinting.

Standard Footprinting – A Summary

LCA, and more broadly the concept of footprints, provides a standardized way of accounting for some of the impacts we conceptualize that we are responsible for, via the interconnections of purchases in product life cycles. It says that:

- The impacts of our purchases include the impacts of all of the activities which our purchases cause to occur, via these activities' direct requirements for the outputs of other activities.
- The (only) kind of activity-to-activity causal influence that we pay attention to in mainstream LCA and currently standardized footprinting is the influence that arises because economic activities require the use of outputs of goods and services from other activities.

Thus, within the conceptual framework of footprints, our purchase of a product is seen as requiring, and thus being responsible for, the activity of producing that product; and so our footprint includes the pollution released and resources consumed by the product's producer in producing the product we purchased. But our responsibility does not stop there. By requiring their production activity, we are seen as requiring this activity to obtain the inputs it needed to produce its output. So our footprint includes the impacts of the production of those inputs and so on, up the supply chain, which ultimately spans the globe.

The set of direct requirements of materials, energy, infrastructure and services which we address in footprinting and mainstream LCA can include those which are physically required by a product system, even if not purchased directly by a process in that system. Thus, for example, the more thorough assessments account for the construction and maintenance of the road on which trucks drive (but for which truck operators do not pay directly or fully), when assessing the full footprint of a life cycle involving truck transport.

In mainstream LCA we explicitly ignore all other sorts of potential influence that our purchases may have, based partly on the assumption that our purchase decision is small in the scheme of the whole economy. For example, we ignore several potentially important price-related effects. First, we generally ignore any impact of changes in demand upon prices, and the subsequent impacts of any such price changes upon other demand. We also ignore 'technological learning': The impact of changes in demand or output upon the technological maturity and thus the costs of production, which can – especially early in the development of a technology – bring down the cost of production, and the selling price.

This practice of ignoring price effects is seen as a safe simplification when we consider the impacts of micro-decisions, such as one consumer's purchase of one product. Consistent with the fixed-price assumption in static input/output economic modelling (and input/output LCA which is based upon it), we estimate the input requirements per unit of output based on data for a process's total inputs and outputs over a given (ideally recent) period.

MULTIPLE ATTRIBUTION OF RESPONSIBILITY

As described above, footprinting attributes responsibility for a given impact to multiple actors. For example:

- the steel producer's footprint includes all of the pollution from their factory;
- the footprint of a car producer includes that portion of the steel producer's pollution which is attributed to producing the steel purchased by the car producer;
- the footprint of the car buyer includes one car's worth of the steel producer's pollution as well.

Thus, in footprinting, we routinely say that many actors are each responsible for the same impact. Putting this another way, the same unit of pollution – let's say 1 kg of carbon dioxide (CO_2) from operating a truck to carry lettuce to a grocery store – is part of the footprint of many different actors in the economy. In the trucked lettuce example, the truck transport emissions of CO_2 are part of the trucker's footprint, the grocer's footprint and the salad-eater's footprint. This sort of accounting implicitly takes account of the fact that events can have multiple causes, and that some events cause other events, so that there arise long chains of causal influence.

This sharing and multi-attribution of responsibility has the positive characteristic that footprinting can motivate every actor whose decisions could improve (reduce) impacts to do so. But if we are trying to understand the footprint of a group of people, or a group of organizations (for example, everyone in a family, or every organization in a city), we need to exercise some care in our accounting. This issue rarely comes up in LCA because we tend to use it to support a specific single decision by a single actor. Nor does it generally arise in footprinting, because we tend to use footprinting to assess the impact and responsibility of a single company, operation or product.

Because of multiple attribution, when we want to assess the footprint of a set of actors, we cannot just sum their individual footprints. Instead, we need to calculate the footprint of the union of their activities. The difference between a 'union' and 'sum' is that a union takes account of the unique identity of each event whose impacts we are summing, and counts the impacts of each unique event only once. The purchases made by the steel producer in a year include those which are stimulated by the car producer to whom they sell steel. Therefore, the collective footprint of the steel and car producer as a group would sum the impacts of the steel producer (and its supply chains) plus the impacts of the car producer and of all of its non-steel purchases – since the impacts of the steel purchases were already accounted for when addressing the footprint of the steel producer.

Handprint Accounting

Handprinting is analogous to footprinting, but there are some major differences as well. First, the similarities:

- Handprinting in general addresses the same comprehensive set of sustainability-related impacts, potentially both 'environmental' (human health, ecosystem quality, climate change, resource depletion) and 'social' (poverty, human rights, working conditions, community impacts).
- Handprinting addresses the full supply chain and life cycle consequences of actions.
- Handprinting can thus draw very heavily on the same LCA-based databases, software and IT systems, calculation methods and even portions of the relevant international standards.

The two principle differences between handprinting and footprinting are:

- handprinting is all about changes to the future; and
- handprinting includes accounting for changes which occur outside of the scope of the footprint of the handprinter.

HANDPRINTING INCLUDES CHANGES TO THE FUTURE

The first major difference between handprinting and footprinting is that by its nature, handprinting focuses on assessing the impacts of efforts to change something in the world, individually or collectively, rather than on assessing the impacts of purchases or purchasing scenarios. We might say that handprinting addresses the impacts of 'intentional events', some of which have the nature of projects.

Assessing the impact of an attempted change is different from assessing the impact of a purchase. On the surface they may sound equivalent. We might even say that handprinting requires comparing two future purchasing scenarios, and calculating the difference between them. However, when we are trying to change the way the future unfolds, we cannot observe both scenarios as actually occurring ones. One of the scenarios is thus hypothetical, and unobservable. Assessing a change requires a characterization of what would have happened without the attempted change – a 'business as usual' (BAU) forecast, either implicit or explicit.

If the explicit goal of handprinting is to assess the impact of a change, this begs the question: Why not make use of consequential or 'change-oriented' LCA? It is a good question, but recent standardization efforts on footprinting have tended to emphasize the use of attributional rather than consequential methods. We can in fact perform handprint assessments using either attributional or consequential LCA.

HANDPRINTS INCLUDE REDUCTIONS TO OTHER PEOPLE'S (AND OTHER COMPANIES') FOOTPRINTS

A second difference between handprinting and footprinting is that actors influencing product life cycles, both individuals and companies, can exert significant influence on the footprints of other actors, both people and companies. This means that handprint modelling needs to take account of causal pathways in addition to those of changing the upstream and downstream direct requirements of their own consumption (in the case of individuals) or their own goods and services (in the case of companies). Let's consider this more concretely, for individuals first, and then for companies.

The scope of footprinting for an individual is the life cycle impacts of the individual's consumption. The scope of handprinting for an individual generally includes changes to their footprint (more on this below), and it can also include:

- changes they influence in the consumption and impacts of other individuals;
- changes they influence in the consumption and impacts of other organizations, such as their employers, the schools they attend, organizations in their community and so on.

The scope of footprinting for a company includes the supply chain impacts of their direct requirements, and it may optionally also include the life cycle impacts of the goods or services which they produce (WRI/WBCSD 2009). The scope of handprinting for the company includes changes to their footprint, and it can also include:

- changes which they influence in the consumption and impacts of individuals, besides those directly associated with the goods and services they produce;
- changes which they influence in the consumption and impacts of other organizations, such as businesses in their supply chains, organizations in their host communities and so on.

A SIMPLE HANDPRINT ILLUSTRATION

A friend of mine named Denise decided that she wanted to reduce, not increase, the risk of climate change, with her own consumption and actions. So, she began by estimating her carbon footprint – the full global warming potential caused by one year of all of her consumption. Next, she did her best to reduce her footprint, by carpooling, insulating her house and replacing her incandescent lightbulbs with compact florescent lightbulbs (CFLs). The handprint associated with her footprint reductions in that year was still smaller than her remaining footprint. This meant she was still responsible for more global warming emissions than she was able to prevent or reduce, that year. So next she set about enlarging her handprint. She did this by calculating how many additional incandescent bulbs would need to be replaced by CFLs, in order to fully cover her remaining (carbon) footprint. At this point, if she'd had the money, she would have purchased the required number of CFLs and then contacted her neighbours and friends and offered to come to their homes or apartments and install CFLs for free. Since she did not have the money for the required number of CFLs, she contacted a local business, explained her plan, and persuaded them to sponsor her purchase of the CFLs. Then she indeed contacted her neighbours and friends and installed the CFLs in their homes for free.

In summary, her handprint in this example consisted of two components:

- the reductions she brought about in her own footprint (relative to the year before);
- the reductions she brought about in the footprints of her friends and neighbours (relative to what would have happened without her influence and initiative).

Note: In the discussion above, we have neglected the important topic of the 'rebound effect', the footprints associated with the economic savings that Denise and her friends and neighbours achieved through increased energy efficiency. We will return to this later in the chapter.

COUNTING OUR OWN FOOTPRINT REDUCTIONS AS HANDPRINTS

The goal of handprinting is to guide actions that make us a net benefit to the world, as people and as organizations. 'Net benefit' means that you bring the world more than you take from it; the benefits of a year of your consumption (if an individual) or your operation (if a company) are greater than the cost of the same year's activity.

A key question is: Do we get handprint credit for reductions we make in our own footprint? Do we get credit for cleaning up our own mess? It all depends on whether we consider our lives (as individuals), or our existence (as a company) to be a legitimate part of BAU.

It certainly seems logical to consider our existence as part of the baseline scenario, since we are indeed alive, or if we are doing an organizational assessment, our organization does indeed exist. When we take our existence as a given, we then establish the rules for handprint accounting to help us answer the following question: How do I make the world better off this year, how to I provide net benefits to the planet, environmentally and/or socially? The answer is simple: Add more than you subtract, give more than you take, reduce more pollution than you cause. If with conscious action you reduce any pollution, yours or someone else's, relative to what would have happened without your actions, these are real benefits to the planet. From this perspective, it makes perfect sense to count the footprint reductions you achieve as part of your handprints.

However, another perspective is possible. A slightly different motivating question or perspective is: How do I make the world better off *with* me than *without* me? In this case, one scenario has you (or your organization) absent from the earth, while the other has you present, both polluting and making reductions in the footprints of others. If you did not exist, then you'd have no footprint at all. So from this second perspective, you do not count reductions in your footprint as part of your handprint.

We will refer to the first perspective, where our existence (as an individual or an organization) is part of both scenarios, as the 'Standard' perspective. And we'll refer to the second one as the 'Contingent Existence' (CE) perspective.

SCOPE OF IMPACTS IN HANDPRINT ACCOUNTING

As mentioned earlier, handprinting in general addresses the same comprehensive set of sustainability-related impacts as footprinting. It can address 'environmental' (human health, ecosystem quality, climate change, resource depletion) impacts as well and 'social' (poverty, human rights, working conditions, and community) impacts.

ESTABLISHING BUSINESS-AS-USUAL FOOTPRINTS

Our handprint will include the impacts of conscious changes to our own footprint (when using the Standard perspective), and changes we bring about in the footprints of other people and organizations. Thus, both individual and organizational handprinting rely on projections of both individual and organizational BAU footprints. Actually, to be precise, we do not necessarily require a complete forecast of the BAU and a complete forecast of the future with our handprint actions. It is often possible to simplify the modelling significantly, by only modelling the ways that the future will change, between the BAU and the actual. But even in this simpler case, we need to be visualizing implicitly the BAU future.

For an individual, the BAU footprint this year consists of the total footprint impacts of all the purchases they would make and activities they would perform this year without any conscious action by anyone to make those impacts better, without creatively trying to change their footprint. And for an organization, it consists of the total impacts which all of the organization's activities would create this year, without conscious attempts to reduce them.

BUSINESS-AS-USUAL FOOTPRINTS FOR INDIVIDUALS

For individual BAU estimation, we make a very simple – and simplifying – assumption, which we call the 'flat BAU assumption'. It says that last year provides a relevant prediction of this year's BAU.

Of course, the flat baseline assumption can be argued with. Indeed, any prediction about the future is virtually guaranteed to be at least a little wrong. Our impacts without making special efforts next year would be larger than this year if we end up making and spending significantly more money next year than this year, for example. An individual's housing impact changes if they move in with someone else, instead of living alone. A couple's impact gets larger if they have a child. Our unconscious, BAU footprints go up and down at different phases of our life, due to all sorts of factors.

We could try to figure out a more complex prediction for this year's BAU footprint than the flat BAU assumption. But really, why go to all the trouble? After all, healing means making things better tomorrow than today. If we can make this year better than last year, we're healing. It will be harder in some years than others to achieve this balance, but these challenges tend to balance out over our lives, and over populations of people. The point of handprint accounting is to provide a guideline for actions that will truly heal the planet. The flat BAU assumption is reasonably accurate much of the time, and eminently practical.

If, for our individual handprinting, we decide to adopt the CE perspective, then we would not be counting reductions to our own footprint as part of our handprint. But even in this case, we should be interested in a projection of our footprint this year, because our goal is to create a set of handprints which is larger than our footprint. And regardless of whether we adopt the Standard or the CE perspective, we will still need to have BAU footprint projections for any other individuals and for organizations whose footprints we act to reduce.

BUSINESS-AS-USUALS FOR ORGANIZATIONS

The output of company is a response to, and also an influence on, what economists call 'final demand'. Final demand is the total consumption by all consumers or households, plus consumption by government agencies, plus exports. You could say that final demand is total demand from 'outside' the economy being considered; it is demand by entities other than the companies whose output meets this demand. The output of the economy to serve final demand includes both the production of the goods and services sold directly to final demand, plus the production of the goods and services needed by the companies to enable their production, directly or farther up supply chains, so that the economy as a whole is able to supply total final demand.

How does the economy partially shape final demand, if this demand comes from outside the economy? First, payments to workers by companies are what enable most of the consumer spending which makes up a big portion of final demand. Next, payments of taxes by companies provide funding to governments which enables them to operate in providing their own goods and services, and to purchase required inputs from the economy. And third, companies play a role in shaping demand through advertising, product development, innovation and pricing. Thus, while the economy clearly responds to, or is driven by, final demand, we also see that the economy and final demand are situated together in a 'feedback loop' relationship with one another.

As we have seen, the footprinting perspective traces ultimate responsibility for the impacts of economic activity to final demand. We build on this perspective in defining the BAU footprints for companies, by simplifying the modelling to ignore the feedback influences from company to final demand described above, and focusing on the ways that the economy responds to final demand. Specifically, we assume that each individual company responds to, but does not itself influence, the demand for its goods and services. We express this by saying that firms are 'demand-takers', that forces beyond their control determine the quantity of good or service they sell this year. They can still influence the footprints of what they sell, because companies design their production processes and their products, and they select their suppliers (and thus the whole supply chains) for the inputs they require to operate.

In BAU modeling for companies, we do take account of the fact that for many of them, the demand for their products can rise and fall significantly from year to year, more so than the income and spending of most households. What can also be dynamic for companies who sell a diverse set of goods or services is the *mix* of different goods or services sold. For these reasons, we do not presume a purely 'flat' BAU in the case of companies.

The BAU for this year for a company is one in which the company serves this year's demand with last year's product models, produced using last year's production methods. That is, BAU involves companies meeting this year's demand the same ways they met last year's demand.

Considering the output of companies as resulting from final demand makes modelling company handprints from the CE perspective quite interesting, and more complex (data-intensive) than the Standard perspective. Recall that the CE perspective calls on us to make the world better off with us than without us, while the Standard perspective calls on us to do more good than harm. This difference leads to the result that for individual handprinting, in the CE perspective we do not count reductions to our own footprint among our handprints.

If final demand is not influenced by the company, then if the company were not in existence, the demand for its output would be met by output from other companies. Which other companies would replace our company's output, and with which impacts? This is often difficult to estimate. We might assume, in the most general case, that the demand for our output would be met by the average producers serving our market.

In this case, if our company produces products which have lower-than-average footprints, then the existence of our company is reducing total impacts. For example, say a company produces computers which are more energy-efficient than average. Without our production, buyers would be buying average – and higher impact – products. In our example, consumers would be buying computers which will require more electricity to operate over their lifetimes. Thus, company handprinting from the CE perspective requires an estimate of the difference between our footprint and the average footprint of producing our quantity of output. This requires data on the footprint of average production of the goods and services which we produce. This in turn also begs questions about how we define the geographic scope(s) of the market(s) into which we supply our goods and services, against which our footprints will be compared.

If a company makes improvements this year, to its products or its production processes or its supplier shares, so that it has a lower footprint, this influences its handprint in the CE perspective because it changes the footprint (its own) which is compared to that of average production. To this first portion of its handprint, we would add the impacts of any changes to other entities' footprints which the company is responsible for.

Corporate handprinting from the Standard perspective is simpler, in that we do not need any data about the average production of the goods and services that serve the markets into which we sell. We simply need to keep track of how our own products, and supply chain impacts and production processes, are changing from year to year. As noted earlier, we simply calculate the benefits from meeting this year's demand differently this year than we did last year. Then, as with corporate handprinting from the CE perspective, we add the impacts of any changes to other entities' footprints which our company is responsible for.

CREDIT FOR FOOTPRINT REDUCTIONS, PART 1: CHANGES TO OUR OWN FOOTPRINTS AS INDIVIDUALS

Every event has multiple causes or enablers. When we change our own footprint as an individual, for example, we could be giving credit in all sorts of directions. Let's say we install a low-flow showerhead. We could give credit to the inventor of the showerhead, the company that made it, the company that sold it to us, and to our friend who inspired or encouraged us to start paying attention to our handprints. It does not stop there! We could also give credit to the authors of the books or articles we have read that have inspired us to live more sustainably, and to the publishers and sellers of those books. Maybe we even give credit to our high school ecology professor, our inspirational neighbour or aunt or uncle, or to our parents for raising us to become someone who cares about these issues.

In addition to giving credit, we can take credit for our own actions. In handprint accounting, when operating from the Standard perspective, we take full credit for the impacts of actions we take to reduce our footprints relative to our BAU. 'Taking full credit' does not mean we're the only people or organizations getting credit for the impacts of our actions – more on this point below in the section on handprint credit overlap. Rather, it means that the full impacts of our actions are counted within our handprint.

CREDIT FOR FOOTPRINT REDUCTIONS, PART 2: CHANGES TO OTHER ENTITIES' FOOTPRINTS

Above we discussed action influences such as awareness and inspiration. To take an action, we need to be aware of the possibility, and motivated to act. Motivation can come from information about the impacts of our action, from persuasion or cajoling or inspiration provided by a friend, from our tendency to imitate or emulate the behaviour or others, from the desire to impress our friends, and so on. In all of the causes above, information is involved. That includes information of all kinds (not just 'data'), conveyed by all routes of information sharing (written, verbal and so on).

Some handprints are created by very basic events or decisions. This will often be the case for handprints arising from individual choices and changes in consumption or lifestyle. For example, a person may decide to start biking to work, or walking to work, or adopting a vegetarian diet. These handprints appear to depend purely on information (in its many forms, from many sources), in order to occur.

Assigning partial credit to the different informational causes of an event is highly problematic, because it is essentially impossible to measure or even accurately estimate the degree to which different informational contributions have influenced an action, other than in the simple relationship where the information was necessary. In the case of being necessary, it makes sense to give full credit. Since overlapping or shared credit is possible in handprinting, and since any non-full estimates for informational credit allocation are essentially impossible and would thus be arbitrary, the simple (and simplifying) approach recommended here is to give full credit to all informational contributors that are known to have helped enable or cause an event.

Sometimes the simple and individual handprint actions require some investment by the individual, as when purchasing higher-efficiency appliances. But generally this funding comes 'out of the pocket' of the individual themselves.

Other handprints will result from larger efforts, which we might call 'projects'. Projects tend to require the input of two additional resources in addition to information: These additional resources are labour, and investment funding (or 'capital'). An interesting thing about both labuor and capital inputs is that their proportion of contribution can be readily measured. For this reason, it is recommended that proportional credit be given to the contributors of these resources. It is further recommended that the labour credit share for a project be equal to the share of total labour hours contributed by all contributors of labour to the project; and that the capital/funding credit share be proportional to the economic value share of total funding required to fund the project.

When an enabler or cause of an event or project is instrumental in causing or enabling the event, this means that the event would not have happened without the input. The impacts of an event can be fully credited to each instrumental input or cause; this is how we acknowledge that without them, the event or project (and its impacts) would not have happened. For project-style events, each type of resource is instrumental. The project would not happen without the required funding, nor without the required labour, nor without the required informational inputs.

Based on the above, the total labour credit apportioned among all labour contributions will equal 100 percent of the project impacts. Likewise, the total investment credit apportioned among all funding contributions will equal 100 percent of the project impacts. Finally, total informational credit given to all informational contributors can often exceed 100 percent of the impacts.

It makes no sense to give credit for more than 100 percent of a project's impacts to any contributor of any resources, including contributors of multiple resources. Thus, someone who contributes 10 percent of a project's funding requirements and 15 percent of a project's labour-hour requirements would receive handprint credit equal to 25 percent of the project's impacts. However, if they contributed 70 percent of the labour and 70 percent of the funding, they would receive handprint credit equal to 100 percent of the project's impacts.

The information above is summarized in Table 8.1.

Table 8.1   What's in Your Handprint?

	Individual handprinting	Organizational handprinting
Standard Perspective	Changes to your FP relative to your BAU (which is your last year's FP), plus changes to other's FPs relative to their BAU	Changes to your FP relative to your BAU (which is supplying this year's demand as you did last year's demand) plus changes to other's FPs relative to their BAU
Contingent Existence Perspective	Changes to other's FPs relative to their BAU	The benefits of your existence (which are the impacts of your production minus the impacts of average production) plus changes to other's FPs relative to their BAU

HANDPRINT CREDIT OVERLAP IN CUSTOMER CHAINS

As in footprinting, there is shared responsibility. That is, the total handprint of a set of actors can be less than the sum of their individual handprints, if there is any overlap in their responsibilities – meaning, if their handprints include any of the same unique events. As with footprinting, accounting correctly for their shared handprint is done by avoiding double-counting of the impacts of the same event, which can be done by preserving information about the uniqueness of each event, and counting the impacts of each event only once.

Our footprint is made up of the footprints of everything we buy. So one way to reduce our footprint is by buying less. Another way is to purchase low-impact products – including products sold by companies which have a handprint that is large compared to their footprint. But there is the potential for some double-counting of benefits which needs to be paid attention to in handprint accounting.

For a company to be net-positive, the handprints of the company must be greater than the total footprints of the company in a given year. In this case, from a handprinting perspective, the company's products are net-positive too. One domain of impact over which companies have a lot of control is the life cycle impacts of their own products. If they innovate in order to make this year's footprint of their products' life cycles lower than last year's, this innovation is part of their total handprint this year.

For some products, a major portion of the life cycle impacts occurs during the usage phase. How are handprint and footprint accounting affected for the buyer of a product, when the product's handprint includes the effect of reductions to its usage-phase energy? If our goal is to estimate the total handprint of the product manufacturer and the customer together, we would avoid double-counting the usage-phase innovation benefits, as we do in all cases of footprint and handprint aggregation, by finding the union of the handprints in ways that maintain the unique identity of the event of reduced usage-phase energy.

Consider the buyer of an energy efficient computer. If the manufacturer has completely offset its footprint with its handprint, then its products have no net footprint, meaning that the buyer's footprint is not increased by buying the computer. Part of the computer's positive impact stems from the fact that it is more energy efficient than the prior-year equivalent model sold by the company. This benefit is not part of the consumer's footprint changes however, so counting it does not involve double-counting a benefit. If the computer is more energy efficient than the buyer's previous computer, then this provides a reduction in the consumer's footprint which was not already accounted for in the computer's footprint.

HANDPRINT GRATITUDE

Because most events have multiple causes, handprints will tend to be very social. Imagine a group of 10 people, in which each person's annual footprint is 1,000 kg. Then, imagine that together they collaborated on a project that reduced total emissions by 2,000 kg, and that the project would not have been successful without the efforts of each person in the group; that is to say, each person's contributions were instrumental to the project in some way. In this case, each person can accurately say that without their efforts, there would have been 2,000 kg more emissions. So each person can say that they are 'net-positive' this year: Their individual footprint minus their individual handprint is 1,000 - 2,000 = -1,000kg. But their individual impacts cannot be added to estimate the net impacts of the group. The total group impacts are $(10 \times 1,000) - 2,000 = 8,000$ kg, which is a net pollution footprint, not net-beneficial at all.

Setting the goal to be a healer as an individual person or company is an important start. But we need to also set collective goals, shared goals. For example, we might aspire that we as a family, or as a community, will also be healers. When we do the accounting for the impacts of the full group, we need to account for the unique identity of each event or project. Indeed, we need to look at our collective project impacts in a new way.

In the hypothetical case described above, we as a member of the group could accurately say both of the following:

- without my efforts, the 2,000 kg of CO_2 emissions would not have been avoided;
- without the efforts of each of my handprint partners, my efforts would not have had an impact.

Thus, while my project partners are thankful to me, I too owe gratitude to them. We can accurately claim that without us, everything we have helped cause would not have happened. But for everything we co-cause, we are also indebted to the other co-causers. Tools for handprint accounting need to enable us to identify our 'handprint partners': All the people or organizations whose contributions made it possible for us to have the handprint we do. This will help us to be mindful – and grateful – for all the ways our interdependence helps create the positive impacts we are a part of achieving.

ACHIEVING HEALER STATUS

Next, let's consider how we can be net healers at all. The conceptually simplest way of approaching handprinting is to focus our efforts on making changes to our own footprint, changes in our own life (obviously, we are operating from the Standard perspective in this case, because from the CE perspective, reductions to our own footprint do not count among our handprints). In this case, we will be a healer if we make enough reductions in our life's impacts that this year's footprint is a bit less than half of last year's. Why is this the case? Imagine that last year we had 10 units of negative impact on the planet. Living unconsciously this year, the flat baseline assumption says we would have 10 units of impact again. If we can have just under five units of impact instead, while 'cleaning up' or preventing five units of impact that would otherwise have occurred, we are net-positive – we have been a net healer or net contributor this year. And to be a healer again next year, we are going to need to cut this year's impacts in half again.

That is some pretty intense reduction in impact, is not it? If last year's footprint was 10 units of impact, this year needs to be at least a bit less than five units, and next year needs to be under 2.5 units. Our third year footprint needs to be below 1.25 units. And after five consecutive years of being a healer based solely on reductions to our own personal footprint, we will have reduced our footprint to about 3 percent of its original size!

Now, you may be thinking that there is just no way we can reduce our own footprint to 3 percent of its initial size in just 5 years. I have the same feeling, but here are three pieces of good news that make being a healer – for multiple years – quite conceivable.

- First, our handprint can be anywhere in the world. It need not only include reductions to our own footprint. Just as our footprint is composed of lots of small impacts, our handprints can be composed of lots of small reductions in impact.
- Second, we are all connected. Our footprints are influenced by the footprints of tens of thousands of businesses and activities spread across the earth. This means that other people's handprints, eventually, will start to reduce our own footprints too. These do not count in our handprint, but they will reduce the size of handprint we need in order to be net-positive.

- Third, humanity is intensely creative. This creativity, plus the ability of all people to share ideas, plus the fact that our footprints are connected, tells us that maybe, every person and every company or organization which wants to be a healer in a year will be able to do so, and that over time, this desire and ability to be healers can scale. By the time that even one-quarter of humanity is trying, we will have truly healed humanity's relationship with the earth, in a deep and lasting way.

References

Corriero, J. 2004. *Role of Youth Survey*. Available at: http://research.tigweb.org/roleofyouth/ (accessed 15 May 2012).

Hertwich, E. and Peters, G.P. 2009. Carbon Footprint of Nations: A Global, Trade-linked Analysis. *Environmental Science and Technology*, 43(16): 6414–6420.

Hoekstra, A.Y., Chapagain, A.K., Aldaya, M.M. and Mekonnen, M.M. 2011. *The Water Footprint Assessment Manual: Setting the Global Standard*. London: Earthscan.

Joint Nature Conservation Committee (JNCC). 2009. *The Biodiversity Footprint of UK Foreign Direct Investment*. Available at: http://jncc.defra.gov.uk/pdf/pub09_biodiversityfootprint.pdf (accessed 15 May 2012).

Liroff, R. 2009. *Don't Know Your Company's Toxic Footprint? Ignorance Will Not be Bliss*. Available at: www.greenbiz.com/blog/2009/05/13/dont-know-your-companys-toxic-footprint-ignorance-will-not-be-bliss (accessed 15 May 2012).

McCann Group. 2011. *The Truth About Youth*. Available at: http://www.scribd.com/doc/56263899/McCann-Worldgroup-Truth-About-Youth (accessed 15 May 2012).

Oxfam. 2010. Oxfam Poverty Footprint: Understanding Business Contribution to Development. *Briefings for Business* 4, 1–16. Available at: http://www.oxfam.org/sites/www.oxfam.org/files/oxfam-poverty-footprint.pdf (accessed 15 May 2012).

Pew Research Center. 2010. *Millennials: Confident, Connected, Open to Change*. Available at: www.pewresearch.org/millennials (accessed 15 May 2012).

Slavery Footprint. 2012. *About Us*. Slaveryfootprint.org/about/#aboutus (accessed 15 May 2012).

World Resources Institute(WRI)/World Business Council for Sustainable Development (WBCSD). 2009. *Product Life Cycle Accounting and Reporting Standard*. Available at: http://www.ghgprotocol.org/files/ghgp/ghg-protocol-product-life-cycle-standard-draft-for-stakeholder-review-nov-2009.pdf (accessed 12 October 2011).

9 *Revisiting the Classic Tension Between Hierarchy and Freedom*

LAURENT BIBARD

Introduction

Questioning the ways leaders lead, in the horizon of a renewal of humans' and organizations' attitude and behaviour towards diversity is urgent. The legitimacy of authority and grounds upon which it is based are in question. It is evident that people need authority. As the current worldwide financial crisis shows, humans cannot live without any kind of control concerning the possibility of a political –for example, par excellence, collective – life. The tension between business and the notion of a possible common good is nowadays in question (Bibard 2012); authority and leadership are inescapable if humans are to live a bearable collective life (Hobbes 1985, 1982). It is nevertheless quite uncertain how to reach such a 'bearable' collective life through authority and leadership.

Authority and leadership may appear radically ambiguous, ambivalent, and sometimes harmful, to say the least. Authority is unfortunately quite often perverted into a coercive behaviour and system, which sooner or later enslave people. A critical aspect of such slavery is the reduction of people to robots aimed at serving taken-for-granted ideologies. In this horizon, the respect for diversity – in other words the capacity to lead people taking into account their variety – is crucial. A leadership which respects people diversity is most probably a non-tyrannical leadership, yet also an efficient one.

I will start by showing to what extent respect and recognition of people's diversity are crucial on a managerial perspective. But the leadership issue – whatever the starting point of enquiry – needs a philosophical detour through political philosophy. This is why I introduce the demanding issue of tyranny. Using such a detour, I will be able to address the leadership issue from the most relevant point of view, which concerns education. Even if avoiding tyrannies looks actually impossible, educating humans certainly favours tyrannies' scarcity. I will terminate our enquiry questioning the conditions for an efficient and genuinely humanizing education.

On Some Currently Fundamental Issues Concerning Leadership

The current worldwide situation is quite difficult for organizations to tackle – as well as for individuals. Organizations are embedded in a chaotic environment, the main characteristics of which are: 1) increasing uncertainty;2) the possible appearance of sudden and overwhelming events in any domain, such as finance, geopolitics and the natural environment and; 3) the seemingly overwhelming consequences of small decisions. Complexity and managerial difficulties do not come only from outside of organizations; they also come from inside. This has been identified by Perrow (1984), and deepened by many authors including Weick (1988). Weick and many other authors particularly question the sudden emergence of catastrophic conditions for a plant, a system or organization and its potentially dramatic consequences. Studying such conditions make clear some leadership issues which deserve to be studied in detail. Before describing some of them, it is necessary to further clarify the point.

Extreme situations are not that exceptional. As reminded above, the current global economic, social and political context, fundamentally generate uncertainty. Second, lessons on catastrophes are not limited to the events themselves. Most often, organizations do work the right way, dampening crises and problems, and ensuring an apparently 'normal' running while continuously being confronted with radical obstacles and uncertainties (Bibard 2007). Yet knowing about catastrophes is spontaneously easier than knowing about working organizations and people. People talk much less about so-called 'normal' situations, or organizations which work without any visible problem despite catastrophe.

Consequently, understanding disasters' dynamics may not only help understanding exceptional and extreme situations, but due to a refraction effect, ordinary ones as well. When things work, they go 'without saying'. Organizations and people that function well generally keep silent; they do not need to talk and to put anything in question in order to run their operations. In fact, everything works as if people did not know about them. To the contrary, when things do not work anymore, they are sooner or later put into question and no longer go 'without saying' (Bibard 2005); they need a reset.

Let us now describe and analyze some peculiar features concerning leadership in organizations on the basis of understanding catastrophic situations. Many empirical studies have been made on extreme if not catastrophic situations. Many others have been made concerning what has been called 'High Reliability Organizations' (HRO; cf Weick and Roberts 1993). As an example, I briefly present the Weick analysis of the Bhopal disaster. This disaster was studied twice by Karl Weick (Weick 1988, 2010); these two publications are taken into account on the Bhopal case.

A first specificity of the Bhopal plant situation before the catastrophe is, in Weick's perspective, the lack of managerial accompaniment following the announcement of the Union Carbide plant closure (Weick 1988). The corporation hierarchy decided to close the plant without accompanying the workers to do so. This had deleterious consequences on the general employees capacity of vigilance. These consequences may be described as decreasing or eliminating people motivation. As a consequence, after the announcement that the plant was to close, workers simply waited to be fired formally.

This deleterious general atmosphere is visible through three main characteristics, which Weick understands as strong and unquestioning commitment (Weick 1988). These three facts are the following:

- First, the refrigerator system had been switched off as a result of the cost of keeping it functioning. Apparently, nobody resisted the switch-off, despite the decisive role the system could play in case of any problem in the plant until its closure.

- Second, many devices did not work anymore in the plant, among which were a number of gauges. In normal situations, gauges are fundamental indicators for security. When the concerned employees observed that one of the gauges in the control room showed an exceptional pressure of one of the plant tanks, only one wanted to raise the alarm while others convinced him not to worry about (Weick 2010).
- Third, once the alarm was activated, the employees' decided to switch off the alarm and to wait for the chief manager before alerting nearby inhabitants of the plant. The gas leak lasted 90 minutes before people were informed. Many of them became direct victims of this decision.

These three facts are together interpreted as employees showing too strong a commitment towards their company and their superiors. Revisited by Weick himself (Weick 2010), the point may be understood the following way: The remaining employees stuck too much to their corporate policy. They did not question the way things were managed, they consciously or unconsciously adhered completely to the decisions and to the evolution of the company and the plant. Not that they were enthusiastic with this choice; rather, they resigned themselves to the plant shutting down and their jobs disappearing. The consequence was a lack of sense of responsibility and active commitment – a form of commitment quite different from the loyalty transformed into a silent and unconscious, progressively inescapable routine.

Yet the most interesting fact is the one at the very root of the accident. During a shift change at 3 pm on December 2, two employees told their two newly assigned colleagues in this sector of the plant that they should clean the water circuits of the plant. These two new employees in this sector of the plant were supposed to do so by turning the dedicated tap. This slight but indispensable operation of circuit cleaning consisted of blocking water with specific metal cylinders, in order to avoid a water leak in the concerned tanks. This very simple operation, being quite evident to the two employees from the earlier shift, was not communicated to their incoming colleagues. Furthermore, the subsequent shift employees were newly assigned to the concerned sector of the plant. They were not at all familiar with the cleaning operation; they were all the more unfamiliar with the blocking aspect of it concerning the tanks. As such, the shift members missed this important step.

A specific point must be briefly made clear about the transaction between the two shifts. For the first two members, the blocking operation was so evident, that it went without saying. For the second group, it did not even exist – they did not even imagine that something should be added to the command to clean the circuit. Ignoring the necessary operation makes the two new employees ignore they are ignoring it. From their point of view there was no problem with the cleaning operation. The radical importance of the two new employees' bounded rationality is now visible to us because it had the huge and awful consequence we subsequently witnessed. During the very transaction, this invisibility is precisely structural thus patently invisible. This last conclusion may draw our attention to the second Weick (2010) article on the accident. In this article Weick insists on the mix of thought and operations, and on the continuously reiterated tension between awareness, decision making and action during regular management operations as well as during crisis situations. The stake may be described the following way.

Spontaneously, action and thought are not the same. To the contrary: They are qualitatively different if not opposed. Their opposition may be sketched underlying the radical opposition between short term and long term. In the short term, people are demanded to contribute immediately, constantly, to the best of their abilities and in a visible way to their organization (whatever the organization to which they belong and contribute). In the long term, people are asked to take distance with action, with their taken-for-granted practices, with evidence, in order to be able to innovate, to behave creatively, to show the necessary flexibility towards their environment changes. In the long term, people are asked to think of unknown options and to remain vigilant to weak signals. The long-term attitude looks quite close to a theoretical attitude, a cognitive attitude, while the short-term one is structurally based on ongoing practices. Everybody knows that what is true in theory may not be true in practice (Kant 1970): On a managerial and an organizational perspective, theory and practice contradict each other. Such a contradiction may prove to be a fundamental one, an ontological one (Strauss 1989, Bibard 2007). Let us examine the consequences of the Karl Weick analysis of the Bhopal situation to deepen our understanding of the tension between theory and practice in real time – in other words while people are embedded in the decision-making dynamics.

The significance of Karl Weick's insistence on mixing action and thought is made quite clear when taking into account with utmost seriousness the spontaneous discrepancy between them. If theory and practice, action and thought, short-term and long-term logics are frontally contradictory, observing that they mix when people are deciding means that something quite important occurs beyond actors' access while deciding – intellectual as well as practical access. While deciding, action and thought interact without any possible a priori understanding, grasping or coping of what is happening by the actors themselves. Something occurs which is superior to actors' rationality while they are making their decisions. This is what Weick apparently has in mind when quoting the poem: 'How can I know what I think till I see what I say?' (Weick 1995: 12, cf. Wallas 1926). What does such an inaccessibility consist of?

The tension between thought and action, discussed on the very basis of pragmatic philosophy in the second Weick article on Bhopal (Weick 2010), may be understood as a tension between actors' competencies and actors' vigilance. Actors' competences and contribution level depend on actors repeating operations the best they can, until they integrate and internalize them as taken-for-granted, evident reflexes, skills and routines. Nevertheless, in doing so they progressively forget about their knowledge and capacities. They just 'do it' – their actions go 'without saying'. Their actions potentially go without any relevant awareness. Now, actors are reasonably demanded to keep aware of what they are doing. They are demanded to keep aware of their actions, and of the consequence of others' actions and behaviours. They are not only demanded so by their hierarchy and colleagues and so on, but by constant environmental changes and evolution. If they do not remain aware of what they are doing, they take a risk of slight – or less than slight – problems.

The main managerial and organizational tension which results from these observations is the two-fold necessity to favour at once people's competencies and awareness, which are patently contradictory (competence supposing training and routines, vigilance supposing radical capacity to question and doubt). Such a contribution supposes favouring people experience and know-how, as well as their capacity to take distance from their jobs and its context (Weick 1988). Competencies are highly favoured by experience. Awareness is more than highly favoured by diversity, in other words by an individual as well as collective capacity to question each others' attitudes and actions and to doubt. Simultaneous integrated competencies and awareness – if not mindfulness

– hugely depend on organizational leadership. A leadership which makes people believe they are not competent or useful dangerously engenders a lack of vigilance, of relevant commitment and of experience. Leadership which succeeds in making people feel responsible and accountable for their actions, in making them feel alert on their operations and on what generally happens in their close and remote environment, in making them proud of their jobs and know-how; a leadership which favours a general admitted respectful nevertheless demanding capacity to doubt, positive networking, and a high level of vigilance as well as of positive reactivity contributes to best decision-making conditions. Indeed, what is at stake here is the content and the form of the relations between leadership and respect for people. This deserves a dedicated examination, which must be but philosophical.

On a Political Philosophy Approach to Leadership

Taking the above for granted, leadership favours efficiency when it favours people's sense of responsibility as well as confidence – to themselves, to their colleagues, to the hierarchy. Sense of responsibility and confidence may be reached but through a minimum of freedom. The classic tension on leadership concerns the extent to which people are free to live the way they want in a society (Strauss 1952, 1968). This tension is a classic one, which concerns politics in general. The general question on politics concerns the extent to which people should be entitled to live the way they want versus the extent to which they should legitimately be expected to obey common laws. Two main understandings shape political philosophy; the so-called 'ancient' political philosophy and the modern political science. The origin of our understanding of politics takes for granted that people be led due to an imbalance in competence. Some people are able to lead others; some are only able to obey the rules and commandments (Aristotle 1998). Ideally, the best ones are to govern the others (Plato 1968). If this is so, common sense may make people imagine that politics will create or favour the conditions for efficient justice. Justice is incompatible with freedom to innovate any way: A certain degree of censorship or control on innovations should complete an efficient and just policymaking (Plato 1968); otherwise, no political stability is possible. Now, political stability is indispensable to politics. People need stability and order, for no order, hierarchy and stability sooner or later means civil wars (Hobbes 1985). This is so because wars are the spontaneous deepening or dramatic intensification of politics (Clausewitz 2004). The ancient political philosophy approach of politics is deeply grounded on authority – if not authoritarianism. Some are supposed to know everything if not what is good for everybody. The extreme or unbalanced expression of the ancient political philosophical understanding of politics is an excessive authority of the leaders. This spontaneous tendency frontally contradicts what we deduced from Weick's examination of leadership and crises management: Leadership needs to dominantly tolerate if not radically favour people's freedom and spontaneous sense of responsibility and initiatives if organizations are to avoid catastrophic – in other words 'bad' – decision making. Such defence of people's sense of responsibility, confidence and initiative is to be found in the roots and developments of the modern political science – of the modern political understanding of politics.

Modern political science is broadly inaugurated by Thomas Hobbes. Thomas Hobbes anthropology presupposes human's equality, rationality and freedom (Hobbes 1985).

An equally distributed rationality is exceptionally compatible with Weick's teaching on leadership. Such an assumption does not mean that on the basis of their day-to-day life and work, people know the same as everyone: The division of labour is at once necessary and spontaneous and organizations do automatically separate actors, tasks and objectives, thus resulting in bounded rationalities (gathering the right information in order to guarantee the necessary common knowledge of organizations is to be continuously started afresh) (Bibard 2007). Contrary to what ancient political philosophy assumes, this means that people are supposed to be potentially as competent as everyone else when it comes to responsibility, decision-making dynamics and vigilance. This amounts to a shared responsibility, to confidence and shared expertise. This is notably convergent with Weick's approach of leadership and managerial issues concerning crises management in particular. This is the defended option here.

Nevertheless, due to the interest in individuals, the so-called modern political science shows vulnerability to private interest as a unique and exclusive kind of interest to defend. This may sound quite dangerous for decision-making processes and leadership efficiency. One of the most important goals of Hobbes when making clear the roots of the new political science is to make sure that grounded anew, political life will prove stable. Stability is essential to humans' collective life, for without stability, political life transforms itself into a civil war. In order to guarantee political stability, Hobbes grounds political life on people's choice or fundamentally free and rational decision. More precisely, it is based on humans considered as individuals, who are supposed to be free, equal and rational. Humans are supposed to be spontaneously such individuals, the 'natural' state of humans being a state of individuals who enjoy a natural right to live, and who are supposed to defend themselves to preserve from violent death (Hobbes 1985).

The Hobbes' 'natural' state of nature is nevertheless sooner or later a state of violence, for individuals will sooner or later long for the same resources. They will sooner or later fight for resources, and resources are structurally finite and lacking when compared to humans' desire. Humans' desire is infinite, while resources are limited. The humans' state of nature is a state of violence and omnipresent humiliations. Hobbes deduces that consequently humans – as free and equally rational individuals – sooner or later decide to delegate their right to preserve from death to a unique authority, which will not only be entitled, but which will have the duty to defend and preserve them from violent death. Such a delegation cannot of course be partial or result from only some individuals' decision. To ensure a real security of each individual, this decision must result from every individual – Hobbes assumes that each individual rationally anticipates other individuals' anticipations. An economical rationality grounds the constitution of the 'modern' State, called the *Leviathan* (Hobbes 1985).

We can look at Economics as being at the root of modern political science. The modern political science is actually economics-oriented, or reducible to economic science. The modern political science is reducible to economical theory, due to its foundation. It presupposes that humans are but individuals, radically independent from their natural features (such as sex, ethnic groups, age and so on). Such an assumption is of course artificial; the Hobbes' notion of 'state of nature' is an artificial one, or the 'state of nature' is an artefact – nevertheless, an artefact which orients even if discretely most of the current policies; an artefact which conditions the dominant paradigm of contemporary action. The main implicit and taken-for-granted assumption concerning collective life results from the liberal interpretation of Hobbes by John Locke.

Locke assumes that the State's principal role is to guarantee individuals' freedom and rights, which mainly consist in private property (Locke 1988). Having created his artefact in order to contribute to a coming political stability in England, Hobbes insists that individuals cannot change their government, due to its origin; they cannot but recognize themselves in the *Leviathan*. Should they revolt against it, they would deny their own initial choice, which is impossible; this would amount to self-destruction. And what has been constructed through the 'social contract' is a reasonable – the only possibly reasonable – political world. Contrary to this, Locke admits people rightly revolt when the governor does not comply with his duty to ensure individuals protection particularly by protecting their private property.

Private property is at the root of modern political thought, to the point that private property limits the current understanding of collective issues (Bibard 2012). Collective issues cannot nowadays be tackled the right way, due to their inaccessibility to people exclusively dominated by the modern political science paradigms. The current worldwide crisis may be interpreted as a crisis of the modern political science crisis. It is needless to be reminded that when modern political science is not interpreted in the horizon of Locke's liberal interpretation, it may be the occasion for the most radical tyrannies. Modern political science's tentative effort to ground politics on a new stability proves to provoke a general disorder due to the exclusive supremacy of individual interests to the detriment of collective action and interest. The modern political science suffers from quite problematic limits as the ancient political philosophy does. The modern political philosophy limits are dominantly the limits of an unlimited freedom. Unlimited freedom has as a major inconvenience to prevent adults from the possibility of educating their children. Education is potentially illegitimate in the context of modern political science due to the assumption of equality of each individual to the others. As children are individuals as all the other ones, they deserve the same a priori respect and consideration as everyone. If they do so on the basis of an immediate and spontaneous existence, the question arises sooner or later about the relevance of educating them – for they are supposed to be structurally 'already' equal and as rational as adults.

Ancient political philosophy's radical limit results sooner or later in an irrelevant authoritarianism. Meanwhile, the modern political science sooner or later devolves into an excessive respect to individuals considered as immediately equal to each other. Before shifting to our fundamental questioning on leadership, let us underscore the following point. Hobbes's so-called 'state of nature' is an artefact, and clearly identified as such by himself. It thus is a normative and theoretical artefact which nevertheless progressively became a perspective of empirical reality, or on the point of view of action, an implicit assumption concerning empirical reality. This may be well-exemplified by the huge consequences that Milton Friedman's statement on profit-making had in practice (Bibard 2012). The stake is the following: Practices are quite slow and do not change fast (Nelson and Winter 1982, Argyris and Schön 1996, cf Aristotle 1985). They depend on time irreversibility. Theories are reversible: People may be wrong and retract their ideas, and this is not that problematic. But what is problematic and somewhat irreversible is scholars' influence on practice, by publishing research results. This happened as well with Hobbes. Hobbes assumed theoretically that humans were equally rational and free individuals. People nowadays believe, in a structural and immediate way, that humans are actually equally free and rational individuals. Doing so, they forget about the difficulties of education, and they forget about the common good, or any notion related to the notion of a possible common good as well as a notion of a real, personal, intimate progress due to education. They have poorer and poorer access to the specifically political problematic. They potentially could not care less about politics understood on the noble sense of the word. People could care less and less about politics or collective interest for the sake of collective interest.

THE LINK WITH LEADERSHIP

Leadership has to do with authority. Leaders are supposed to orient followers towards a right way, right action, right society, right future and so on. Doing so, leaders necessarily favour unbalanced relations between themselves and their followers. The potential evolution of leadership is always that leaders progressively reduce their followers' liberty, autonomy, sense of responsibility and self-esteem. Modern political science made room for a new understanding of leadership, based on people's freedom, equal capacities and rationality. Modern politics spontaneously makes room for people's spontaneous and voluntary contributions. Making such room proves potentially as dangerous as the first option, which nevertheless prevented humans from creating really 'democratic' and efficient collective structures and dynamics.

Here we are with the classic political tension, politics being confronted to the two potential extremes, collective sense and sense of a common good, but no freedom, and freedom without any sense of a possible common good. The truth is of course in-between; we need to understand how. To make some progress towards our understanding of modern leadership and new ways to favour an efficient respect of people as potential leaders – or at least as competent and vigilant followers – without creating the conditions for negative (for example, 'anarchic') political consequences, we need to revisit our examination of the very roots of the two political models which are the modern political science on one hand, and the ancient political philosophy on the other hand. Actually, the two models are relevant when taken into account together. They are thus relevant through their very frontal contradiction.

On Education: Back to a Tension Between Business and the Common Good

Let us go straight to the point. For many reasons, and particularly due to its potential 'authoritarian' shape, the ancient political philosophy model looks a masculine one; whereas the modern political science one looks a feminine one. Apart from the probable agreement on this first superficial understanding of the two models based on the relation to authority, a second reason may be of some interest here. The second model amounts to a release of individual interests which are coherent with the release of a free economy, in which the basic anthropological assumption is one of a free, rational and equal to all others, individual economic agent. The origin of economics must be traced back to the classic 'family' or private life, which was supposed to depend on women. The shape of the modern political model results from the initially radical yet persistent issue of women's freedom. The modern political science model makes room for one of the most important current worldwide phenomena, women's liberty and sovereignty, to be formally recognized and at last stabilized by laws. Dealing with the leadership issue through an examination of political philosophy issues drives a consideration of gender relations through the recognition of the importance of the current worldwide feminine revolution. Let us deepen our understanding of the two models on the basis of these previous observations.

EQUALITY AND THE EDUCATION STAKE

In opposing ancient political philosophy on the basis of his understanding of humans' 'natural state', Hobbes opposes the classic common sense, which admits that politics begin by the family, or by heterosexual bond between men and women (Aristotle 1998). It may be stated with no great risk of error that the heterosexual relation was, for a long time, a fundamental means for humans to protect themselves from enemies and secure daily life. During a period when weapons essentially consisted of the number of humans composing communities, and when procreation was not 'medically assisted', it is of a common sense to assume that producing citizens or community members was one of the most secured way to guarantee communities' security and prosperity. In other words, sex was an indomitable means for making war when necessary, as well as for ensuring the day-to-day life of the community and developing it. Such a context favoured an utmost attention to sexuality considered as the basis of any community sustainability.

This is of course radically different nowadays, due to the technological capacity to produce tremendously powerful weapons (not only on the basis of their destruction power, but as well on the basis of the capacity to run them with so few people), as well as agriculture, industry and biotechnologies. Thanks to progress in agriculture and industry, people do not need to be numerous in order to ensure a sufficient production of goods and services. Second, thanks to progress in biology and genetics, procreation is more and more favoured independently – or quite independently – of heterosexual intercourse. People do not necessarily need any more to make love in order to reproduce.

Modern economics, modern sciences and technologies favour the possibility of a world where sex is of no use – not other than pleasures which it still makes possible. Contrary to what used to be the case previously, in such a world, homosexuality, celibacy and impotence are not any more of any 'political' importance. It is quite coherent that in such a context, morality changes about sex, if morality long depended on politics as used to be the case in contexts close to the ancient political philosophy descriptions and prescriptions.

Based on empirical observation, the ancient political philosophy duly represented by Aristotle's one, admits that humans spontaneously live in communities, and that communities' fundamental roots consist of families, built on the basis of heterosexual bonds. Even if differentiating clearly between a father and a king is crucial for a correct understanding and leading of political life (Aristotle 1998), from families through clans, villages, cities, to nations and empires, there is a continuous growth of an initial entity which is built on the basis of the indomitable sexual intercourse needed for human procreation.

Not only did Hobbes make possible a new way of understanding politics, he as well fought against the ancient understanding of humans' differences or variety. Following Machiavelli's teaching on the same topic (Machiavelli 1981), Hobbes contributed dramatically to the progress towards a world shaped by the desire to get rid of nature, its limits and cruelty. The very notion of the so-called 'state of nature' that Hobbes shapes prepares the understanding of humans as individuals potentially independent from any natural pre-condition: Sexual, ethnic, related to age and so on. As alluded to, this may have huge problematic consequences concerning education. For, if children are considered as immediately equal to any other individual, they are considered as immediately equal to grown ups and consequently to their parents. In such context, there is no reason why parents should teach anything to their breeds: Children are supposed to spontaneously know the difference between good and bad, between justice and injustice, between right and wrong, as they may know the difference between truth and error. Needless to say they are supposed to master – whether now or later on – any technical expertise. Nevertheless, techniques are of no difficulty at all compared to the sense of justice, of goodness and so on. A child may understand many technical and rational problems, he or she may solve many difficulties in mathematics, physics and so on, without acquiring or showing the necessary maturity to solve any ethical problem (Aristotle 1985). To be understood, ethics need experience. Ethics are a question of practice, and suppose training. Ethics – as politics – needs education (Aristotle 1985, cf Aristotle 1998). More generally, human affairs may not be solved without experience. Nevertheless, education does not depend only on experience. Education depends on trusting already grown people, who show how things work and should work. Education supposes trusting grown ups who are supposed to show young people how the world works, what may be changed, what should be changed and so on. Now, the very radical responsibility of parents or grown ups is not only to teach about expertise or any kind of knowledge. Education is about responsibility. Responsibility needs sovereignty. People who do not master themselves nor their actions cannot take any responsibility nor be considered as being accountable for their actions and deeds. Freedom presupposes responsibility. Given that freedom is not immediate – in other words that children are not immediately as free and equal as grown ups (whereas they may be as rational as them) – it must be experienced to be understood, appropriated and developed. Ages to a certain extent evidently differentiate children from grown ups. Educating children amounts at least to make them feel their future is a grown up life. Adults are responsible for showing children that their world is the future one, and that there is a future.

These two points would need to be deepened by themselves. Let us nevertheless limit our investigation to the following one. Children should be taught there is a world which makes sense despite all its limits, and that in the future children will be able to find and shape their place, or that it is as well possible to understand and shape it better than it used to be so far, and that they will contribute to such changes. At any rate, be the world the same or improved, children should feel they are welcome. This is not an easy task; sooner or later children revolt against grown ups' authority. The other reason is that grown ups do not necessarily spontaneously admit that their children – that children in general – may know, understand, talk and do better than they themselves did, regardless of similar positions and social roles.

These stakes may be put the following way. Ancient political philosophy was quite risk averse, conservative, authority grounded and 'masculine'. Modern political sciences favour innovation, freedom, equality; in this perspective they look rather 'feminine'. Supposing 'classic' heterosexual families, we may deduce that education always involves a tension between 'masculine' (or authoritarian) versus 'feminine' (liberal) ways. Leadership results from tradition if not strength on one hand, and from a taste for innovation and the assumption of universal equality, competences and responsibilities on the other hand. It is observed that none of these two options may work apart from the other. In this context, gender differences play a decisive role in children's education. I consider this role on the basis of a brief understanding of gender differences, and conclude coming back to the initially dealt with leadership issue – whatever management situations considered.

GENDERS DIFFERENCES AND EDUCATION

For various reasons (of which the details cannot be presented now), women are spontaneously future-oriented, towards the unexpected, and the sentiment of freedom, whereas men are dominantly security, identity and stability-oriented (cf above on the analogy between the two main political philosophy models and genders). Actually, this is to be nuanced, on the basis of four observations:

1. So far, only women get pregnant. And despite the extraordinary amount of new available technologies helping humans' reproduction, humans are still all born of a woman. This makes a clear – if not 'natural' – difference between men and women.
2. Taking into account the very negativity of desire, it may be assumed that each spontaneously given sexually conditioned apperception prepares its denial if not its destruction as such – in other words the desire of its contrary. Be this true, the spontaneously identity-based sexual identity of women would drive them towards difference and newness, while the spontaneously difference-based constitution of men would drive them towards a securing identity. On the basis of a taken-for-granted identity (due to their capacity to repeat what their mothers did, in other words, pregnancy), women would favour children due to future-oriented longing and freedom. On the basis of a longing for identity (due to them losing their origins when born), men would educate children in a fundamental and original conservative way, trusting laws, structures and rules.
3. Now, every human is born of a woman, on the basis of a previous heterosexual intercourse. Be such intercourse heterosexual indeed, or medically assisted, it supposes the meeting of the two sexes, male and female. This amounts to saying that, being the result of a heterosexual meeting, every human bears both of them: A man, is never exclusively masculine, nor a woman exclusively feminine.
4. As a consequence, individuals' behaviour is much more ambivalent and varied than what could initially be expected when taking into account our investigation and examination of the two political philosophy models. Men may behave much more in a feminine way and women in a masculine way than initially suggested. Such observation would favour a positive consideration for homosexual families, if not families with a unique parent and so on. Nevertheless, the difference between male and female initial apperception of reality may help understanding the leadership issues described first part of this article – particularly, due to the consequences of 'education' in general on leadership capacities as well as sense of responsibility – life-long education as well as the initial one.

BACK TO THE ISSUE OF LEADERSHIP

Education cannot from now on but be approached on the basis of life-long learning projects and attitudes. Being graduated – from any level from any institution – does not any more suffice to ensure professionalism and efficiency as it was once supposed. Only through their experiences do people show how they adapt to new circumstances, new environments, new challenges and so on in their professional lives. Fortunately enough, diplomas are no longer considered as 'proof' of competence and skills; experience is from now on the radical criteria.

The necessity of life-long learning of course always existed. But its visibility is irregular. Crises situations make it more clear than stable situations. The current globalization dynamic, considered as depending on a continuous negotiation between control and non-control (Bibard 2005), makes necessary if not urgent that people learn how to adapt to increasing worldwide changes – this was alluded to beginning of this chapter. People no longer need to learn skills and competences; they need to learn how to constantly learn.

While learning about expertise and techniques is indomitable, learning about how to learn continuously is even more indomitable. Learning constantly makes necessary the capacity to unlearn skills and competences which were so far considered as relevant if not evident; organizational life makes people rest on some taken-for-granted skills and routines which spontaneously emerge from day-to-day life (see above). Sometimes – crises situations show it dramatically – routines and skills must be questioned if people are to tackle real, new, unexpected problems. Such problems do not concern only highly-complex industrial systems, medicine or air transportation. Due to the chaotic current evolution of the worldwide economy (Bibard 2007), new problems may loom ahead of any sector, in a non-predictable way. It is nowadays crucial to learn how to unlearn in order to be able to re-learn.

Such competence – the competence of awareness – is frontally contradictory to any previously internalized expertise, routine, know-how, which so far ensures actors' efficiency. The tension between competence and vigilance is to be deepened on the basis of a learning to learn process. Education begins by school, it continues sometimes with executive education, and always with experience and experiences.

Given that people should learn to learn, it is evident that leaders should do the same. A leader who learns and is able to learn constantly – added to this, a leader who is able to communicate about such constant learning is able to question his/her very leadership. Accepting to question the leader's leadership amounts to recognizing people limits, and the indomitable necessity for everybody to rely on others in his/her job. Leadership should be understood on new bases. Leadership is no longer a question of a unique, omnipotent and omniscient leader. Leadership is a question of sharing information, sharing expertises, sharing common understanding of situations and decision-making dynamics. On the other hand nevertheless, decisions must be made, and people need to feel responsible if not accountable for them: Leadership understood as resulting from structures, hierarchy and power cannot structurally be eliminated. People, organizations and communities need leaders in the classic sense of the notion. But leaders need from now on, to rely on followers, who are absolutely not only followers in the traditional sense (people executing orders from leaders and conforming to their vision, wishes and so on). Leaders and followers must converge in coherent dynamics which favour balance between expertise and vigilance.

Taking into account what has been said on gender, the best leadership dynamics mix positively masculine and feminine logics, individually and collectively. Favouring a positive balance between competence and vigilance while making decisions amounts to balancing power, expertise, experience on one hand, and the capacity to question, to doubt, to listen to each other on the other hand. This amounts to balance the feminine and masculine understandings of leadership and collective dynamics – which amounts to balance masculine and feminine sentiments on what education consists of.

References

Argyris, C. and Schön, D. 1996. *Organizational Learning: A Theory of Action Perspective*. Boston: Addison-Wesley Longman.

Aristotle. 1985. *Nicomachean Ethics*, translated by T. Irwin. Indianapolis: Hackett Publishing.

Aristotle. 1998. *Politics*. New York: Oxford University Press.

Bibard, L. 2005. The Ethics of Capitalism, in *Ethical Boundaries of Capitalism*, edited by D. Daianu and R. Vranceanu. Farnham: Ashgate, 3–24.

Bibard L. 2007. Towards a Phenomenology of Management: From Modelling to Day-to-Day Moral Sensemaking Cognition, in *Moral Foundations of Management Knowledge*, edited by M.L. Djelic and R. Vranceanu. Cheltenham: Edward Elgar Publishing, 3–30.

Bibard 2012, is the text published on internet for the ESSEC conference on Business and the common good – "Business and the Common Good : A Genealogy of a Confusion", (Business and the Common Good), ESSEC, 8 & 9 mars, 2012.

Friedman, M. 1970. The Social Responsibility of Business is to Increase Its Profits. *New York Times*, 13 September.

Hobbes, T. 1982. *De Cive: Or The Citizen*. Westport: Greenwood Press.

Hobbes, T. 1985. *Leviathan*. London: Penguin Books.

Holy Bible King James Version. 1990. Iowa: Riverside World Publishing.

Kant, E. 1970. *Political Writings*. Cambridge: Cambridge University Press.

Locke, J. 1988. *Two Treatises of Government*. Cambridge: Cambridge University Press.

Machiavelli, N. 1981. *The Prince*. New York: Penguin Books.

Nelson, R. and Winter, S. 1982. *An Evolutionary Theory of Economic Change*. Cambridge: Harvard University Press.

Perrow, C. (1984). *Normal Accidents: Living With High Risk Technologies*. Princeton, NJ: Princeton University Press.

Plato. 1968. *Republic*, translated by A. Bloom. New York: Basic Books.

Strauss, L. 1952. *Persecution and the Art of Writing*. Columbus: The Free Press.

Strauss, L. 1968. *Liberalism, Ancient and Modern*. Chicago: The University of Chicago Press.

Strauss, L. 1989. The Problem of Socrates Five Lectures, in The *Rebirth of Classical Political Rationalism*, edited by L. Strauss and T.L. Pangle. Chicago: The University of Chicago Press, 104–187.

Wallas G. 1926. *The Art of Thought*. New York: Hartcourt Brace.

Weick K. 1995. *Sensemaking in Organizations*. Thousand Oaks: SAGE Publications Inc.

Weick, K. 1988. Enactment Sensemaking in Crisis Situations. *Journal of Management Studies*, 47(3): 551–580.

Weick, K. 2010. Reflections on Enacted Sensemaking in the Bhopal Disaster. *Journal of Management Studies*, 47(3): 537–550.

Weick, K. and Roberts, K.H. 1993. Collective Mind in Organizations: Heedful Interrelating on Flight Decks. *Administrative Science Quarterly*, 38(3): 357–381.

PART V

The Role of Educators

10 *Management Education: How Can We Develop a Generation of Business Leaders to Act for the Common Good?*

ISABEL RIMANOCZY

In the last decade the number of corporations that have started to pay attention to corporate social and environmental responsibility has significantly increased (Hollender and Fenichell 2004, Edwards 2005, Benioff and Southwick 2004). However, given the dimensions of our planetary challenge, there is still an insufficient number of business leaders who have shown their willingness to champion initiatives that could have a positive impact on communities and on the environment. As observed by Campbell (2006) and Waddock (2008), the drivers for introducing and implementing corporate social responsibility (CSR) initiatives are people, individual leaders, and not 'organizations'.

A few years ago I found myself wondering why so many business and political leaders devoted themselves to philanthropic causes only after they had retired from work. Why, I asked myself, did their interest in initiatives that address the common good become manifested after they left their influential positions in business or politics? I questioned if they had indeed been aware of the potential impact on the environment and communities of their daily decisions at the time they made them, but for some reason they had not acted on that awareness.

I was further intrigued when I met several business leaders who in fact were championing initiatives that had a positive impact on the environment or on people, even though these initiatives were not a stipulated part of their role. This made me curious to explore why they behaved as they did, what they knew about the environmental problems, how they thought, and what had motivated them to take action. If we could understand why these 'unusual' leaders acted the way they did, I reasoned, we might be able to be more intentional in our management education efforts, and to focus on developing a new generation of business leaders who would actively incorporate the dimension of 'common good' into their daily decisions.

As such, we developed a qualitative case study of 17 organizations engaged in CSR initiatives that explored the connection between leadership and sustainability. The results suggested that there was 'the need for leadership theorists to better understand the factors prompting certain leaders to adopt a focus on sustainability' (Quinn and Dalton 2009: 27). Similar recommendations were made by Siegal (2009), who called for empirical studies of the role played by corporate leaders in both the formulation and implementation of CSR initiatives. A careful literature review conducted by Visser (2007) indicated that academic research on CSR is only two decades old (Elkington 1994, Gladwin, Kennelly and Krause 1995), yet the role of individuals affecting environmental change in organizations has been under-researched (Sharma 2002). The focus has been mostly on the economic justification of CSR (Margolis and Walsh 2003, Basu and Palazzo 2008) but the motivation behind the implementation has remained a 'black box' (Linnenluecke, Russell and Griffiths 2007). I found myself in agreement with this need to explore the values and leadership behaviours that triggered social and environmentally responsible responses in corporations (Waldman, Siegel and Javidian 2006, Waldman, Sully de Luque, Washburn and House 2006, Basu and Palazzo 2008).

This research gap was further raised at the first forum of 'Business as an Agent for World Benefit', convened by Case Weatherhead School of Management, the Academy of Management and the United Nations Global Compact in Cleveland, 2006. The Forum attracted over 400 leading scholars and business leaders from 40 countries. With the aim of engaging the audience, a selection of corporate leaders shared stories of how their organizations were currently contributing to the betterment of society or environment. It became clear to the attendees that there were too few such efforts, and the awareness grew that the world needed many more similar leaders championing initiatives that could shape a better planet for all.

The question that emerged at the forum was: What is the role of management education in developing these new leaders? A task force led by Dr Manuel Escudero, Head of Global Compact Network and Special Advisor to the United Nations Global Compact, was thus established to create a set of principles that could provide guidance to the field of management education as it aims at greater social and environmental responsibility. A year later, the commission presented the UN-sponsored PRME, Principles for Responsible Management Education. The six Principles address the purpose of business education, and the values, methods, research, partnership and dialogues that need to be created between the different stakeholders: Educators, students, business, government, consumers, media, civil society organizations and other interested groups and stakeholders, on critical issues related to global social responsibility and sustainability. PRME invites management schools from around the world to become signatories, commit to set yearly goals to implement the principles, and to be part of a growing learning community.

These Principles signalled the understanding that educators had a potentially significant role in influencing and guiding new generations of leaders, by helping them gain the knowledge they need, to develop the mindset that is required, and to foster their awareness of the personal footprint they leave. The Principles indicated that educators had a new responsibility and opportunity to shape and support the change needed for the return to a sustainable world. The next question was what to teach.

The Research

While individuals learn spontaneously by trial and error – through experience and by interacting with others – the assumption was that there is room for furthering the learning, and adult educators could play a significant role in this (see Figure 10.1). The purpose of my study was to understand and explore the processes that business leaders go through as they learn to identify and champion sustainability initiatives, to understand and describe the knowledge and supports they found, and to identify the mindset, competencies and attitudes that helped them in that learning process. This understanding, I believed, could assist adult educators to develop recommendations in promoting the concept of sustainability and to develop leaders to champion similar initiatives.

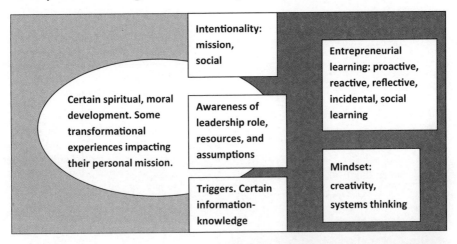

Figure 10.1 Assumed Context of Leaders and Opportunities for Adult Educators'
Methodology

The research design was based on a descriptive exploratory approach in the qualitative tradition. To study the insufficiently explored phenomenon of business leaders fostering sustainability initiatives, the multiple case method was used to gather data from a group of outstanding individuals (Denzin and Lincoln 1998: 90, Creswell 1998: 55). Biographical and phenomenological techniques were used in semi-structured interviews. Furthermore, the study was framed within the constructivist paradigm (Guba 1990), which makes the findings of an inquiry not a report of what is 'out there' but 'the residue of a process that literally creates them … it depicts knowledge as the outcome or consequence of human activity; knowledge is a human construction, never certifiable as ultimately true but problematic and ever changing' (Guba 1990: 26). This constructivist approach was meant to enrich the knowledge on this topic by triggering readers to find new ways of looking at the phenomenon, and of gathering data based on, derived from, or different from those stated here.

A comparative cross-case analysis was used (Creswell 1998: 63, Yin 2003: 46). Sixteen exemplary individuals were selected, based on the following criteria: 1) they were currently or had been in the past in leadership positions; 2) they were championing – or had in the past personally championed – sustainability initiatives inside their organizations; 3) their efforts in this regard were not at the time a stated part of their job description. Table 10.1 presents the data of the participants, using pseudonyms.

Table 10.1   Demographics of the Individuals Studied

Name	Gender		Industrial area	Age	Position	Currently
	M	F				
Anthony	x		Retail	75	CEO*–Founder, medium size US MNC	Chairman and speaker
Jack	x		Technology	70	Former VP Product Development, large US MNC	Faculty
Raul	x		Technology	66	Former CEO, small US MNC	Transitioning to a new job connected with sustainability
Stephen	x		Food	61	Chairman, large US corporation	Retiring, starting a major philanthropic initiative
Harry	x		NGO	60	President–Founder, association of corporations, NGOs and government	Same
Malcolm	x		Household products	56	VP, medium size US corporation	Corporate Social Consciousness Director
Diego	x		Coffee	56	President–Founder, small US corporation	Same
Howard	x		Apparel	53	Director, medium size US corporation	Same
Kevin	x		Pharmaceutical	53	VP, large European MNC	Same
Ronald	x		Restaurant	53	Global Senior VP, large US MNC	Same
Daisy		x	Apparel	53	Former Global Director Research, Design and Development, large US MNC	Starting sustainability consulting firm

Table 10.1 Demographics of the Individuals Studied *concluded*

Name	Gender		Industrial area	Age	Position	Currently
	M	**F**				
Shani		x	Food	49	Director, Legal Affairs, large US MNC	Same
Barry	x		Coffee Coop	47	President–Founder, small international cooperative	Same
Stanley	x		Restaurant	45	Former President and Owner, large US Franchises in Europe	CEO/Founder of a sustainability investment fund
Janine		x	Food	39	VP, R&D, large European MNC	Same
Nelson	x		Food	37	VP, Investors Relations, large US corporation	Same

Literature Review

When approaching the topic of business leaders fostering sustainability initiatives, a number of areas seem to tangentially surround or impact this phenomenon: What leads a person to be motivated to contribute to the common good? What supports, and what learning experiences help to develop the initiative? What is the connection between the leaders' legacy and corporate responsibility; specifically how does intentionality impact these initiatives, and how can leaders be best supported?

For the purpose of this study I reviewed books, magazines and newspaper articles, unpublished papers submitted by colleagues, trade and professional conference papers and presentations, dissertations from the ProQuest database, digital dissertations from Columbia University Teachers College, ABI/INFORM Global database, Ethnic NewsWatch (ENW) database, ERIC dissertation abstracts and internet searches, especially articles and information presented on websites of not-for-profit organizations related to CSR as well as educational institutions addressing CSR through their offered programmes.

I sought to find all the aspects that could be related to the phenomenon and that could guide my analysis. Progressively, some categories emerged that grouped these different factors. I finally identified two aspects, for the purpose of analysis. The first was the readiness of the individual to engage in CSR initiatives. What makes a person ready to consider engaging in something that is not part of his or her role, yet has a major impact on common good? The iterative process of reading, reflecting and discussing with individuals connected to the field of CSR led me to search specifically within certain sub-themes (Table 10.2)

The purpose of this section of the literature review was to understand what creates and contributes to develop the readiness of the individual to act in a sustainable way. The second aspect was related with the action, the planning and the implementation of initiatives, with the engagement in championing or fostering them. How does a person learn about CSR opportunities? How does an individual learn to identify, plan and implement such initiatives?

Table 10.2   Sub-themes Contributing to the Readiness to Engage in CSR

Intentionality related	Intentionality and personal mission
	Intentionality and social sensitivity
Self-awareness related	Awareness of leadership role
	Awareness of resources, knowledge, skills
	Awareness of assumptions
Triggers	Inspiration by personal events and by others
	Learning about current problems
	Learning about opportunities

In this group I identified the following sub-themes: The umbrella framework of CSR learning, comprising proactive, reactive, reflective, incidental and social learning, and the mindset that makes it possible (Table 10.3).

Table 10.3   Sub-themes Related to Action

CSR Learning	Proactive Learning
	Reactive Learning
	Reflective Learning
	Incidental Learning
	Social Learning
Mindset	Creative thinking and CSR
	Systems thinking and CSR

Summary of Aspects Influencing the Readiness

The literature review on the concept of life mission shows a connection of a personal mission with the human and universal need of making meaning. The 'Why am I?' is a core question for which individuals seek answers in different ways and at different stages of their life. Several development theorists incorporated the concept of mission, suggesting it is a key part of adult development (Gould 1978: 78, Levinson 1978: 91, Fowler 1981: 290, Belenky, Clichy, Goldberger and Tarule 1986: 16, Cochran 1990, Tisdell 2003). Others (Jarvis, 1983, 1993, Kroth and Boverie 2000) observe that most people struggle to understand the larger questions of existence, purpose and reasons for being over a lifetime. These questions are embedded in human nature and challenge, perhaps even haunt each of us as we continue upon our life journey.

While perhaps not clearly linked to a certain developmental stage, the need to find a purpose – a meaning for one's own life – seems to be a major human task. Kroth (1997) studied the relationship between personal mission and adult learning, in order to establish if adult educators could help in the development of personal missions. This study suggested that adult educators can improve the adult learning process by helping learners understand their life mission, by providing a learning environment which supports life mission explication and exploration, by connecting with their own mission as educators, and by linking individuals with community mission.

In terms of intentionality, Kroth and Boverie (2000) suggest that individuals would be able to keep a stronger motivation when they are conscious about their purpose, when they had reflectively come to think that their purpose is their life mission. Also, Dobel (2005) indicates that when the public office leaders ask themselves 'What do I wish to leave, or what have I left behind?' it adds a strategic dimension to the legacy. The focus upon legacy underlines moral responsibility and emphasizes the consequences of being in the public office position.

In contrast, most of the subjects of Kovan and Dirkx's (2003) research were not intentional, but became aware of what their life mission had been only during the interviews. The authors suggest that without challenging assumptions, the mission and learning may remain limited. When there was a clear focus – an intentional sense of mission – the motivation was steadier.

This is also indicated by Cohen and Greenfield (1997), co-founders of the environmentally and socially responsible ice-cream business Ben & Jerry's. They began their business following a spontaneous need to be generous with the community, to make a social impact, and later included the environmental impact. They slowly evolved into a values-led business, although they didn't realize they were doing it until they heard Anita Roddick, founder of another socially and environmentally responsible business (The Body Shop), refer to it as 'value-based leadership'. After realizing that, Cohen and Greenfield indicate they became much more focused, aware and intentional, which helped them in identifying new initiatives of common good, in making choices and decisions, and in facing obstacles. This resonates with accepted concepts like visioning, goal setting, strategic planning and management by objectives as different ways to focus the attention and the energy on specific outcomes in order to achieve them more efficiently – something with which business leaders are very familiar.

With regard to the awareness of one's own resources, impact potential and responsibility of the leadership role as factors influencing the readiness for CSR causes, the literature indicates only a very recent interest in the area of business ethics. While this was an unattended topic up until the 1990s, the corporate scandals of the last decades drew attention to it (Koehn 2005, Trevino, Brown and Harman 2003, Cordeiro 2003). The crisis in ethics and values is also seen as an opportunity for change (Louisot 2003, Mendonca 2001). Personal mastery (Senge 1990) becomes important as a way to develop ethical leadership, although values also need to be manifested into actions. Studies indicate a discrepancy between the self-perception of the leaders, their awareness of their impact potential and how employees see leaders in terms of ethics.

In trade literature there are testimonials from corporate leaders who mention their interest in using their resources for common good (Cohen and Greenfield 1997), their sense of responsibility (Anderson 1998) but little is found about the initial awareness or how that awareness was developed. The literature presents a variety of stories about the business cases of CSR initiatives, but no information about the skills, knowledge or individual journeys of the leaders.

While assumptions are known to play a significant role in changes of perspective (Mezirow 1991), I did not find information in the literature about the role of assumptions when becoming interested in sustainability initiatives. In terms of triggers that play a role in creating readiness, age, reminders of mortality and personal events are important, as well as traumatic or disorienting dilemmas (Dobel 2005, Mezirow 1991, Brookfield 1994). Research reports that some individuals have transformative learning experiences, while others learn to develop their purpose more gradually – with or without reflection. The role of mentors and communities is indicated, both for challenge and support (Daloz, Keen, Keen and Parks 1996).

A study of environmental activists (Kovan and Dirkx 2003) found that while the environmental activists had a perspective transformation, it didn't happen in a dramatic or epiphanic shift. Instead, they observed a gradual process occurring over an extended period of time, which parallels the findings of Daloz (2000), suggesting that the 'change or shift was long in coming and it is possibility prepared for in myriad ways, generally across years' (Daloz 2000: 106). If this is the case, adult educators may have a valuable opportunity to help individuals reflect and progressively identify their life mission.

Role models are an uncharted territory (Schutz 1991), but can be seen from the perspective of social learning theory (Bandura 1986) as having an influence on readiness. Actions that have a social or an environmental impact provide a greater sense of connectedness with the community or with the 'whole'. Participation in social movements or exposure to marginality is an important source of learning, as both develop social sensitivity; they help by clarifying beliefs and values and constitute motivators to act. The literature indicates the responsibility of adult educators lies in supporting the individuals in finding meaning, identifying their purpose through reflection, and also helping to convert the personal mission into concrete actions (Lindemann 1926, Kroth 1997, Elias 1993, Mezirow 1991, Jarvis 1993).

Summary of Aspects Related to Engagement in Actions

Since I wanted to assess opportunities for adult educators to foster sustainability minded leaders, I explored the aspects related to the planning and implementation of CSR initiatives. The literature indicated different types of learning, and the umbrella concept of 'entrepreneurial learning' (Maples and Webster 1980, Rae and Carswell 2000, Duffy 2006), was selected as possible framework, since entrepreneurs and leaders championing CSR have many characteristics in common.

Entrepreneurs utilize proactive learning to find information or skills they realize are missing, with a preference for informal settings. This has its roots in andragogy and self-directed learning (Knowles 1970, Brookfield 1994, Garrison 1997). In addition entrepreneurs use reactive learning as they face unexpected, unplanned events, which parallels with experiential trial and error learning (Dewey 1938, Lewin 1947, Kolb 1984), also with critical incidents (Brookfield 1993) and disorienting dilemmas (Mezirow 1991). Reflective learning is also used by entrepreneurs, both to learn from mistakes and to look at the future anticipating what can happen (Marsick and Watkins 1990, Reuber and Fischer 1999). Through incidental learning (Burgoyne and Hodgson 1983, Stokes and Pankowski 1988, Marsick and Watkins 1990, Watkins and Marsick 1992), entrepreneurs learn as they extract learning from accidental opportunities where the learning was unintended originally. This is similar to peripheral learning by observation or by being present in situations where something is happening that can be learned from (Wenger 1998, Seger 1994).

As entrepreneurs characteristically prefer to learn from other entrepreneurs, networks play a critical role (Aldrich and Zimmer 1986, Birley 1985, Smith 2000, Sexton, Upton, Wacholtz and McDougall 1997). This is also found to be the case with individuals committing to causes for common good (Daloz, Keen, Keen and Parks 1996), and it connects with the theories of learning through modeling or exchange (Bandura 1986, Wenger 1998). Emancipatory learning theories also indicate the importance of mutual learning (Freire 1970, Habermas 1971, Belenky, Clinchy, Goldberger and Tarule 1986). The expectations and feedback received from others play a significant reinforcement role for individuals committing to common good causes (Kroth and Boverie 2000, Daloz, Keen, Keen and Parks 1996, Dobel 2005).

In terms of mindset to help in the planning and implementation of CSR initiatives, empirical studies indicate that innovation and creativity are key for scanning the environment for opportunities and for valuing new ideas (Antonites 2004). The trade literature is filled with anecdotes reporting on innovative solutions (Cohen and Greenfield 1997). Also the printed media offers a daily increasing number of corporate examples of creativity: Gap Inc., Patagonia, Interface, GE, WalMart, Chevron and many more.

Systemic thinking is found in the literature as a key mindset to understand the interconnectedness of all things, as opposed to Western fragmented thinking (Bohm and Edwards 1991, Senge 1990, Senge, Scharmer, Jaworski and Flowers 2005). Relations that are not linear, but cyclical and web-structured, with long-term cycles, as well as the ability to cooperate and to think in terms of patterns are essential to address complex and ambiguous challenges (Capra 2002, Kegan 1994).

Research Needs

Based on the literature review, the following questions related to the readiness to consider CSR initiatives needed to be answered: 1) In what ways did the concept of personal mission and social sensitivity impact the intentionality of business leaders considering initiatives for common good? 2) In what ways did the self-awareness of the potential impact as a leader influence the readiness of business leaders to consider initiatives for common good? 3) What was the impact of events, of influences of other people, of information about problems or about opportunities as triggers for considering those initiatives?

With respect to engaging in actions, the following questions needed to be answered: 1) What did leaders learn about implementing their initiatives? 2) What types of learning and supports helped the business leaders when engaging in planning and implementation? 3) What mindset was conducive, important, or helpful in enabling action?

Findings

The study sought to explore the following questions:

1. What initiatives can a business leader champion that contribute to the common good in communities or in the environment?

2. How do business leaders learn to implement those initiatives?
3. How can educators or coaches support the process?

In this section I will specifically share the findings that provide input into how management educators could develop a generation of sustainability minded leaders.

GETTING READY AND DEVELOPING INTENTIONALITY

The question was, 'What does a business leader need to initiate or champion that contribute to the common good, be it communities or environment?' This question refers to what makes the leader 'ready'. The researcher explored the role of a personal mission, social sensitivity, and awareness of the impact potential as factors that develop intentionality, and the role of triggers that may have been of influence.

While the concept of a mission, a calling, leaving a legacy, or the urge to act are mentioned by 14 of the individuals interviewed, it seems to be less of a linear process, and only in three cases (Diego, Raul and Malcolm) was it present prior to starting the initiative. The intentionality implicit in the thought of carrying out a mission or making a personal contribution seems to evolve and develop over time, having a reinforcing effect. Spirituality in its diverse manifestations appears to play a major role in both creating readiness and in reinforcing the initiatives for 14 individuals. Several participants advocated for different models of business that introduce spirituality into the corporate world. Table 10.4 presents the comments related to personal mission and spirituality.

Table 10.4 Individual Comments Related to Personal Mission and Spirituality

	Anthony	Kevin	Howard	Daisy	Malcolm	Diego	Shani	Raul	Harry	Stanley	Nelson	Ronald	Stephen	Janine	Jack	Barry
Personal Mission																
Mission				x	x	x	x		x	x			x	x		x
Need to act	x	x			x	x	x	x	x		x	x	x	x	x	x
Social mission				x		x		x		x			x			x
Personal contribution	x	x		x	x	x		x	x	x	x			x		x
Legacy	x	x		x		x			x	x				x	x	
Life dream			x	x		x				x	x			x		
Spirituality																
Purpose, own role				x	x	x	x		x	x				x		x
Spirituality and religion			x	x	x	x	x	x	x	x	x	x	x		x	x

Table 10.4 Individual Comments Related to Personal Mission and Spirituality *concluded*

	Anthony	Kevin	Howard	Daisy	Malcolm	Diego	Shani	Raul	Harry	Stanley	Nelson	Ronald	Stephen	Janine	Jack	Barry
Spirituality																
Strong values								X			X	X		X	X	
Fragmented life					X	X	X			X				X		X
Connect spirituality with business			X		X	X	X	X	X	X					X	X

SOCIAL SENSITIVITY

Within the factors that contribute to create readiness to act, the intentionality developed by social sensitivity was explored: What is it that helps individuals develop social sensitivity? I am sharing here the findings that allow for influence by educators. The findings were grouped into early development of social sensitivity and adult awakening (see Table 10.5).

Table 10.5 Individual References to Early Development of Social Sensitivity

	Anthony	Kevin	Howard	Daisy	Malcolm	Diego	Shani	Raul	Harry	Stanley	Nelson	Ronald	Stephen	Janine	Jack	Barry
Upbringing Context																
Learning about religions		X			X	X		X								
Learning about social issues, politics, world		X				X				X						
Experienced poverty, self		X						X								
Experienced poverty, others									X							
Learned by reading			X		X	X		X								
Role Models																
Parents								X	X				X		X	

Table 10.5   Individual References to Early Development of Social Sensitivity *concluded*

	Anthony	Kevin	Howard	Daisy	Malcolm	Diego	Shani	Raul	Harry	Stanley	Nelson	Ronald	Stephen	Janine	Jack	Barry
Role Models																
Teachers		x				x										
Mentors		x	x	x				x	x					x		
Others, not close						x		x				x				x

The upbringing context was only influential for six out of 16 individuals in developing their social sensitivity. In those cases, it was through the influence of teachers, outside mentors, natural curiosity toward world events, reading and experiencing poverty.

Ten individuals had some kind of adult awakening, either through reading, personal encounters where they learned about problems of the planet, or through experiences while travelling. Table 10.6 presents the comments related to triggers of adult awakening.

Table 10.6   Individual References to Triggers of Adult Awakening

	Anthony	Kevin	Howard	Daisy	Malcolm	Diego	Shani	Raul	Harry	Stanley	Nelson	Ronald	Stephen	Janine	Jack	Barry
Parenting	x	x									x			x	x	
Fragmentation					x	x	x			x				x		x
Information																
Travelling				x		x										x
Reading	x	x				x	x				x	x	x	x		
Listening											x	x		x	x	
Learning about problems	x			x		x					x			x	x	x
Learning about opportunities		x					x			x	x		x	x	x	
Transformational, traumatic event	x				x	x	x	x		x	x	x			x	x

	Anthony	Kevin	Howard	Daisy	Malcolm	Diego	Shani	Raul	Harry	Stanley	Nelson	Ronald	Stephen	Janine	Jack	Barry
Pushed into it	x								x	x		x		x		
Feelings																
Pain, sadness, despair	x			x		x	x		x	x		x				
Shocked, concerned				x		x		x	x					x		x
Debt, guilt	x	x	x							x				x	x	
Anger, drives me crazy			x		x	x		x		x				x		

Information was an important trigger: Seven leaders learned about problems and this provoked a strong reaction in them, while seven reacted to opportunities that could be capitalized, such as embarking on initiatives that improved the company efficiency or strategy, or the morale of the employees. Interestingly, five individuals were pushed into the opportunity by others, and soon after developed their own passion and interest in an initiative.

Feelings played a major role as triggers, and were mentioned by 14 of the 16 individuals. The range of emotions covered deep anger, shock, profound concern and fear, pain, sadness, despair and guilt. Positive feelings such as joy and satisfaction were connected with a reinforcement of what they were doing, coming as a result of their actions, but not as triggers for action.

All but two individuals indicated being aware of the responsibility of occupying a leadership position or being in a decision-making role in an organization that had resources, or having the potential to make a major impact on the world. Fifteen out of 16 individuals mentioned that they were aware of knowing something that others did not and that they needed to tell, teach, share and spread the information. In one case it became a personal crusade: To influence other corporations around the world by showing a successful business case, and sharing how it was achieved. Five individuals mentioned that being aware of their gifts and talents created the need to act for the benefit of others. The awareness of impact potential, knowing something others did not, and having certain skills contributed to their intentionality and motivated them to act. Table 10.7 presents the comments of the participants related to awareness of their responsibility, knowledge and skills.

IMPLEMENTATION AND LEARNING

I wanted to explore how the individuals learned to implement initiatives that were different from their usual business, and what learning strategies they found helpful. In addition, I explored what mindset and attitudes they found useful. The purpose was to identify elements that adult educators could consider in order to support other leaders, or to develop and foster other individuals, for example in management education

Table 10.7 Individual References to Awareness of Responsibility, Knowledge and Skills

	Anthony	Kevin	Howard	Daisy	Malcolm	Diego	Shani	Raul	Harry	Stanley	Nelson	Ronald	Stephen	Janine	Jack	Barry
Responsibility																
Leadership role							x	x		x				x	x	
Sense of responsibility and contribution	x	x	x	x	x		x		x	x	x		x	x	x	
Awareness of resources		x				x	x	x								
Awareness of impact potential		x				x	x	x		x	x			x	x	
Knowledge																
Need to share, teach	x	x	x	x	x	x	x	x	x	x	x	x	x	x		x
Awareness of skills																
Skills, talents, gifts								x	x	x	x			x		

programmes, to implement initiatives for common good. I am sharing here the findings that have more relevance for management educators.

The participants repeatedly mentioned that they embarked into unchartered territories and had to innovate since there were not many similar experiences from which to learn. This required that they experiment and try out their ideas and learn from feedback received from colleagues or beneficiaries. Thirteen individuals sought to form partnerships or learning communities to support each other, and 11 mentioned drawing on available experts to help them and learn from them. Seven found role models very valuable, when they were available. Self-directed learning strategies, such as finding books to read, and writing, were definitely important, as were reflective practices, although these seemed more connected to deepening self-awareness than reflecting on the implementation as such.

The individuals collected a large number of lessons related to implementation strategies, both around what worked and what did not. Inspiring others by connecting the environmental concerns with operations was the most frequently cited strategy (eight participants), followed by the idea of leading a movement (seven), and providing a higher vision (six). Challenging assumptions (six) and creating new paradigms (five) was also mentioned as necessary. Eleven individuals mentioned their educational role, telling or writing about what they knew. They communicated it through harsh but compelling facts or by touching the hearts, using stories and metaphors.

The biggest surprise for 13 individuals interviewed was the immense enthusiasm and passion they found in the employees, who literally 'jumped on it', finding in the different initiatives a meaningful purpose that they seemed lacking, or did not even know they needed. Table 10.8 presents the comments of the participants related to the different learning strategies.

Table 10.8   Individual References to Learning Strategies

	Anthony	Kevin	Howard	Daisy	Malcolm	Diego	Shani	Raul	Harry	Stanley	Nelson	Ronald	Stephen	Janine	Jack	Barry
Self-directed Learning																
Reading	x	x		x			x		x	x		x			x	
Writing	x	x		x												
Reactive Learning																
Trial and error	×		×	×		×	×		×	×	×	×			×	×
Lonely			×	×	×	×	×		×	×			×			
Inventing		x	x	x	x	x	x		x	x				x	x	x
Reflective Learning		x		x	x	x	x	x	x	x					x	
Social Learning																
Asking experts	x		x	x		x				x	x	x	x	x	x	x
Role models	x		x			x						x		x		x
Seeking support	x	x		x		x	x	x	x	x	x	x	x		x	x

MINDSET

The findings related to what mindset they found helpful are organized in the following emergent categories: Systems thinking, innovative thinking and being orientation (see Table 10.9).

Systems thinking was a recurrent theme among 13 of the participants, relating a holistic, integrative worldview, understanding the interconnectedness of all things and the oneness of self and the universe. Long-term thinking, understanding the cyclical flow and complexity were also emergent themes. Since they were all navigating in new territories, innovative thinking and creativity became a very important way to process and think. Eight individuals made comments that indicated a qualitative value-based approach to life, centered on being as opposed to having. Nature was a factor repeatedly mentioned: Seven individuals commented how their experiences of Nature have shaped their thinking and their actions.

Table 10.9 Individual References to Mindset

	Anthony	Kevin	Howard	Daisy	Malcolm	Diego	Shani	Raul	Harry	Stanley	Nelson	Ronald	Stephen	Janine	Jack	Barry
Systems Thinking																
Holistic, interconnected			x	x	x		x	x					x			
Non-linear, cyclical	x	x	x	x			x									x
Long term	x				x	x						x				x
Complexity	x		x	x		x										
Inclusive				x	x			x							x	
Innovative Thinking																
Inventing		x	x	x	x	x	x		x	x				x	x	x
Creativity		x	x	x	x	x								x		
Being Orientation																
Qualitative versus quantitative				x		x		x								x
Nature	x			x				x	x				x	x	x	

Findings Related to Adult Educators

The question was, 'How could educators or coaches support the process?' This question addresses what advice the individuals would have for adult educators and coaches, given their own experience of what they had, what they sought, or missed. Fourteen participants responded to the questions related to their advice for adult educators.

The results were disparate. The most frequently mentioned aspect was incorporating ethics and discussion of values into the whole curriculum and into all technical subjects, to really embed it. Personal growth through spiritual practices, learning about religions, and deep self-contemplative work were recommended by four individuals as valuable for understanding the greater questions and getting a bigger picture. Information about environmental damage, climate change and social inequity that is destroying our planet was mentioned by four individuals, and also four suggested using real stories and life examples to learn from what is already being done.

Several mentioned the importance of transmitting a message of knowing yourself, thinking of the other, seeing the systemic interconnections of all things and 'getting outside the bubble'. This was also mentioned in a few cases as learning more about other cultures and perspectives, to expand the understanding. Some individuals highlighted the importance of adult educators become an inspiring example themselves, creating a habit of service to others and belief in the good.

With respect to learning methods, participants suggested to find innovative methods, such as experiential learning, faculty acting as learning facilitators, reflecting, dialoguing, and engaging both the right and left brain. Table 10.10 presents the comments for adult educators.

Table 10.10 Individual References to Advice for Adult Educators

	Howard	Daisy	Malcolm	Diego	Shani	Raul	Harry	Stanley	Nelson	Ronald	Stephen	Janine	Jack	Barry
Contents														
Study the classics					x									
Personal growth, spirituality				x	x			x	x					
Values, ethics		x		x		x					x		x	x
World perspectives				x	x				x					
History											x			
Team work											x			
Anthropology, cultures					x									
Statistics and biology	x													
Info about environment, climate change, social issues		x					x			x		x		
Messages														
Know thyself		x	x	x										
Think of the other			x						x					x
Change frameworks of thinking			x				x							
Keep an open heart			x											
Connected, get outside of your bubble		x					x	x						
Habits														
Innovation, creativity, risk taking		x	x											
Engaged, lifelong learning		x	x											

Table 10.10 Individual References to Advice for Adult Educators *concluded*

	Howard	Daisy	Malcolm	Diego	Shani	Raul	Harry	Stanley	Nelson	Ronald	Stephen	Janine	Jack	Barry
Challenge beliefs			X								X			
Inspire by example				X				X						
Serve others, be helpful								X	X					
Inspire teams to be their best							X							
Learning methods														
Different methods, no tests			X											
Reflection			X											
Meditation			X											
Travel, learning journeys				X	X									
Host foreign students				X										
Success stories, life examples								X	X			X	X	
Be a learning facilitator							X						X	
Internship in bus. and NGOs							X							
Work left and right brain								X						
Dialogue		X												

Conclusions and Implications

This study contributed to the current knowledge by providing a detailed picture of the elements that play a role for leaders championing sustainability initiatives. The elements covered issues such as what prepares the leaders to take such a stance; what are their learning strategies for implementing the initiatives; what they learned about the implementation process and – most importantly – the mindset that they found helpful in supporting their efforts. The study provided suggestions and recommendations particularly for management education, and it identified the critical competencies that should be developed to achieve what I named 'the sustainability mindset'. Chief among these competencies – some of which are still foreign to our traditional business education – are systems thinking, introspective practices, scrutiny and expansion of one's world-view, reflective practices, exploration of spirituality, increasing awareness of humans' oneness with nature, cross-functional and cross-cultural collaboration, and innovative thinking.

Based on the findings of the research, I was invited to design a course to develop the sustainability mindset for graduate students, which is currently being run at Fordham University, New York (for MBA students) and at Fairleigh Dickinson University, New Jersey (in the Masters Program of Hospitality and Tourism).

Developing the Sustainability Mindset

This programme has been designed to achieve three objectives which are discussed in more detail below:

1. To develop awareness of the challenges.
2. To develop the sustainability mindset.
3. To develop action.

DEVELOPING AWARENESS

In this programme we address the planetary changes that are impacting our life. We cover the areas of water, energy, waste, consumption, social inequity, climate change, wildlife, pollution. Then, we identify the values, paradigms and beliefs that got us here.

DEVELOPING THE SUSTAINABILITY MINDSET

Through exercises and dialogue we aim at developing the three pillars of the sustainability mindset: The systemic perspective, the collaborative action and the 'being orientation'. Within systems thinking, we focus on interconnections, long-term thinking/planning, both/and versus either/or thinking, oneness with nature, non-linear thinking. Within the being orientation, we focus on identity: Who am I? What is my role? What is my purpose? What are my values and how do they influence my decisions? Within the collaborative action, we focus on tools and processes to generate ideas with others, to develop innovative solutions, to support each other. As reflected in the findings of the research, awareness and mindset find a natural follow up in action. Therefore in this programme both serve one purpose: To move into action.

DEVELOPING ACTION PLANS

During the programme the participants are invited to identify a 'passion project' – something relevant and significant for them. They develop a plan designed to support their project, a plan that they will follow up with actions. This is their way to convert the programme experience into an opportunity to make a difference in the world.

Learning Methods

It has been repeatedly recommended over the past few years that developing a generation of CSR-minded leaders required innovative and different learning methods.[1] Several participants of this study equally suggested a more experiential and self-directed learning approach. The programme has therefore been designed following the adult learning methodology Action Reflection Learning (Rimanoczy 2007, Rimanoczy and Turner 2008). The sessions are planned according to the following ten learning principles, to optimize the learning:

- Relevance: The course is designed to ensure that participants own their learning, via personal learning goals, participative sessions and a self-selected project.
- Social Learning: Learning opportunities are maximized through multiple activities such as learning in pairs, working in small teams and large group exchanges.
- Reflection: Guided reflection, journaling, reflective writing and dialogue constitute some of the processes used to develop a critical reflective habit of mind.
- Paradigm change: Unfamiliar situations are created to challenge participants' assumptions and mental models.
- Self-awareness: Introspection, self-examination, exercises to understand self and others are used to develop self-awareness.
- Integral: The course addresses participants from a holistic, integral perspective combining physical, emotional, intellectual and spiritual dimensions.
- Systemic: A systems perspective pervades the course – from the contents to the interconnectedness of the modules.
- Repetition and Reinforcement: Time is used as an ally to help participants travel the road of discovery and growth; the course is rooted in an appreciative philosophy that seeks to build upon the best everyone has to contribute.
- Tacit Knowledge: Activities are planned and designed to help participants bring out their tacit knowledge and connect it with the knowledge in the room plus the inputs of the faculty.
- Facilitated Learning: The course uses blended learning techniques and the faculty alternates roles of learning facilitator, coach and expert instructor.

Final Remarks

This course is designed to promote personal transformation and development. Personal growth and insight cannot be mandated, only encouraged, facilitated and supported. This means that differently from traditional courses, participants are invited to take full ownership of their developmental process. They identify their personal learning goals in the beginning and review them as needed; the criteria to measure progress are collectively constructed as well as the evaluation criteria.

These characteristics require a different approach from the faculty too, who do not play the traditional authority role, registering attendance, setting grades, but a coaching role, more akin to executive coaching within an organization.

---

[1]   See Principle # 3 of UNPRME.org.

Some challenges ahead to be addressed are how does this developmental programme connect within a traditional MBA programme, where the grades of the students may have an impact on the job opportunities. Also, the willingness of faculty to explore a different approach than the traditional teaching role.

Beyond this programme, as also Waldman and Siegel (2008) suggest, more cross-level research is needed to clarify links between leadership behaviours, motivations and CSR. As sustainability becomes a more popular concept and more widely built into corporate strategies and operations, the contents of this programme may need to be adapted to continue presenting developmental challenges and opportunities of growth for the participants.

References

Aldrich, H. and Zimmer, C. 1986. Entrepreneurship through social networks, in *The Art and Science of Entrepreneurship*, edited by D.L. Sexton. Cambridge: Ballinger, 154–167.

Anderson, R.C. 1998. *Mid-course Correction*. White River Junction: Chelsea Green Publishing Company.

Antonites, A.J. 2004. *An Action Learning Approach to Entrepreneurial Creativity, Innovation and Opportunity Finding*. Pretoria: University of Pretoria.

Bandura, A. 1986. *Social Foundations of Thought and Action: A Social Cognitive Theory*. Englewood-Cliffs: Prentice-Hall.

Basu, K. and Palazzo, G. 2008. Corporate Social Responsibility: A Process Model of Sensemaking. *The Academy of Management Review*, 33(1): 122–136.

Belenky, M.F., Clinchy, B.M., Goldberger, N.R. and Tarule, J.M. 1986. *Women's Ways of Knowing*, New York: Basic Books.

Benioff, M. and Southwick, K. 2004. *Compassionate Capitalism: How Corporations Can Make Doing Good an Integral Part of Doing Well*. Franklin Lakes: Career Press.

Birley, S. 1985. The Role of Networks in the Entrepreneurial Process. *Journal of Business Venturing*, 1(1): 107–117.

Bohm, D. and Edwards, M. 1991. *Changing Consciousness: Exploring the Hidden Source of the Social, Political and Environmental Crisis Facing the World*. San Francisco: Harper.

Brookfield, S. 1993. Self-directed Learning, Political Clarity and the Critical Practice of Adult Education. *Adult Education Quarterly*, (4394), 227–242.

Brookfield, S.D. 1994. Adult Learning: An Overview, in *International Encyclopedia of Education*, edited by T. Husen and N. Postwhite. Oxford: Pergamenon Press, 163–168.

Burgoyne, J.G. and Hodgson, V.E. 1983. Natural Learning and Managerial Action: A Phenomenological Study in the Field Setting. *The Journal of Management Studies*, 20(3): 387–400.

Campbell, J.L. 2006. Institutional Analysis and the Paradox of Corporate Social Responsibility. *American Behavioural Scientist*, 49, 925–938.

Capra, F. 2002. *The Hidden Connections*. New York: Anchor Books-Random House.

Cochran, L. 1990. *The Sense of Vocation: A Study of Career and Life Development*. Albany: State University of New York.

Cohen, B. and Greenfield, J. 1997. *Double Dip: Lead with Your Values and Make Money, Too*. New York: Simon & Schuster.

Cordeiro, W. P. 2003. The Only Solution to the Decline in Business Ethics: Ethical Managers. *Teaching Business Ethics*, 7(3): 265.

Creswell, J.W. 1998. *Qualitative Inquiry and Research Design: Choosing Among Five Traditions.* Thousand Oaks: Sage.Daloz, L.A. 1999. *Mentors: Guiding the Journey of Adult Learners.* San Francisco: Jossey-Bass.

Daloz, L.A. 2000. Transformative Learning for the Common Good, in *Learning as Transformation: Critical Perspectives as a Theory in Progress,* edited by J. Mezirow and Associates. San Francisco: Jossey-Bass, 103–124.

Daloz, L.A., Keen, C.H., Keen, J.P. and Parks, S.D. 1996. *Common Fire: Leading Lives of Commitment in a Complex World.* Boston: Beacon Press.

Denzin, N.K. and Lincoln, Y.S. 1998. *Strategies of Qualitative Inquiry.* Thousand Oaks: Sage.

Dewey, J. 1938. *Experience and Education.* New York: Collier Books.

Dobel, J.P. 2005. Managerial Leadership and the Ethical Importance of Legacy. *International Public Management Journal,* 8(2): 225–247.

Duffy, S.G. 2006. *Entrepreneurial Learning: Exploring Unexpected Key Events in the Post-startup Period.* Washington: George Washington University.

Edwards, A.R. 2005. *The Sustainability Revolution: Portrait of a Paradigm Shift.* Vancouver: New Society Publishers.

Elias, D.G. 1993. *Educating Leaders for Social Transformation.* Unpublished doctoral dissertation. New York: Columbia University.

Elkington, J. 1994. Towards the Sustainable Corporation: Win-Win-Win Strategies for Sustainable Development. *California Management Review,* 36(2): 90–100.

Freire, P. 1970. *Pedagogy of the Oppressed.* New York: Seabury.

Fowler, J. 1981. *Stages of Faith: The Psychology of Human Development and The Quest for Meaning.* San Francisco: Harper and Row.

Garrison, D. 1997. Self-directed Leaning: Towards a Comprehensive Model. *Adult Education Quarterly,* 48: 16–33.

Gladwin, T.N., Kennelly, J.J. and Krause, T.S. 1995. Shifting Paradigms for Sustainable

Development: Implications for Management Theory and Research. *Academy of Management Review,* 20(4): 874–907.

Gould, R.L. 1978. *Transformations.* New York: Simon and Schuster.

Guba, E. 1990. The Alternative Paradigm Dialog, in *The Paradigm Dialog,* edited by E. Guba. Newbury Park: Sage, 17–30.

Habermas, J. 1971. *Knowledge and Human Interests.* Boston: Beacon Press.

Hollender, J. and Fenichell, S. 2004. *What Matters Most: How a Small Group of Pioneers is Teaching Social Responsibility to Big Business and Why Big Business is Listening.* New York: Basic Books.

Jarvis, P. 1983. The Lifelong Religious Development of the Individual and the Place of Adult Education. *Lifelong Learning: The Adult Years,* 6(9): 20–23.

Jarvis, P. 1993. Learning as a Religious Phenomenon. In *Adult Education and Theological Interpretation,* edited by P. Jarvis and N. Walters. Malabar: Krieger, 3–16.

Kegan, R. 1994. *In Over Our Heads.* Cambridge: Harvard University Press.

Koehn, D. 2005. Integrity as a Business Asset. *Journal of Business Ethics,* 58(1–3), 125–136.

Knowles, M. 1970. *Informal Adult Education.* New York: Association Press.

Kolb, D. 1984. *Experiential Learning.* Englewood Cliffs: Prentice-Hall.

Kovan, J.T. and Dirkx, J.M. 2003. 'Being Called Awake': The Role of Transformative Learning in the Lives of Environmental Activists. *Adult Education Quarterly,* 53(2), 99–118.

Kroth, M. 1997. *Life Mission and Adult Learning.* Unpublished doctoral dissertation. Albuquerque: University of New Mexico.

Kroth, M. and Boverie, P. 2000. Life Mission and Adult Learning. *Adult Education Quarterly*, 50: 134–49.

Levinson, D.J. 1978. *The Seasons of a Man's Life*. New York: Ballantine.

Lewin, K. 1947. Frontiers in Group Dynamics. *Human Relations*, 1: 5–41.

Lindeman, E.C. 1926. *The Meaning of Adult Education*. New York: New Republic.

Linnenluecke, M.K., Russell, S.V. and Griffiths, A. 2007. Subcultures and Sustainability Practices: The Impact on Understanding Corporate Sustainability. *Business Strategy and the Environment*, 18(7): 432–452.

Louisot, J.P. 2003. The Implications of 'Could I?' *Risk Management*, 50(9): 56.

Maples, M.F. and Webster, J.M. 1980. Thorndike's Connectionism, in *Theories of Learning*, edited by G.M. Gazda and R.J. Corsini. Itasca: Peacock.

Margolis, J.D. and Walsh, J.P. 2003. Misery Loves Companies: Rethinking Social Initiatives by Business. *Administrative Science Quarterly*, 38(3): 268–305.

Marsick, V.J. and Watkins, K. 1990. *Informal and Incidental Learning in the Workplace*. London: Routledge.

Mendonca, M. 2001. Preparing for Ethical Leadership in Organizations. *Canadian Journal of Administrative Studies*, 18(4): 266–276.

Mezirow, J. 1991. *Transformative Dimensions of Adult Learning*. San Francisco: Jossey-Bass.

Quinn, L. and Dalton, M. 2009. Leading for Sustainability: Implementing the Tasks of Leadership. *Corporate Governance*, 9(1): 21–38.

Rae, D. and Carswell, M. 2000. Using Life-story Approach in Researching Entrepreneurial Learning: The Development of a Conceptual Model and its Implications in the Design of Learning Experiences. *Education and Training*, 42(4–5): 220–227.

Reuber, A.R. and Fischer, E.M. 1999. Understanding the Consequences of Founders' experience. *Journal of Small Business Management*, 37(2), 30–45.

Rimanoczy, I. 2007. Action Reflection Learning: A Learning Methodology Based on Common Sense. *Industrial and Commercial Training*, 39(1): 43–51.

Rimanoczy, I. and Turner, E. 2008. *Action Reflection Learning: Solving Real Business Problems by Connecting Earning with Learning*. Palo Alto: Davies-Black Publishing.

Schutz, A.O. 1991. *The Relationship between Creativity and Role-modeling*. Ph.D. Dissertation. Toronto: University of Toronto.

Seger, C.A. 1994. Implicit Learning. *Psychological Bulletin*, 115: 163–196.

Senge, P., Scharmer, C.O., Jaworski, J. and Flowers, B.S. 2005. *Presence: An Exploration of Profound Change in People, Organizations and Society*. New York: Doubleday.

Senge, P. 1990. *The Fifth Discipline*. New York: Currency Doubleday.

Sexton, D.L., Upton, N.B., Wacholtz, L.E. and McDougall, P.P. 1997. Learning Needs of Growth Oriented Entrepreneurs. *Journal of Business Venturing*, 12: 1–8.

Sharma, S. 2002. Research in Corporate Sustainability: What Really Matters?, in *Research in Corporate Sustainability: The Evolving Theory and Practice of Organisations in the Natural Environment*, edited by S. Sharma, and M. Starik. Cheltenham: Edward Elgar, 1–29

Siegal, D. 2009. Green Management Matters Only if it Yields More Green: An Economic/Strategic Perspective. *Jerusalem Institute for Market Studies*, 23(3): 5–16.

Smith, C.A. 2000. *'Market Women': Learning Strategies of Successful Black Women Entrepreneurs in New York State*. Unpublished doctoral dissertation. New York: Columbia University.

Stokes, I. and Pankowski, M. 1988. Incidental Learning of Aging Adults via |Television. *Adult Education Quarterly*, 38(2): 88–100.

Tisdell, E.J. 2004. *Exploring Spirituality and Culture in Adult and Higher Education*. San Francisco: Jossey-Bass.

Trevino, L.K., Brown, M. and Hartman, L.P. 2003. A Qualitative Investigation of Perceived Executive Ethical Leadership: Perceptions from Inside and Outside the Executive Suite. *Human Relations*, 56(1): 5–37.

Visser, W. 2007. Corporate Sustainability and the Individual: A Literature Review. *University of Cambridge Program for Industry* Research [Online], Paper Series No. 1. Available at: http://www. cpi.cam.ac.uk/resources/publications/sustainability_research_papers.aspx (accessed 15 January 2012).

Waddock, S. 2008. Building a New Institutional Infrastructure for Corporate Responsibility. *Academy of Management Perspectives*, 22, 87–108.

Waldman, D.A., Siegel, D.S. and Javidan, M. 2006. Components of CEO Transformational Leadership and Corporate Social Responsibility. *Journal of Management Studies* 43(8): 1703–1725.

Waldman, D.A., Sully de Luque, M., Washburn, N. and House, R.J. 2006. Cultural and Leadership Predictors of Corporate Social Responsibility Values of Top Management: A GLOBE Study of 15 countries. *Journal of International Business Studies*, 37: 823–837.

Watkins, K.E. and Marsick, V.J. 1992. Towards a Theory of Informal and Incidental Learning in Organizations. *International Journal of Lifelong Education*, 11(4): 287–300.

Wenger, E. 1998. *Communities of Practice: Learning, Meaning and Identity*. Cambridge: Cambridge University Press.

Yin, R.K. 2003. *Case Study Research: Design and Methods*. Thousand Oaks: Sage Publications.

11 *Teaching a Common Good in a Business School: The ESSEC Seminar on Water Management*

LAURENCE DE CARLO

The ESSEC seminar on water management was created in 2009. It has two types of objectives, relating respectively to the knowledge the students need to acquire and the stance they will have to adopt as future managers working in a complex, diverse and uncertain environment.

The seminar pedagogy is based on certain principles that will be described, analyzed and discussed in the chapter. It concerns both reality and the symbolic level; it proposes a paradoxical vision of the world, in which both sides of paradoxes are recognized and accepted, and it operates through correspondence between the seminar subject, which is a common good, and the way it is led. The chapter ends with examples of student and professor feedback. The final discussion concludes with some factors that could be picked up by professors and business schools interested in accompanying their students along the path to taking a responsible role in their future mission as managers, and in society at large.

Water as a Common Good and a Human Right: The Related Challenges in the Northern and Southern Countries

In France with its legacy of Roman law, water, like air and sea, is part of the *res communes*, in other words common goods defined by the Civil Code (1804) as 'things that belong to nobody and are used by everybody' (Allain 2011: XLI).

Moreover, on 28 July, 2010 the UN General Assembly declared that 'safe and clean drinking water and sanitation is a human right essential to the full enjoyment of life and all other human rights'. Water, as a common good, becomes a fundamental right that needs to be provided for everyone. There is much progress to be made: Around one billion people in the world have no supply of clean water and 2.6 billion live without sanitation.

Because this theme is not usually considered a priority in the 'Northern' countries, most 'Northern' and 'Western' governments abstained from voting on this resolution. 'Of the 27 European Union States, only 11 voted for it. The legalistic arguments put forward by the abstainers cannot hide the fact, which is regrettable for the Northern countries' credibility in human rights matters, that the resolution was also marked by a North/South divide' (Petrella 2011, our translation). More generally, in the Northern countries, water is also an important issue not in terms of access but in terms of quality, as it is becoming increasingly contaminated with the development of undetected new sources of pollution.

It is also a key management issue, as more and more local Northern authorities want to manage water services themselves these days. Many of them are questioning the renewal of their contracts with private water management companies, following the example of the city of Paris which in 2010 decided against renewal. In the Southern countries, with their less-developed public resources, new types of public–private partnerships are being developed; they are specific to each case and successful to varying degrees (Frérot 2009).

The theme of water, a common good that has seen great changes in its management in recent years, is thus of interest to business school students. This, combined with a personal interest in environmental matters, led me to create an elective seminar on water management at ESSEC Business School in 2009. The collective dimension of this seminar's subject places the students in a responsible stance, working for the good of society at large. This dimension alone is insufficient to accompany them in developing openness to complexity, diversity and uncertainty. But the seminar subject is part of a frame which gives them the opportunity to discover a complex, diverse and uncertain domain.

The Seminar Syllabus

As a professor specializing in multi-party decision processes in planning and environmental matters, I address the subject from a multi-organizational and multidisciplinary perspective. The seminar addresses social matters, economics, geopolitics, public health, history, gender, education, human resources, plus other questions, all of them fundamentally linked.

The seminar is organized with a partner from outside the school. This partner has an involvement in water management on the territory concerned, representing a vision of water as a common good and the real-life situation. The first two seminars were organized in partnership with the Agence de l'Eau Seine Normandie (AESN, the Seine-Normandy Water Agency) and the third one with the Agence Française de Développement (AFD, the French Agency for Development). The AESN is a public establishment that is part of the French ministry of ecology, set up to fund action to protect water resources and fight pollution around a specific area (basin). 'In line with its plan of action defined by the committee for the area (a democratically representative body for water actors, local authorities, the State, and users) it provides financial aid in the form of subsidies and promotes to local authorities, industrial operators, farmers, and associations that carry out work to improve management of resources and fight pollution. The aid is financed by contributions received under the principle of reparations for environmental damage'[1] .

---

1   Source: AESN website, June 2012, our translation.

The AFD, meanwhile, is a 'financial institution … central to the French system for public aid to developing countries … The AFD acts against poverty, supports economic growth and contributes to enhancement of worldwide public goods in developing countries, emerging countries and French overseas territories'.[2] The AFD acts under the supervision of, and in close collaboration with, the ministries it reports to: The ministry of Foreign and European affairs, the ministry of the Economy, Industry and Employment; the ministry of the Interior, Overseas Territories, Local authority and Immigration. Through the large range of financial instruments it has developed and enhanced, the AFD supports public authorities, the private sector and local charity networks, to set up a wide range of economic and social projects. Its action for economic growth and environmental protection relates directly to the Millenium Goals, which were defined in 2000 by the United Nations with the aim of halving poverty in the world by 2015.

These partnerships mean that the overall syllabi are discussed with the partners, to make the key issues facing these organizations accessible for the students. Where necessary, the professor makes the final decision, as pedagogical objectives come first. The partners are actively involved in the seminar: Their CEO and some experts take part in different sessions. These experts are specialists in different disciplines necessary to understand the stakes of water management: Economics, sociology, geopolitics, agronomy and so on. Also, the organization partner provides a budget to enable the students to do field work. For the first two seminars, the students visited a water treatment plant and for the third they had the opportunity to attend the sixth World Water Forum in Marseille, and report on certain sessions for the Forum organizers. To thank them for their support and input, the partners receive a collective report after the seminar consisting of research work done by the students in groups of three or four. Depending on the seminar, this work may be analytical and/or prescriptive, answering specific questions asked by the partner. Students can propose recommendations on small-scale questions, but large-scale recommendations are beyond them in view of the complexity of the subject and the expertise of the guest speakers. The students are in a more modest position, like the vast majority of the professionals in this field – but this by no means prevents them from posing new questions, and/or posing them in a new way that can help the experts.

The seminar fosters dialogue between guest experts from different disciplines and organizations, and between those experts and the students. The participating experts come not only from the partner organization, but also from diverse horizons such as private companies, research laboratories and non-governmental organizations (NGO). Whenever possible, two experts from different organizations attend the same session so that the students encounter two different, legitimate and often divergent positions on a specific water management issue at the same time.

This dialogue between diverse positions is not only direct, but is also conducted through problematization of their contribution by the students afterwards, in debriefings led by the professor at the beginning of the next session, and in their research work for the collective report.

Like all the courses of the ESSEC MSc in Management, the seminar comprises ten sessions of 2.5 hours a week. The students choose to participate in the seminar, and numbers in previous years have varied between 20 and 30. The seminar participants have

---

2   Source: AFD website, http://www.afd.fr/home/AFD/afd_recrute, June 2012, our translation.

diverse backgrounds in terms of education, qualifications, practical work experience and participation in NGOs. They are also driven by diverse motivations: Some are simply curious about a topical theme, most are interested because they have recently discovered and become involved in environmental matters and/or developing country problematics. Their motivations range from an interest in understanding these themes, to a desire to be useful somehow in the field through a future placement and/or job.

The Seminar Concerns Both Reality and the Symbolic Level

Being involved in the reality level chiefly means recognizing the subject's complexity and uncertainty, and the real but limited power of its actors. In the classroom too, the power of the participants is conceived as limited and the groupal illusion (Kaës 1976, 1993) – that is, the process in which a group thinks it is omnipotent and can create miracle solutions – is avoided. This conception of the seminar in the reality level, in other words the consideration that the seminar participants' power is at the same time limited and shared, echoes the preoccupations of De Anca et al. in this book:

> *In management literature as early as 1924, Mary Parker Follet recognized the holistic nature of community and advanced the idea of 'reciprocal relationships' which conveyed the dynamic aspects of the individual in relationship to others. Follett was an advocate of what she called the 'integration' principle. This was based on non-coercive power sharing ruled by the notion of 'power with' rather than 'power over'.*

(De Anca, Aragón and Galdón 2013)

The same authors also stress that:

> *If the traditional paradigm of leadership emphasized individual attributes and characteristics, the growing paradigm of collective leadership emphasizes the community and groups within which different leaders emerge for different tasks and then step back to leave the leadership role to others.*

(De Anca, Aragón and Galdón 2013)

The concept of dialogue between diverse positions, and of limited and shared power in the seminar, is consistent with such a collective leadership concept, which means accepting and moreover valuing differences in visions and legitimacies between participants and guest experts. Conflicts between these positions and legitimacies can appear. Potential conflicts must therefore be managed constructively, in order to enrich participants' reflections. Following Mary Parker Follett in the 1920s (1995), a conflict simply means a difference, which does not have to be pre-judged as good or bad. She defined three ways to deal with conflicts: Domination, compromise and integration. The third of these is constructive (because its result is positive for each party) and needs creativity. This means each party must recognize its own desires, and each party's desires must be taken into consideration.

De Anca, Aragón and Galdón observe in this respect that:

> *The study by Carson, Tesluk and Marrone (2007) focused not only on the effectiveness of shared leadership but also on the necessary pre-existing conditions for it to emerge. They found that the emergence of shared leadership is more probable in the presence of an adequate internal environment, with a shared goal, social support, and where everybody's opinions are heard. Also, external coaching was a relevant predictor of the emergence of shared leadership. Arnone and Stumpf (2010) also moved beyond measuring effectiveness and focused on identifying specific success factors of shared leadership relations among co-CEOs. According to their findings, the success of such shared leadership relies on trust among the leaders, continued communication and respect among other elements.*

> (De Anca, Aragón and Galdón 2013)

This is why the seminar operates not only on the reality level but also on the symbolic level, as:

> *The symbolic arises when we must pronounce, elect, commit, give our word. These opportunities, more than others, make it possible to have this specific dimension alive in oneself. It is a new conception of the symbolic. Its gives it a much greater autonomy and importance, connects it to language and particularly the act of speaking. 'The symbol is human reality.'*

> (Juignet 2003)

Operating on the symbolic level means here that the seminar rules and the professor give the students space to engage with the seminar as human beings with specific desires and commitments, willing and able to connect with others through dialogue. As we have seen, dialogue is emphasized in the seminar (the participants' and professors' stance in these dialogues will be defined more precisely below). And students can express their own desires, in the framework of the seminar, by forming groups of three or four and choosing a theme for their research work, validated by the professor.

The Seminar is Linked to a Real Territory

The territory concerned was the Seine Normandy Basin in France for the first two seminars, and developing countries for the third. A territory is seen as the real place in which people experience several common goods. Water may or may not be rare there, but it is always at stake for different stakeholders of the same territory as it must be shared by people, including individuals, communities and companies, operating under certain rules that have yet to be defined.

As a reality to be taken into account, the territory and its many different actors represent the field that the experts' concepts and methods are designed to understand and improve. This means that the concepts and methods developed by the experts are both valuable and limited tools at the same time. Concepts and methods are by no means considered as omnipotent miracles applicable to all contexts and able to solve all problems. For example, economic studies assessing water projects in developing countries are explained in their own right, but also put into perspective regarding their relevance and role in decision-making processes. Giving such status and tools to methods and concepts seems particularly important in the management education field. Over-formalization and excessive modelling of the kind taught in management schools have been criticized, especially after the economic crisis of 2008 (L' Institut de l'Entreprise, le Cercle de l'Entreprise et du Management et la FNEGE 2010: 38). One of the proposed ways to bring about change in this situation is to reintroduce the uncertainty inherent to the human contexts in which the concepts and methods developed are to be applied (L' Institut de l'Entreprise, le Cercle de l'Entreprise et du Management et la FNEGE 2010: 38). The authors propose to reintroduce human sciences into management teaching, so that students can step back and take a critical view. While certainly relevant, this is not apparently enough. The very status of knowledge, in other words concepts and methods, needs to be revised, to move from the status of predefined knowledge for direct application to the status of instruments that must be adapted and possibly even reinvented as appropriate to the situation, whatever concepts and methods are concerned, whether in human sciences or the exact sciences. This would appear to require teaching that is not only cross-disciplinary, but takes place in project mode like this seminar, focusing on real issues. This type of work in a research approach is in fact proposed in the same report (42–43). In our seminar, the recommended 'research laboratory' consists of all seminar speakers, students and the professor.

Taking into Account the Technical Constraints and Potentialities

In the seminar, students not only discover the multi-organizational and multi-actor governance that exists in water management. They are also made aware of the technical constraints and potentialities of the projects studied. This technical dimension is linked to the other dimension, not seen as separate or simply ignored, as the success of a project depends on all these dimensions: The choice of a relevant technical solution, linked to a relevant governance approach and a relevant process for participation of local actors. These projects could for example concern supplying safe drinking water to inhabitants of a city or a village, or organizing a sanitation system in a city in order to protect the quality of the water at the beach, or implementing a water treatment system for an agglomeration of several cities. Taking the technical dimension into account appears important for business school students. First, it places them in the realm of reality. They do not develop a vision of water management that only involves different types of contracts and financing problems and solutions. Financing questions take on the status of means used to solve real problems involving environmental, technical and human dimensions. Such an approach seems even more necessary after the 2008 economic crisis. It has been shown that the 'artificial fascination' for a 'financial and managerial doctrine' imported from US business schools played a role in that crisis (L' Institut de l'Entreprise, le Cercle de l'Entreprise et du Management et la FNEGE 2010).

Accompaniment of Students in Their Learning Process

An 'accompanying' professor's stance is perhaps more necessary in teaching a common good than for other courses: The students need to build their own vision of the common good rather than learning the professor's view, as they all are and will be actors in the common good processes, even if only at an individual citizen and user level. In an accompanying stance, the professor puts the means in place to develop the students' learning process.

In a first phase, when listening to and discussing matters with the experts, judgment is suspended. The students and the professor listen carefully to the different, divergent expertise and experiences of the guest speakers, and talk with them to understand better. In the case of the seminar, suspension of judgment at this phase appears easy. There are many reasons for this, including: Students choose the course and are by definition interested in understanding water management; the experts present themselves in a modest way, emphasizing the complexity of their job and decisions without proposing 'ready-made' solutions; they themselves really listen to and answer the students' questions; the professor asks questions and makes comments without judging the experts or the students.

The second phase (usually at the beginning of the next session) consists of debriefing between the students and the professor, in order to step back from the discourses heard, contextualizing the views expressed and identifying links between them. In particular, this is a very good time to recognize 'where each person is coming from', this being a way to understand their vision. Judgments may appear in this phase. They are often put into context to make them more constructive, searching for the value added of even a criticized idea. After this process, the criticisms generally evolve. This does not mean that students have no right to be critical, but it does mean that their criticisms should be rigorous and respectful of people, facts and contexts.

Next, with further reading and after other sessions, students progressively build their point of view as a new expert and a citizen, in that they become engaged in Lacan's symbolic level. This means they do not consider the seminar as a set of knowledge external to them which must be integrated, but as a set of complex problems in which they are, and will be, involved and committed. The symbolic level of commitment is also at stake when, at the beginning of their interventions, the experts present their background and explain the history of their own commitment to water management. Their career paths are very diverse. At this point in the proceedings, the experts are giving space for each student to develop his/her own type of commitment.

French experts in management education have criticized the case study method (L'Institut de l'Entreprise, le Cercle de l'Entreprise et du Management et la FNEGE 2010: 41) as used in France because it offers a mix of extreme simplicity and extreme theorization. They argue that the main beneficiary of this mix is the professor, who can appear both pragmatic and learned at the same time.

In the water management seminar, the students' critical thinking skills develop by using human science concepts conceived as tools. The specific dynamic of the seminar, in which students have the status of actors rather than consumers or appliers of knowledge, also seems necessary for them to develop their critical eye, and moreover their own way of thinking. Another key factor is that the professor does not present herself as dominating water management knowledge. She is more experienced than the students, with more knowledge of contents and methods in some fields, while at the same time she is learning through the seminar with the students. This type of professor's stance gives the students more space and brings them to learn in their own way, as there is no single model of expertise to attain.

For effective involvement in such a learning process, the students must be cared for. Part of this caring is accompanying them and giving them space to develop their own reflections. For some students, caring also means giving reassurance, as the professor's stance is unfamiliar for the students and may cause anxiety in some, who can be reluctant to accept that a professor is not omniscient. Such a mix of caring and development of critical thinking, in his words the reconciliation of an ethic of care and an ethic of criticism, has been advocated by Yiannis Gabriel (2009) in management education as not only interesting but also socially useful.

The Seminar Proposes a Paradoxical Vision of the World

In the proposed paradoxical vision of the world, both sides of paradoxes are recognized and accepted (Lewis 2000, Smith and Lewis 2011, Winnicott 1971, 1986): Economic and social, private and common interests, public and private management, global and local, short term and long term, and so on. Such a perspective avoids the simplistic visions and quick judgments that are often developed more to reassure the thinker (professor and students) than to understand reality. In real-life settings and in terms of management, such simplistic contrasts are sometimes used by certain actors defending public management against private management or the reverse, independently of any context.

But water management offers situations of paradoxical phenomena. For example, different, potentially contradictory systems of regulations exist in the field of water management: Resource use limitation objectives set by environmental public policies co-exist with guarantees of usage rights awarded to users of these resources, through private property rights and also by other public policies (Nahrath, Gerber, Knoepfel and Bréthaut 2011).

STUDENTS HAVE TO TAKE INTO ACCOUNT BOTH SIDES OF THE REALITY AT ONCE

Taking into account both sides of the reality at once can create anxiety in some students when they cannot distinguish clearly, choose between and judge the two sides of the paradoxes. This anxiety must be accepted and worked through. Students are accompanied and cared for as they confront paradoxes and uncertainty. In some courses, the professor him/herself is responsible for this 'accompaniment' (de Carlo 2012).

In this seminar, the guest experts themselves unconsciously accompany the students, because they present their concepts, methods and cases assertively and modestly, not defensively – in other words they do not claim to know only the right methods and succeed in all cases. They develop narratives in which they talk about the methods they used in the field, and their successes and failures in applying them; they explain the new methods they tried to implement, and so on, accepting their own successes, failures and limits. As they are recognized experts, they give the students the possibility to accept their own successes, failures and limits in trying to work on a complex subject. Paradoxically, when students accept their own limits and failures, they tend to be more open-minded and so therefore better understand the complexity at stake.

THE ACCEPTANCE OF PARADOXES ALLOWS CREATIVITY TO EMERGE

The acceptance of paradoxes allows creativity to emerge (Weick and Sutcliffe 2006, Winnicott 1971, 1986). This creativity is expressed in discussions, and new visions of parts of the issue. In particular, students can make new links between points of views and visions not previously brought into contact. They can polish the governance schemes proposed by the experts for different projects, introducing new dimensions. For example, the participation of all stakeholders is often advisable in these schemes. This participation can be specified further by defining which stakeholders are consulted and at which phase, although there is no guarantee their opinions will be taken into account, and which stakeholders are involved in specific phases of decision-making processes according to status or other criteria. Thus we see that sometimes, paradoxically, consulted actors play just as important a role as actors who are officially part of the decision-making processes. Students can then give their point of view on these decision-making processes.

Such reflections are not enough to offer space for creativity in the seminar. The evaluation of the students' work, in other words their grades, must take this creativity into account. That is why most of the grades are based on research work carried out in groups of three or four. The students choose their subjects on the basis of the themes covered in the seminar. Their subjects are validated and commented on by the professor during the seminar. They fine-tune their problematization during the seminar, also through questions to the experts and reading. At the end of the seminar, they write a first draft of their work which is also submitted to the professor, and propose a new version following the professor's comments. There are further exchanges between the professor and the group of students during the seminar and during the month after it ends. With this approach to evaluating students' work, the objective is not to achieve a good grade by solving a known problem. It is not a one-shot evaluation. Evaluation here is conceived as the result of a reflection and creativity process. The management education experts of the Institut de l'Entreprise also encourage this type of evaluation (L'Institut de l'Entreprise, le Cercle de l'Entreprise et du Management et la FNEGE2010: 32) in their recommendations. Such an approach is certainly an important factor for encouraging reflection and creativity in students. But it is much more time-consuming for the professor than the traditional system. These shifts in pedagogy therefore concern not only professors at the individual level, but also their schools and universities at the organizational level, as they will have to take account of professors' commitment if they are aiming for change in management course pedagogy.

Correspondences Between the Seminar Subject and the Students' Learning Processes

First, in the seminar, water is acknowledged as a common good (that should be accessible to everyone), while recognizing different needs depending on users and contexts. In the seminar, the knowledge is common to all students, the professor and the guest speakers at once, and it also belongs to each individual, who develops that knowledge based on his identity, requirements and context. Second, water as a common good should be managed at both collective level and individual level, in order for everyone to be able to receive enough water. Similarly, the students' learning process is both collective and individual, and the benefit is received at both these levels. Third, one of the complexities of water management is the different levels of understanding of the issue among the population. For one thing, it is a very technical subject and many people do not know how water is actually distributed, yet specialized public authorities and NGOs would like to extend water-related knowledge in the general population. Similarly, students in the classroom know different amounts about water management and the related issues at the beginning of the seminar. The professor and the group must deal with these differences and make space for everyone.

Conceiving these correspondences between the students' learning processes and stances in the seminar with the theme of the seminar has several objectives and results. First, it gives the students a feeling of congruence which is part of the 'professor's caring'. In particular, the definition of water as a common good shows that the common dimension of water (its availability) is essential, and also that everyone as a human being should benefit from water services, but differently, according to possibilities and needs. These principles also apply in the seminar as students' collective reflection and initiatives are given space and value. The proposed student groups' research work subjects are discussed in front of the whole class at the beginning of sessions in order to give these reflections the status of collective thinking, related to others and interesting for all. Meanwhile, the students' individual ways of being involved in these reflections in the seminar are respected, as long as they respect the collective rules of the seminar. For example, some want to work on cases they have heard about during work placement or travels. This is generally possible, subject to certain conditions regarding the relevance of the cases for the collective reflection.

Student Feedback

The official evaluations tend to show that the students felt the seminar gave them very diverse perspectives on water management and an overview of the principal stakes in the field and potential career orientations. It must be noted that with this type of pedagogy that makes space for students' constructive critical sense, evaluations are never 100 percent uncritical. Students can say they learnt a lot in the seminar and still propose ways of improving it. There are also generally one or two students who have not appreciated the seminar dynamic in that they would have preferred more certainty, with knowledge imparted rather than discussed, and a more directive and 'omniscient' stance by the professor, taking a dominant position regarding knowledge. This can be interpreted as an indication that more such pedagogy is needed in business schools, to bring students to consider that uncertainty is part of their learning process and will be part of their working environment. It can also be interpreted as reflecting the need for a collective, institutional reflection on student evaluations and the way they are used (the standard attitude being that the higher the evaluations, the better the course or seminar, with 100 percent uncritical and positive evaluations considered the best).

As a student assists me in organizing the seminar each year, I also benefit from informal feedback the assistant hears from the participating students. In particular, 'off the record', students find it difficult to work on writing several drafts of their research work. They are used to producing just one version of their work, and having it graded so that they can 'get it behind them'. But here, there are several drafts and exchanges, through the operation in project mode rather than traditional academic lecture or class mode, involving reviewing their problematization, reading additional references, asking experts questions and so on. Therefore, they must begin to involve themselves in this research work very early on, without leaving it until the last minute, then continue for up to one month after the end of the seminar. This comes easily to some, but others need reminders of the type of pedagogy that is being implemented. Such students' perceptions are rational in a traditional conception of pedagogy, which does not require this type of significant commitment from students. It is also rational because traditional one-shot evaluations give students (and the professor) a feeling of certainty. My interpretation of why the students concerned did not write this feedback in their formal evaluations is that they have ambivalent feelings about it. I believe that they more or less consciously understand that the work asked of them is meaningful for acquisition of management skills and knowledge, but would nonetheless like to spend less time on it.

Professor Feedback

One specific episode helped me to reach a certain evaluation of the learning students achieved through the seminar. This is not a specifically rigorous or representative evaluation, but it gives an interesting reflection of one type of skill learned in the seminar.

One year, a partner representing a public service concession operator offered to organize a film showing a debate with students about a controversial film that was highly critical of the company he belonged to. This was a brave proposal, made possible by the relations of trust built up previously with students when this partner had visited as guest speaker. I invited other students likely to be interested in the issues to this film and debate. The discussion after the film was very interesting, and it was noteworthy that the only questions posed in a relatively abrupt manner, with little critical distance from the film, were asked by two or three students who had not attended the seminar. The students who had attended the seminar asked contextualized, nuanced questions that the partner was willing to hear. I interpreted this phenomenon through the two interrelated dimensions: The incorporation of complex stakes, and respect of others whomever they may be, even when they express views that do not agree with our own.

The dynamic of the debate brought non-seminar students to awareness of their lack of nuance, and the difficulty of constructive discussion when a relatively accusatory stance is taken. After the debate, they went to speak to the partner individually, to better understand the stakes he was confronted with, leaving aside any polemic.

Discussion and Conclusion

Much apparently remains to be done in terms of pedagogy if business school students are to be helped to work in a changing and diverse environment and adopt a more responsible stance regarding societal matters. As shown in the Institut de l'Entreprise report (2010), the 2008 crisis obliges us – collectively as management education institutions and individually as professors – to ask ourselves about the type of skills and stances management students must develop in order to avoid another similar crisis.

There are many critics of non-contextualized teaching that leaves little room for pluralism and nuances (L'Institut de l'Entreprise, le Cercle de l'Entreprise et du Management et la FNEGE 2010). As shown in this chapter, water is a particularly relevant subject in this regard, being a common good that is difficult to transport. Its presence and distribution depend on the condition of the ground and underground areas of the territories concerned, as well as the cultures, customs and ancestral representation of the local inhabitants. Therefore, contextualization of reflection is essential for the theme of water, arguably more so than for any other theme.

As a professor, it is important to foster a multidimensional understanding of complex phenomena in students, systematically placing the situations studied in their institutional, historical, cultural and relational contexts. In other words, it is up to us, the professors and guest experts, to regain space for analysis of complex situations, and thus to call on human sciences to approach decisions, concepts and managerial instruments in their contexts.

In this chapter, I have pointed out that while new types of knowledge must necessarily be taught, this in itself is not enough to enable students to work in an uncertain, diverse and complex environment. A specific dynamic of learning for students also appears necessary, to help them be actors rather than consumers of knowledge and skills. Approaching the complexity of phenomena and ensuring that students are actors in their classes contributes to placing managerial decisions in relationships of power that is real but limited. This is in contrast to the assumption of omnipotence, which can happen if oversimplified cases are offered that simply require application of known concepts and methods. Within the dynamics of the seminar, students learn to suspend their judgment in an initial phase in order to listen with an open mind to different actors. They then identify connections between the different positions expressed and read (in other words, they problematize) and give their own, more subtle positions.

In the dynamic of courses and seminars, it is also essential to accompany the students and encourage reflexivity, in the sense of a capacity to analyze and question their own behaviour, choices and decisions. It is by developing reflexivity that students will become increasingly congruent, and will not develop discourses that are disconnected from their acts, or at least not develop them to the same extent. It is by developing reflexivity that they can examine their autonomy in the organizational situations they will experience, and will be able to develop a relationship with reality that takes their environments into account.

This seminar is an example of pedagogies that can be applied to this end. Elaboration of this reflexivity dimension can also be carried out in the long term in a confidential manner, through individual accompaniment of students of the type offered by ESSEC's tutorship system. It appears that this mode of learning and personal development should be made a priority and encouraged in the face of the challenges raised by the current crisis.

The chapter also highlights that professors must be willing to work using different pedagogies, and that these initiatives must be supported by their institutions. The pedagogy developed in this seminar and others designed to meet the same objective could easily attract more students than currently, if it were more widespread and more valued in business schools, and in their students' experiences before they arrive at business school.

The example seminar presented in this chapter also shows that such a shift in pedagogy needs in-depth collective reflections in business schools on their course evaluations, which need to evolve with the pedagogy and/or be interpreted in a way that makes space for new pedagogies.

The ESSEC water management seminar is analyzed not as a model but as an example of a pedagogy that offers students the experience of working and learning in a complex, diverse and uncertain environment – something they will have to do in their future jobs. It shows interesting learning processes in the way students consider knowledge and other people. But it remains a modest contribution. Other similar seminars are being developed, and many more should follow in business schools and universities if we want our students to play a significant, constructive role in their organizations and in society.

References:

Allain, S. 2011. Négocier l'Eau comme un Bien Commun à Travers la Planification Concertée de Bassin (Negotiating Water as a Common Good Through Basin Concerted Planning). *Nature Sciences Sociétés*, XL–LIII.

De Anca, C., Aragón, I. and Galdón, C. 2013. Leadership in Multi-identity Contexts: A Mediterranean Framework, in *Uncertainty, Diversity and the Common Good: Changing Norms and New Leadership Paradigms*, edited by S. Gröschl. Farnham: Gower Publishing Ltd.

De Carlo, L. 2012. Teaching Negotiation Through Paradox. *Negotiation Journal*, 28 (3): 351–364.

Follett, M.P. 1995. Constructive Conflict, in *Mary Parker Follett:Prophet of Management*, edited by P. Graham.Washington DC: Beard Book, 67–95.

Frérot, A. 2009. *L'Eau – Pour une Culture de la Responsabilité (Water – For a Culture of Responsibility)*. Paris: Autrement.

Gabriel, Y. 2009. Reconciling and Ethic of Care with Critical Management Pedagogy. *Management Learning*, 40(4): 379–385.

Juignet, P. 2003. Lacan, le Symbolique et le Signifiant (Lacan, the Symbolic and the Signifier). *Cliniques Méditerranéennes*, 68(2): 131–144.

Kaës, R. 1976. *L'Appareil Psychique Groupal – Constructions du Groupe* (The Groupal Psychic Apparatus–Buildings of the Group). Paris: Dunod.

Kaës, R. 1993. *Le Groupe et le Sujet du Groupe (The Group and the Subject of the Group)* , Paris: Dunod.

Lewis, M.W. 2000. Exploring Paradox: Towards a More Comprehensive Guide. *Academy of Management Review*, 25(4): 760–776.

L'Institut de l'Entreprise, le Cercle de l'Entreprise et du Management et la FNEGE. 2010. *Repenser la Formation des Manager (Rethink Managers Training)*. Paris: L'Institut de l'Entreprise.

Nahrath, S., Gerber J.D., Knoepfel P. and Bréthaut C., 2011. Gestion des Ressources Communes en Suisse: Le Rôle des Institutions de Gestion Communautaire dans les Politiques Environnementales et d'Aménagement du Territoire (Common Resources Management in Switzerland : The Role of Community Management Institutions in Planning and Environmental Policies) . *Nature Sciences Sociétés*, May 2011: 17–24.

Perez de Pablos, S. 2012. Formemos Directivos Menos Arrogantes (We Train Less Arrogant Managers). *El Pais*, 17 February.

Petrella, R. 2011, July 28. *Interview*, Institut Européen de Recherche sur la Politique de l'Eau (European Research Institute on Water Policy). Available at:www.ierpe.eu, June 2012

Smith, W.K. and Lewis, M.W. 2011.Toward a Theory of Paradox: a Dynamic Equilibrium Model of Organizing. *Academy of Management Review*, 36(2): 381–403.

UN General Assembly. 2010. *The Human Right to Water and Sanitation*, (Resolution A/RES/64/292). New York: United Nations.

Weick, K.E. and Sutcliffe, K.M. 2006. Mindfulness and the Quality of Organizational Attention. *Organization Science*, 17(4):514–524.

Winnicott, D.W. 1971. *Playing and Reality*. London: Tavistock.

Winnicott, D.W. 1986. *Home is Where we Start From*. New York and London: W.W. Norton and Company.

Concluding Remarks

STEFAN GRÖSCHL

Throughout this book, for some readers maybe more questions have been raised than answered. This shows the complexity of the theme, but also the possibilities for each manager, business leader, employee, consumer and any other stakeholder to decide for themself what role they want to play in addressing the current and urgent global challenges we all face. Each of us has to decide for ourself what we define as the common good and what are our responsibilities and obligations, individually and as part of an organization, towards society and the socio-environmental context in which we live and work. Each of us has to set the boundaries of our responsibilities.

The different contributions have highlighted the diversity of sources from which future leaders could emerge – from newly formed groups such as the transnational capitalist class to historically marginalized bi-cultures. New leadership models seem to develop around the world, led and formed by ethical, legal, social and transcultural norms and requirements. Certain movements in the Middle East have shown how the idea of individuals as leaders can be questioned, and, that groups, tribes and other collective forms can create new, organic leadership models.

Regardless from where these new leaders emerge, educators might want to review their existing teaching methods and aims to better help future decision makers understand and address their responsibilities and obligations. Business leaders who want to respond to today's complex challenges in a sustainable and responsible way might need a more holistic perspective and education, and an understanding and appreciation of the multitude of functional areas concerned with the rapidly changing, unpredictable and ambiguous environment in which we live. Some business schools have started to address these needs by developing interdisciplinary programmes, putting socio-environmental subjects on the agenda, and by reviewing current business practices from an ethical perspective. But as in the business world, many educational initiatives remain embryonic. A greater collective effort by both the business world and business schools is needed to do well and to do good at the same time.

Index